Workers and Dissent in the Redwood Empire

Workers and Dissent in the Redwood Empire

Daniel A. Cornford

Temple University Press

Philadelphia

Temple University Press, Philadelphia 19122
Copyright © 1987 by Temple University. All rights reserved
Published 1987
Printed in the United States of America

The paper used in this publication meets the minimum
requirements of American National Standard for Information
Sciences—Permanence of Paper for Printed Library Materials,
ANSI Z39.48-1984

Library of Congress Cataloging-in-Publication Data

Cornford, Daniel A., 1947–
Workers and dissent in the redwood empire.

Bibliography: p. 261
Includes index.
1. Trade-unions—Lumbermen—California—Humboldt County—History.
2. Lumbermen—California—Humboldt County—History.
3. Humboldt County (Calif.)—Politics and government.
4. Humboldt County (Calif.)—Economic conditions.
5. Humboldt County (Calif.)—Social conditions.
I. Title.
HD6515.L92H853 1988   322'.2'0979412   87-6526
ISBN 0-87722-499-4 (alk. paper)

to my parents, Hugh and Jean Cornford

and Lynn Helton

Contents

Acknowledgments

Writing a book is both a solitary and communal experience. Space does not permit me to acknowledge either the diversity or extent of the debts I have incurred to relatives, friends, and colleagues. I wish briefly, however, to express my gratitude to those whose contributions to this book were especially important.

Two people have been closely involved with this study from its inception as a doctoral dissertation in the late 1970s to the completion of the book manuscript. My greatest debt is to my friend Jeffrey Stine, who devoted countless hours to editing and critiquing my work. He combined rigorous criticism with sustained moral support and encouragement in a manner which few friends could have done. Carl Harris, my dissertation supervisor, also read the manuscript at various stages and gave me valuable advice. The following scholars have given generously of their time to comment on all or parts of my manuscript: JoAnn Argersinger, David Brody, Elliot Brownlee, David Brundage, Robert Cherny, Patricia Cohen, Joseph Conlin, Otis Graham, Jr., William Issel, Kerby Miller, William Robbins, and William Wrightson. My editor at Temple University Press, Janet Francendese, was a constant source of support and encouragement, while Mary Capouya graciously and efficiently supervised the production of the book in its final stages.

I have also been the beneficiary of the hospitality and assistance of many inhabitants of the Redwood Empire. Donald and Marilyn Murphy provided both, as did Noel and Ina Harris. Authors Lynwood Carranco and Frank Onstine kindly shared their knowledge of lumber and labor in the redwood lumber industry and guided me toward important sources. My special thanks to Erich Schimps and the staff of the Humboldt Room at the Humboldt State University Library. The excellent local and regional history collection greatly facilitated my work, and Erich's efforts on my behalf were above and beyond the call of duty.

I am also grateful to the staffs of the libraries at the University of California, at Santa Barbara and Berkeley, and especially to their interlibrary loan departments. The Forest History Society showed great interest in my work from the outset, and I made considerable use of its facilities while it was still located in Santa Cruz, California. In particular, Ronald Fahl, former editor of the *Journal of Forest History*, provided me with invaluable archival and bibliographic information. A fellowship from the Bancroft Library at University of California, Berkeley in 1980–1981 helped support my research at a crucial stage, and librarians at the Bancroft have for many years responded courteously and efficiently to the many demands I have made on them. A grant from the American Association for State and Local History in 1985 assisted in the completion of this work.

On a more personal level, the close friendship of Dave Freedman, John Herman, and Pepita Herrandiz has been a source of stability and for many years has sustained my morale and sense of humor during difficult times. I have fond memories of my late grandmother, May Allardyce, in Devon, England. Her reading Charles Dickens to me as a child kindled whatever historical imagination and compassion that I possess. My parents unfailing love, faith in me, and support of my education is reflected in the book's dedication to them. The book is also dedicated to my wife Lynn Helton, who has been a constant source of support from shortly after my arrival in America in 1972. She sacrificed more than I, or any author, had any right to expect. I know she will appreciate the irony of the dedication to her.

Workers and Dissent in
the Redwood Empire

Introduction

On January 2, 1884, Charles Ferdinand Keller and his family reluctantly boarded the passenger ship *Humboldt* to leave forever the county where they had striven to make a living for ten years.[1] Following Keller's disclosure of one of the largest timberland frauds in American history, a boycott of his shop in Eureka left him no alternative but to depart the land of the giant redwoods.[2]

Keller had arrived in Humboldt County, California, in the mid-1870s, and after filing a homestead claim, began farming 15 miles south of Eureka. Within a few years, he became one of the county's most articulate dissenters. Deeply troubled by both local and national developments, he joined a branch of the Greenback Labor party. At an Independence Day celebration in 1880, he reiterated his support for the party and deplored the inequities that he believed characterized the American political system:

The rights of the majority are being prostituted to the money mighted minority. Mammon dictates the laws that are to govern the nation. There is an aristocracy exempt from taxation that feeds upon the vitals. . . . These wards of the nation have everything their own way, and no man has needs they need to respect. . . . We must either take what they offer, or, what is more likely, starve.[3]

In 1883, after the demise of the Greenback Labor party, Keller voiced outrage at attempts by a "Scotch syndicate" to acquire 100,000 acres of redwood timberlands in Humboldt County by fraudulent means and consolidate many of the county's pioneer lumber concerns into a giant enterprise. Faced with the opposition of lumber companies and the county press, Keller founded branches of the International Workingmen's Association (IWA) and sowed the seeds of the county's first labor movement. In spite of impassioned appeals and determined efforts, Keller was no match for the power of the lumber companies. Exiled from Humboldt, he moved to Tulare County, California, where, with other dissidents, he established the Kaweah Cooperative colony and endeavored to build a new moral world in an era that seemed to him dominated by large corporations and a pernicious spirit of acquisitive individualism.[4]

Keller's profound disquiet and his transcendent social vision reflected a strong dissenting tradition in Humboldt County and elsewhere in the United States during the late nineteenth and early twentieth centuries. Keller's tale illuminates important aspects of the social and political conflict that affected Humboldt County and many communities from the redwood forests of the Far West to the Eastern Seaboard.

Since the early 1960s, numerous community studies have greatly enriched our understanding of the American past, particularly our knowledge of the lives of ordinary workingmen and women.[5] The case-study approach has enabled historians to examine in detail particular industries, cities or regions, and social strata often neglected in sweeping national histories. Most community studies have focused on Eastern and Midwestern towns and cities and on the impact of industrialization on the working class of comparatively large metropolises. Although these studies have often explored the main locus of nineteenth and early twentieth century industrial development, and thus the environments in which labor unions and political radicalism often thrived, the majority of Americans lived in different settings during this period. As Steven Hahn and Jonathan Prude have noted, the proportion of Americans living outside cities was five out of six in 1860 and two out of three in 1900.[6] Not until 1920 did a majority of Americans live in an "urban" setting.

The fact that most Americans lived in small towns until well into the twentieth century has far-reaching implications for the study of American social history. The fabric of social relations and the problems of organizing labor and dissenting political movements were not the same in the nation's large cities as they were in the countless mining, lumbering, and textile communities that dotted the American landscape. In the American West, especially, economic development typically occurred in small-town settings. The locus of industrialization was dictated by the availability of raw materials that were usually situated in remote areas. Thus, industrialization often led to the ascendancy of one industry, such as lumber or mining, and the mushrooming of company towns and single-industry communities. By no means unique to the American West, this pattern of development was a pervasive and enduring feature of the industrialization of the region.

Melvyn Dubofsky, and other historians, have argued that the Western working-class experience was distinctive, owing to the conditions under which industrialization occurred there. But the conclusions reached by Dubofsky were based on a broad overview of the American

West extrapolated mainly from findings on the social history of the mining industry in the Rocky Mountain West during the late nineteenth and very early twentieth centuries.[7] Twenty years after the publication of his seminal essay we still know relatively little about the degree to which Western working-class radicalism was the product of rapid industrialization, concomitant changes in technology, and the concentration of capital in many subregions of the West and in industries besides mining. We have yet to explore fully how the remote setting in which industrialization frequently took place affected the labor movement and political activity, and the extent to which there was something qualitatively different about the nature and development of Western working-class radicalism.

The focus on industrialization in large urban areas of the North and Midwest has produced some excellent studies of such industries as textiles, boot and shoe manufacturing, the artisanal trades in the nineteenth century, and some of the mass-production industries such as steel and automobiles, but it has also led to the neglect of more "rural" industries like lumber, which at one time or another played an important role in the economy of virtually every region of the United States. Even in 1900, when the lumber industry in Maine and the Middle Atlantic and Great Lakes regions was declining, lumber stood among the top manufacturing industries whether measured by workers employed, total capital invested, or total value of product.[8] From the late nineteenth century until the mid-twentieth century, the lumber industry employed well over half a million workers each year; it was the major source of employment in nine states and second in importance in ten others.[9] In the American West, the lumber industry was crucial to the economy of many states for half a century. In 1910, lumber workers constituted 63 percent of the wage earners employed in manufacturing in Washington, 52 percent in Oregon, and 20 percent in California. In California, there were twice as many workers in lumber as in any other branch of manufacturing.[10] Invariably, lumbering took place in the context of company or single-industry towns. Thus, as late as 1931, 44 percent of towns in Washington and 40 percent of those in Oregon were company towns or depended on the lumber industry for their livelihood.[11]

Forest historians have written some excellent monographs on the business and environmental history of the lumber industry, but, like many labor historians, they have tended to treat lumber workers and labor relations in an episodic manner, usually from the standpoint of a particular strike. Vernon Jensen's *Lumber and Labor* (1945) was the last major work devoted to lumber workers and labor relations in the industry. Our understanding of the social and labor history of the lumber industry stands to benefit from the case-study approach applied to many other industries, and it permits the detailed examination of questions precluded by the chronological and geographical breadth of Jensen's work.[12] Humboldt County provides an excellent microcosm for such a study. Located in northern California, in the heart of the redwood lumber region, Humboldt was by the late nineteenth century one of the foremost lumber-producing counties in the United States. As recently as 1948, it ranked as the nation's second most important lumber-producing county.[13]

This book examines the political history of one of the country's premier lumbering communities, as well as its social and economic history. The texture of social relations in Humboldt County cannot be seen apart from the politics of the community. Moreover, the county's politics is an important story in itself. The book focuses, in particular, on the emergence of a strong tradition of political dissent in the 1870s that was reflected and sustained by considerable support for the California Workingmen's party, the Greenback Labor party, the Knights of Labor, the Populists, and the Socialists. Throughout the Gilded Age, a radical democratic–republican tradition united many lumber workers, farmers, artisans, and small businessmen and nurtured these movements. The ideology of Humboldt County dissenters reveals that the politics of dissent was not simply a mechanistic response to changing social and economic conditions. As Gareth Stedman Jones has argued persuasively with reference to the Chartist movement, the language of class or dissent can be a major and independent determinant of the parameters of radicalism.[14]

The vibrant democratic–republican ideology that nurtured this dissenting tradition drew on a cluster of ideas that included "equal rights" and the labor theory of value. It upheld the American political system as the world's foremost example of a government founded on pure republican principles. To be sure, this ideological legacy contained contradictions and ambiguities, as well as elements that fostered consensus, accommodation, and a spirit of mutuality. Nevertheless, the more radical features of the democratic–republican tradition provided dissenters with a body of ideas with which to scrutinize Gilded Age America. Humboldt radicals were greatly alarmed by what they saw. They were convinced that economic power was becoming dangerously concentrated and the once pristine American political system was suffering from a serious affliction.

Two points concerning politics in Gilded Age Humboldt County are worthy of particular note. First, although in its geographic location

Humboldt County could hardly have been more of an "island community," to borrow Robert Wiebe's phrase, there was nothing parochial about the political awareness of the county's dissenters. To an important extent, their perception of developments at the national level shaped their critique of Gilded Age American capitalism. Parallel developments at the local and state levels reinforced the dissenters' conviction that the American body politic was suffering from a grievous malaise. Second, while social and labor historians are increasingly recognizing the vital role of a democratic–republican tradition in the politics of dissent in nineteenth-century America, the majority of these studies ascribe this ideology to eastern urban artisans whose culture and workplace experience were being threatened and transformed by the industrial revolution before the Civil War. In Humboldt County, artisans made up a small proportion of the workforce, and technological changes did not significantly affect work processes in the lumber industry or lead to the "de-skilling" of large segments of the workforce. The fact that a radical democratic–republican tradition was by no means the exclusive preserve of artisans and others seriously affected by industrialization suggests that this ideology was more pervasive in Gilded Age America than has often been supposed and helps explain the widespread appearance of third-party movements at the local level noted by such historians as Herbert Gutman, David Montgomery, and Leon Fink.

One of the goals of this book is to elucidate the many problems associated with trying to organize workers in single-industry or company town settings. The tendency of business and labor historians to examine labor relations in the lumber industry from the perspective of strikes has left a misleading impression concerning the militancy and organizability of lumber workers. Studies of the Industrial Workers of the World (IWW) and the Congress of Industrial Organizations (CIO) in particular have tended to portray lumber workers as irreverent, rebellious, radical workers who constituted ideal union material.[15] This assessment has obscured the major logistical problems encountered in organizing lumber workers and requires considerable qualification. From the late nineteenth century until the 1930s, very rarely was more than 5 percent of the lumber workforce organized in any one year. By 1940, after the "turbulent years" of the 1930s, only 11.5 percent of the total lumber workforce was unionized.[16]

Although a strong dissenting political tradition emerged in Humboldt County during the late nineteenth century, attempts to build a trade union movement were less successful. In the mid-1880s, the Knights of Labor became a major force in the community, but ultimately their presence proved to be as ephemeral there as it was nationwide. The turn of the twentieth century witnessed a dramatic renaissance of the union movement, both within and outside the lumber industry. In 1905, Humboldt's lumber workers founded the first international union of lumber workers, and succeeded within a year in organizing half of the county's lumber workforce, making it the strongest bastion of lumber unionism in America at the time. The success of the lumber workers, however, proved to be as short-lived as that of the Knights. The lumber companies, wielding their formidable power in the community and an array of more subtle strategies, virtually eliminated lumber trade unionism in the aftermath of a major strike in 1907. The Humboldt County labor movement, aside from a brief flourish during World War I, ceased to be a major force in the community until the 1940s.

In recent years, a rash of historiographical and review essays has appeared, appealing for a synthesis in the field of labor history, Western history, and American history generally.[17] Although this is desirable (albeit a daunting undertaking), it is, for several reasons, premature. Most important, because of the relative dearth of community studies of the American West, any synthesis of American social history will have to incorporate the findings of local studies of this vast and diverse region of the American continent. I hope this book makes a contribution toward the task.

Chapter 1

From Gold Rush to Lumbering Community

Discovery and Settlement

Humboldt County is situated in northwest California approximately 250 miles north of San Francisco and 50 miles south of the Oregon border. Stretching 108 miles from north to south, it is one of California's largest counties, encompassing an area half the size of Massachusetts. Topographically, rugged mountains hem the county in on three sides against the Pacific Ocean. Humboldt was finally connected to the state and national railroad network in 1914. Before then, Humboldt Bay usually provided access to the county. Humboldt Bay, a large lagoon extending 14 miles in a north–south direction and varying in width from .5 mile to 4 miles, is the most natural harbor between San Francisco and Portland.[1]

Until the mid-twentieth century, a belt of towering redwood trees that stretched the length of the county dominated the landscape. The redwood belt varied in width from 3 to 20 miles and covered more than 500,000 acres. This band of trees was part of a massive tract of redwoods that once ran from north of the Oregon border to south of San Francisco. Coast redwoods are the world's tallest trees, often growing to a height of more than 300 feet.

A substantial population of Native Americans lived in northwest California until the mid-nineteenth century. European and American explorers made a few expeditions to the region in the late eighteenth and early nineteenth centuries, but with the exception of a few Russian trading posts that were defunct by the 1820s, no permanent settlements were established. The California gold rush led to the first white settlement and the disruption and eventual annihilation of most of the region's Native American population. By the summer of 1849, the gold mines in the Trinity Mountains, 50 miles to the east of Humboldt Bay, were among the most productive in California. Because Humboldt Bay is well concealed from ocean vessels by miles of sand dunes, it was not immediately discovered by the argonauts and they had to reach the diggings by means of a laborious overland route from Sacramento. In the fall of 1849, however, a group of miners, led by the famous western explorer Josiah Gregg, stumbled on the bay after an exploratory expedition from the Trinity Mountains.

The news of Gregg's discovery of Humboldt Bay, and the almost simultaneous discovery of Trinidad Bay, 20 miles to the north, led to settlements on the fringes of both bays and new trails to the diggings. The first towns in Humboldt County thus originated as supply stations for the Trinity mines. Arcata, located at the northernmost point of Humboldt Bay, provided the most direct route to the mines and was the center of population and business activity in the early 1850s. For a few years, Trinidad vied with Arcata as the most important settlement, but by 1854 its population had dwindled dramatically in the face of competition from towns on Humboldt Bay. Eureka, which was to become the county's major township, was the last of the early settlements founded on the bay. It was not as well served by trails to the diggings as Arcata and Trinidad, but, unlike its rivals, it was a deepwater port. Eureka quickly became the major lumbering port in the county and one of the most important lumber-producing towns on the Pacific Coast. (*See map.*)

Economy and Politics

Shipments of lumber from Humboldt Bay began in 1850. The close proximity of the forest to the bay, and the great demand for timber in gold rush California, enticed entrepreneurs into the lumber business. The first sawmill was erected in September 1850, and by 1854 nine steam-powered mills operated in the county, seven of them in Eureka. These mills represented a capital investment of over $400,000 and employed 130 workers. The largest mill, capitalized at $100,000, employed 35 men and could cut 60,000 feet of lumber daily. Most of the other mills had a capacity of not more than 20,000 feet per day and employed fewer than 10 men. Approximately 200 workers supplied the mills with logs, and $400,000 was invested in logging operations. A substantial portion of this capital went into building primitive railroads to link Eureka with the gradually receding forest. In 1854, 138 lumber

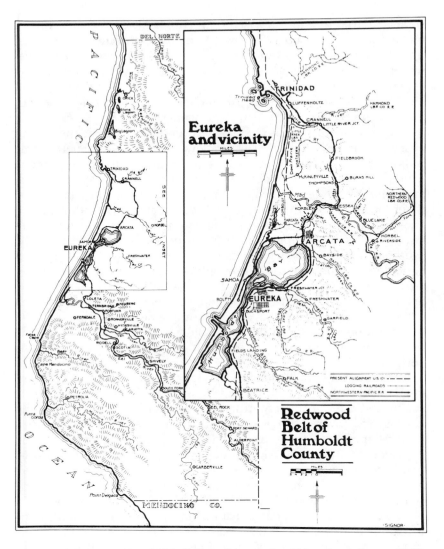

Eureka and vicinity, Humboldt County. From *Redwood Lumber Industry,* 1982; used with the permission of the publisher, Golden West Books, San Marino, California 91108.

vessels arrived in San Francisco from Humboldt County, and the 11 months preceding June 1854 saw 19 million feet of lumber exported from Humboldt Bay. Nevertheless, the progress of the lumber industry was uneven in the pioneer years because its fortunes were highly dependent on the regional and national economies. The depression of 1855 forced a virtual suspension of lumbering operations, and not until 1866 did production levels match the boom year of 1854.[2]

Another feature of the county's early development was the growth of agriculture. Humboldt's river valleys possessed extremely fertile soils. The climate was benign, with temperatures ranging between 45 degrees in winter and 65 degrees in summer and an average annual rainfall of 40 inches. Agricultural pioneers began settling in the Eel River Valley and on the flat and unforested land surrounding Arcata and Eureka in 1850. By the end of the decade, the Eel River Valley, which extended from a point just south of Humboldt Bay to the southern and eastern reaches of the county, was the focal point of agricultural settlement. In spite of labor shortages and problems of internal transportation, agriculture flourished. Wheat, barley, oats, and potatoes were the principal crops; production of them doubled between 1854 and 1860, and over 3,500 acres were under cultivation by 1860. The stock business also developed rapidly in the late 1850s, with the number of cattle increasing from 1,812 in 1854 to nearly 20,000 by 1860.[3]

Humboldt County's pioneers came from many places. People lured by the gold rush were mainly from New England, the Middle Atlantic states, and the Canadian Maritime Provinces of New Brunswick and Nova Scotia. Invariably these migrants took the sea route to California, via the Isthmus of Panama or around Cape Horn. The other main group of pioneers came from the Midwest and the border states. Not surprisingly, the vast majority of them made their way to California overland, and most of them commenced farming on arrival in Humboldt.[4] The county had a very transient population in the 1850s. Of the almost 300 people on the county's first tax list in 1853, only a third were residing in Humboldt when the 1860 census was taken. In spite of the high turnover rate, the origins of the county's population did not change much in the early years. In 1860, 80 percent of the population (2,100 of 2,694) were native-born. Of them, 470 were born in California, and all were under twenty-one years of age. The midwestern states, Middle Atlantic states, northern and southern border states, and New England states contributed roughly equal proportions to Humboldt's population. The majority of the county's 594 foreign-born residents came from the British Isles and Canada.[5]

The distribution of wealth in pioneer Humboldt County was distinctly unequal. In 1860, the wealthiest 5 percent of the population owned 26 percent of the wealth, and the top 10 percent accounted for 40 percent of the community's total wealth. At the other end of the spectrum, the bottom 50 percent owned only 13 percent of the wealth. Income distribution was more skewed in the "urban" townships of Eureka, Arcata, and Bucksport. In Arcata, for example, the top 5 percent possessed 45 percent of the wealth, while the bottom 50 percent held only 9 percent. Moreover, these figures significantly understate the maldistribution of wealth. According to the 1860 census, 486 employed people in the county (out of 1,559) did not own any property or assets worth enumerating.[6]

Issues of state and national concern, especially the growing sectional crisis, dominated the political life of Humboldt County in the 1850s. There was little divisiveness over local political issues. Shortly before the local elections of 1857, the *Humboldt Times* (the county's only newspaper from 1854 until 1858) stated that the outcome would be determined "by the personal propriety of the candidate more than by his political associations."[7] The *Humboldt Times* devoted the majority of its coverage to state and national politics, as did the *Northern Californian*, which emerged briefly to challenge the monopoly of the *Times* in 1858. The *Times* wavered between Stephen A. Douglas Democrats and the Republican party in the late 1850s. In the 1860 presidential elections, Douglas, aided by an endorsement from the *Times*, received a plurality of the votes cast, garnering 445 compared to 335 for Abraham Lincoln, 232 for John Breckinridge, and 20 for John Bell. The Douglas Democrats and the *Times* did not take the South's threat of secession very seriously. However, dismayed and outraged by the South's eventual secession, most of the leading Democrats in the county, with the strong support of the *Times*, urged the formation of a Union party in California, and in June 1862 the Humboldt County Democratic and Republican parties merged.[8] In the interim, Republican Leland Stanford won a majority of the county's votes in the California gubernatorial contest of September 1861. Support for the Union party was so strong by 1863 that the *Times* attributed the apathy of voters to its ascendancy.[9] In the 1864 presidential election, Lincoln trounced George McClellan, receiving almost twice as many votes as his rival in the county.

For most of the 1850s, Humboldt County experienced modest and uneven growth because its population levels and economic vitality were highly dependent on the fortunes of the gold miners and the lumber market. By 1860, the county had a population of only 2,694 people. Nevertheless, by the late 1850s, with the gold rush subsiding, Humboldt had become a relatively stable pioneer community based on the agricultural economy of its hinterland and the lumber industry centered in Eureka. The *Times* proclaimed that "permanent citizens, substantial businessmen and real laborers" were "taking the place of adventurers, town lot speculators, gamblers and their usual associates."[10] By 1860, Eureka with 581 residents was the largest township in the county, followed by Arcata with 524. Both towns possessed a scattering of general stores, craft shops, saloons, and hotels, and a variety of fraternal orders, including branches of the Odd Fellows, Masons, and International Order of Good Templars.[11]

The population of Humboldt County grew steadily during the late nineteenth century, reaching 27,000 inhabitants by 1900. Population growth occurred mainly in the immediate vicinity of Humboldt Bay and in the Eel River Valley. Although logging operations, and to some extent sawmilling activity, began to take place farther from Eureka, the county seat enhanced its position as Humboldt's major city. It contained approximately a third of the county's population by the 1880s, and in 1900, 8,500 people lived in the general township area.[12] The origins of Humboldt's population remained fairly constant throughout the late nineteenth century. Not surprisingly, the proportion of inhabitants born in California rose substantially after 1860. The New England states (especially Maine), the Middle Atlantic states, and the midwestern states, in that order, continued to supply the bulk of the native-born population. Foreign-born residents remained in the minority, fluctuating between 22 and 32 percent of the population. As late as 1900, immigrants from the British Canadian provinces accounted for the largest proportion of the foreign-born population. The Irish and Germans ranked second in terms of their representation among the county's foreign-born from 1870 to 1900, although by 1890, Scandinavians took over second place (*see Table 1*).

For most of the period, Humboldt County agriculture experienced steady growth, especially in the production of cereals, livestock, and dairy products. A depression in the late 1870s and the early 1880s, however, had a serious impact on farming. The cultivation of potatoes, the county's most important crop for years, declined from 19,608 tons in 1879 to 4,714 tons in 1880 and never recovered. The total number of acres cultivated diminished from 27,897 in 1880 to 17,297 in 1881.[13] In the aftermath of the depression, an important shift occurred in the structure of the county's agricultural economy. Production of most cereal crops declined, and more land was devoted to raising livestock. Humboldt became one of the leading wool-producing counties in Cali-

Table 1

Nativity of Humboldt County Population, 1870–1900

Origin	1870	1880	1890	1900
Foreign-born				
British America (Canada)	548	1,349	2,172	1,698
Canada (French)	—	—	—	37
England and Wales	180	289	449	346
Ireland	383	598	735	604
Scotland	51	108	123	108
Germany	138	333	686	726
France	24	58	98	70
Sweden and Norway	41	180	—	—
Norway	—	—	258	314
Sweden	—	—	523	536
Denmark	—	—	342	367
China	34	242	19	6
Mexico	5	9	6	7
Italy	6	—	146	232
Switzerland	15	—	300	409
Austria	—	—	88	77
Russia	—	—	194	15
Portugal	—	—	87	135
Finland	—	—	—	322
Total foreign-born population (including nationalities not in census breakdown)	1,494	3,521	6,378	6,191
Native-born				
California	1,974	7,006		
Maine	354	629		
New York	323	563		
Missouri	182	391		
Massachusetts	120	197		
Ohio	217	451		
Illinois	—	388		
Pennsylvania	—	321		
Iowa	—	301		
Indiana	—	205		
Total native-born population	4,646	11,991	17,091	20,913
TOTAL POPULATION	6,140	15,512	23,469	27,104

SOURCE: U.S. Bureau of the Census, *Statistics of Population*. Data compiled from the Ninth, Tenth, Eleventh, and Twelfth Censuses of the United States, Selected Nativity by Counties (Washington, D.C.: GPO, 1872, 1883, 1895, 1901).

fornia. But the dairy industry became the most important branch of the county's agriculture. By 1900, Humboldt County ranked eleventh in population of California's 58 counties and third in the value of its dairy products.[14] Dairying remained second only to the lumber industry in importance to the county's economy in the late nineteenth and early twentieth centuries.

A Fledgling Lumber Industry

During the late nineteenth century, Humboldt County became one of the most important lumbering regions in the United States. In 1908, the Census Bureau referred to Humboldt as the "metropolis" of the California lumber industry and called its mills perhaps the most technologically advanced in the world.[15] No significant transfer of resources from agriculture to lumber occurred in the last quarter of the nineteenth century. The county's agricultural sector expanded, but did not grow nearly so rapidly as the lumber industry. As early as 1870, while agriculture almost certainly employed more people than lumbering, the annual value of lumber production ($704,100) exceeded that of agriculture ($557,212).[16] By the 1880s, employment in the lumber industry surpassed employment in agriculture; in 1890, lumber accounted for 80 percent ($3.5 million) of Humboldt's exports and agriculture for 20 percent.[17]

The rapid expansion of the lumber industry began in the late 1860s. In 1870, 40 million feet of timber were cut, and the industry employed more than 400 workers.[18] By the late 1870s, lumber production had almost doubled, there were 20 mills in the county (compared to only 8 in 1866), and nearly 1,000 lumber workers in the Eureka area alone.[19] The depression of the late 1870s briefly interrupted the expansion, but the 1880s proved to be a watershed era in the industry's development. There were 22 mills in the county in 1881, and in the next five years 6 large sawmills were established.[20] The most conservative estimates put lumber production at 120 million feet in 1887, and the county's two leading newspapers reported that the industry employed 2,000 men.[21]

Investment by outside capitalists played an important role in the county's lumber industry in the 1880s. The Pacific Lumber Company, owned principally by Nevada entrepreneurs and soon to become one of the giants of the Pacific Coast lumber industry, commenced full-scale operations in 1887. The Korbel brothers of Sonoma established the Humboldt Lumber Mill Company in 1883 at Blue Lake, 5 miles east of

Arcata. Also in 1883, a syndicate financed primarily by Scottish capital attempted to consolidate much of the county's lumber industry. Yet, in spite of the influx of outside capital, the Humboldt lumber industry continued to be owned and operated primarily by local entrepreneurs until the early years of the twentieth century.

The expansion of the county's lumber industry in the last three decades of the nineteenth century reflected a nationwide boom in the demand for lumber. Wood continued to be the major energy source in the Gilded Age, even though coal gradually superseded it. Shipbuilding, railroads, and construction all depended for their growth on an abundant and inexpensive supply of wood. Per capita consumption of wood products in the United States quadrupled between 1850 and 1909.[22] The continued growth of the San Francisco Bay Area and the "instant urbanization" of southern California, beginning in the late 1870s, were major factors stimulating the expansion of the Humboldt County lumber industry. Over half the annual output of lumber went to San Francisco. Some of this lumber was transshipped to the eastern United States and abroad, but most of it was used in the San Francisco Bay Area. Although large quantities of lumber went directly to the ports of San Pedro and San Diego, the southern California market never surpassed the Bay Area as the primary market for redwood lumber. Foreign markets were cultivated as early as the 1850s, but only rarely was more than 15 percent of production exported.[23]

The growth of the lumber industry in the 1870s and 1880s and the receding timber stands in the immediate vicinity of Eureka and Humboldt Bay forced lumbermen to conduct logging operations farther afield and often to establish mills close to these operations. Eureka remained the site of several large mills, but most plants founded after 1880 were situated either north or east of Arcata or in southern Humboldt County in the Eel River Valley. Even by 1880, more lumber workers resided in and around Arcata than in Eureka.[24] A necessary condition for the decentralization of the lumber industry was an improvement in intracounty transportation. Before 1870, the lumber industry depended on rivers and a rather primitive railroad network. Beginning in the mid-1870s, several of the larger lumber companies embarked on extensive programs of railroad construction to link all the major lumber-producing areas of the county with Eureka. By 1887, 14 mills depended entirely or partially on railroads, and by 1892 there were 150 miles of railroad track in the county.[25] Humboldt County businessmen and residents lobbied determinedly for a connection with the state and national railroad network, but the geographic isolation of Humboldt and its rugged topography deterred prospective investors.

Until 1914, when the completion of the Northwestern Pacific Railroad finally integrated the county into the national rail network, the county remained almost entirely dependent on shipping services from Humboldt Bay for the transport of both cargo and passengers. The sea voyage to San Francisco took twenty-four hours, and the twice or thrice weekly passenger service cost $5. Through a combination of primitive wagon roads and railroad connections, overland transportation to San Francisco was possible before the arrival of the Pacific Northwestern Railroad, but the journey usually took two days. Consequently little cargo and few passengers traveled this route.

As the Humboldt County lumber industry expanded during the 1880s, many lumber companies completed the almost total vertical integration of their operations.[26] A few companies used subcontractors to supply their mills with timber, but most relied on their own logging operations. Lumber companies invariably owned their timberlands and rarely paid fees to cut on other people's land. In the 1870s and 1880s, entrepreneurs became increasingly preoccupied with securing vast acreages of strategically located timberlands. Even small concerns possessed several thousand acres, while larger ones owned 20,000 acres or more by the late nineteenth century. Most lumber operators realized that the supply of timber was finite and that the long-term viability of the business depended on securing large tracts of timberland. Many companies acquired all or part of a local railroad and a fleet of sailing vessels and steam schooners. Most had marketing offices in San Francisco, and all large companies operating outside Eureka had company stores.

The redwood lumber manufacturers made repeated efforts to regulate output and control prices. The first such effort occurred in September 1854 with the establishment of the Humboldt Manufacturing Company, but the depression of 1855 ended this experimental venture. A host of lumber trade associations came and went in the late nineteenth and early twentieth centuries. It proved difficult to obtain the cooperation of the less competitive Mendocino redwood lumber businesses. Moreover, competition from other kinds and sources of lumber, and the tendency of the industry toward overproduction, frequently caused lumber capitalists to renege on gentlemen's agreements and trade associations to dissolve within a few years.[27]

The majority of Humboldt County's nineteenth-century lumber entrepreneurs were from relatively humble origins.[28] William Carson, David Jones, Joseph Russ, Daniel Newell, David Flanigan, David Evans, John Vance, Isaac Minor, John McKay, and Frank Graham, to name only the more prominent examples, played pivotal roles in the development of the county's lumber industry, yet all arrived in Humboldt with few means. Two factors account for this pattern. First, most of these men had considerable mechanical or technical skills before coming to the county, some in logging and others in related areas. During the nineteenth century, the efficiency of milling and logging operations depended on the skill and experience of the proprietor. Second, most of the men started their careers in the lumber industry during the 1850s and 1860s, before the capital required for entry became prohibitive for an individual, although many entered into partnerships, at least initially, to raise the necessary capital.

William Carson was born in New Brunswick, Canada, in 1825. As a youth, he worked in his father's small logging business. In September 1849, infected with gold rush fever, he took a ship to San Francisco. There he worked at the mint for a while before proceeding to the Trinity gold mines. Food shortages compelled Carson and his companions to spend the winter of 1850 in Humboldt County. In order to support himself, Carson contracted to supply one of the county's mills with logs. He engaged in logging for several more years before becoming a partner in a lumber mill. During the early 1860s, in partnership with John Dolbeer, Carson established what was soon to become one of the largest lumbering concerns in the county, and by the 1880s, he was one of the county's wealthiest and most revered figures. According to the 1860 census, Carson was worth $11,000. On his death in 1912, his estate was valued at $20 million.[29]

John Vance was born in Nova Scotia in 1817. At age sixteen he began learning carpentry and shipbuilding. He then went to Roxbury, Massachusetts, and worked for a few years in the building industry. Like Carson, he was lured to California by the gold rush. Arriving in San Francisco in 1850, he spent an unfruitful year at the diggings. He moved to Humboldt County in 1852, and while employed as a carpenter and millwright, converted a wrecked steamer into a sawmill. Vance also engaged in merchandising in the 1850s.[30] Humboldt County's first tax list, compiled in 1853, assessed Vance's total wealth at a modest $1,600. By the 1870s, he had become one of the county's wealthiest lumbermen.

Isaac Minor was born on a Pennsylvania farm in 1830. He came to California in 1851 and spent eighteen months at the diggings. Arriving in Humboldt County in 1853, he acquired a pack train and sold goods to miners. In 1859, he settled on a ranch and engaged in stock raising, only to have most of his herd destroyed by Indian raids in 1862–1863. Undaunted, Minor remained in the county and in 1875 entered the lumber business with Noah Falk. In 1881, Minor's career was hailed as proof that "even if unsuccessful at first, by energy a person may attain a competency, and become a useful and productive citizen."[31] By the early twentieth century, Minor was one of the wealthiest men in the county. Early in the new century, he sold 26,000 acres of redwood lands in Del Norte County for $960,000 and another 13,000 acres in Humboldt for $430,000.[32]

Many of the men who occupied the second echelon of leadership in the lumber industry—those who became logging foremen or mill supervisors—rose from the ranks by dint of their wide-ranging experience and technical aptitude. "The foreman is always a man of long experience and broad judgment, who has passed through several grades of the service, and is familiar with the details of the different kinds of work," asserted the *Humboldt Times* in 1889.[33] Lumber entrepreneurs attempted to oversee the day-to-day field operations of their businesses, but as the size of the workforce grew and milling and logging operations spread over a wider area, this task became more difficult. Increasingly, they had to rely on a foreman to make important decisions about the organization of production and the hiring and management of workers.

A large proportion of the rank and file of the Humboldt County lumber workforce had almost certainly worked in the lumber industry before coming to the county and were drawn to Humboldt by a pattern of occupational migration. The 1860, 1870, and 1880 census records show that a substantial number of Humboldt County's lumber workers came from Maine and the Canadian Maritime Provinces. Lumbering had been predominant in these regions in the early and mid-nineteenth century, but during the second half of the century, they ceased to be at the apex of the American lumber industry as the gravitational center of the industry shifted westward. Although the bulk of lumber capital, entrepreneurs, and workers migrated to Great Lakes states up until the 1880s, a significant transfer of lumber resources to the Far West also took place.

In 1860, 27 percent of the native-born men employed in the lumber industry were from Maine, while nearly 80 percent of the foreign-born engaged in lumbering were from New Brunswick and Nova Scotia. Workers from these areas made up half of the total lumber workforce in 1870 and 45 percent in 1880.[34] Women were not employed in logging or milling operations until World War I.[35] During the war, an acute shortage of labor and a booming demand for lumber resulted in the employment of women in some of the larger mills. But this was regarded, and indeed proved to be, a temporary expedient.

A mix of "pull" and "push" factors caused lumber workers from

Maine and the Maritime Provinces to undertake this transcontinental migration. On the push side, the general decline of that region's lumber industry forced many lumber workers and farmers to contemplate migration, and by the 1840s, they were beginning to flock to Boston and other large New England cities and towns. "California fever," as it was called, infected even the remotest parts of the northeastern American continent and accelerated the exodus from many of the region's lumbering and farm communities. In July 1851, the *Frontier Journal* of Washington County, Maine, spoke of "wagonloads" of men who had left the county for California.[36] Out-migration continued steadily throughout the second half of the nineteenth century. Although a majority of the migrants from the Maritime Provinces went initially to New England, a sizable minority went directly to California. The well-developed trade in lumber and other items between the region's small ports and the Far West facilitated the migration of lumber workers. Ship captains or companies catered directly to the Pacific Coast passenger market, and steerage was obtainable for a modest fee.[37]

Like William Carson, the majority of lumber workers were drawn to California by the glitter of gold. When the diggings proved disappointing, the migrants reverted to the occupation they knew best, plying their skills in the fledgling California lumber industry. By the late 1850s, when gold rush fever had subsided, most lumber workers from Maine and the Maritime Provinces almost certainly went west hoping for immediate employment in the lumber industry. The higher wages obtainable in California and the relative ease of transportation to the West Coast sustained this transcontinental migration. Kinship and friendship networks also played a role: Canadians and people from Maine working in the California lumber industry wrote to relatives and friends with glowing tales of life in the Golden State.[38] Frank Fraser, whose parents migrated from New Brunswick in the 1860s, recalls how it was common practice for lumber employers to "send back every year and get a few of the younger fellows" who had experience in the lumber industry.[39] Gilmann Knapp remembers instances of neighbors and friends moving from Canada to Humboldt County to rejoin former neighbors and friends.[40] Many lumber capitalists who migrated to the Great Lakes states returned to Maine and the Maritime Provinces to recruit labor and, in some instances, brought their labor force with them.[41] It is likely that many Humboldt County lumber entrepreneurs did the same thing.

During the nineteenth century in most parts of the United States and Canada, lumbering was an occupation often combined with farming. But the vast majority of men who migrated from Maine and the

Maritime Provinces to work in the Humboldt County lumber industry were full-time lumber workers. By 1850, most lumber workers in New Brunswick were unable to combine farming or other occupations with work in the mills and woods. Low wages and high land prices and rents discouraged employment in agriculture, while the expansion and commercialization of the province's lumber industry necessitated the virtual full-time employment of workers in areas often far removed from their homes. The pattern was similar in Maine and the other Canadian Maritime Provinces.[42] In part, this explains why comparatively few of the first generation of Humboldt County lumber workers combined farming and logging. In 1860, 46 of 168 lumber workers owned some real estate; in 1870, only 68 of 397 did. Seventeen of 46 owned less than $500 worth of real estate in 1860, and in 1870, 24 of 68 fell into this category. These figures include the holdings of lumber capitalists and lumber workers who did not necessarily farm the land they owned.[43]

Lack of farming experience before coming to Humboldt was not the only reason so few pioneer lumber workers engaged in agriculture. As in Maine and the Maritime Provinces, lumbering in Humboldt County generally employed workers for most of the year. Moreover, the lumbering season overlapped more directly with the growing and harvesting season than it did in the Northeast. In the latter region, logging generally began with the onset of winter and lasted until spring; in Humboldt and the Far West, the logging season commenced in the spring and continued until the heavy late-fall rains suspended operations. H. S. Turner, whose father migrated in 1853 to work in the Humboldt lumber industry, stressed two additional reasons the early lumber workers did not purchase more land. First, many of them went west "to make their whack . . . and to return to their eastern home and sweetheart, to marry and settle down in those snow clad states," even though many ended up staying in Humboldt County.[44] Second, only a small amount of the county's land was available for purchase. Much of the land had not been surveyed and was not open for entry; other land had been acquired or taken under squatters' rights.[45]

The Work Process

A considerable degree of labor specialization existed in both logging and milling operations by the late nineteenth century and was especially pronounced in the California redwood lumber industry. In 1886, the wage list of the Excelsior Redwood Company listed 18 occupational classifications in logging and 19 in mill work.[46] Logging camps varied greatly in size, with larger companies employing anywhere from 30 to 100 men.[47] Harvesting redwood trees with average diameters of 12 to 16 feet and sometimes standing 300 feet placed great demands on the ingenuity of lumbermen and heightened the division of labor. So daunting were the technical problems that not until the 1860s did extensive logging of redwoods begin.

How the redwood lumber industry operated can best be conveyed by describing the primary work processes. Two choppers were responsible for cutting down a tree. The head chopper decided how to fell the tree in order to cause the least damage to it and to adjacent timber. On steep hillsides, redwoods were usually felled uphill, and sometimes a soft bed of brush was laid to cushion the giants' fall. Scaffolding was erected from 6 to 15 feet from the base of the tree so that the choppers would not have to cut through the widest part of the trunk. The choppers made a giant undercut halfway through the tree that was often 6 feet high at the periphery. Old logging photographs show as many as 20 men standing in the vast undercut. The choppers then moved to the other side of the tree and began sawing through to the undercut. As the saw progressed, wedges were driven in to relieve pressure on the saw and direct the fall of the tree. It is little wonder that the felling of a large redwood often took a week.

Peelers removed the tough and stringy bark of the redwood tree before buckers began cutting the fallen giant into lengths of 8 to 12 feet. By the late nineteenth century, most camps employed a filer to keep the saws sharp. Next, the logs had to be transported to the mill. From 1850 to 1880, before the construction of an extensive rail network, logs were floated downriver to the mill. By the 1880s, most large logging operations relied on railroads to transport logs and this eliminated many of the uncertainties associated with river transportation. But the logs still had to be transported to rivers or railroads along logging roads that had to be carved through the forest. The most important logging road, the skid road, was reinforced with cross logs in a corduroy pattern so that the heavy, 8- to 12-foot sections of redwood could be slid along them. In the early spring, most of the men in the logging camp worked at building these roads, which cost about $5,000 a mile to construct. A crew of men known as swampers assumed the main responsibility for road construction and maintenance. Teams of horses or oxen pulled the logs over the skid roads. In charge of each team was the most important person in the camp, the teamster, or bullwhacker. It was his responsibility to negotiate the skid roads up hill and down dale with his precious cargo of logs. He was accompanied by a water packer, or slinger, whose job was to throw water in front of the lead logs to make the road more slippery.

In 1881, logging operations in Humboldt County, and before long in the whole United States, were greatly facilitated by Humboldt County lumberman John Dolbeer's invention, which soon became known as the Dolbeer donkey. An upright boiler powered a horizontal shaft, from which ran long lines of thick rope that could be fastened onto logs up to 200 feet away. Logs could thus be mechanically manipulated over rough or steep terrain for a considerable distance. Within a few years, Dolbeer's donkeys were modified so that the most sophisticated ones, using steel cables, could haul in logs at a distance of 2,000 feet. Specialized crews operated the donkeys and attached ropes and cables to the logs. The donkeys did not obviate the need for skid roads and bull teams, but made hauling logs to skid roads infinitely easier.

As with logging, the multiplicity of milling work processes and job classifications were not substantially altered by the continuous introduction of more efficient and adaptable saw machinery. By the 1860s, most sawmilling was done by steam-powered double circular saws, with a third and fourth saw employed in some mills by the 1870s. Logs often had to be cut or split into smaller sections by Mulay or sash saws before being fed into the circular saws. By the 1880s, however, almost all logs could be floated directly into a small channel that led from the mill pond to the sawing assembly line. The log was placed on a slip carriage and perfectly aligned by a "carriage setter" before it was drawn into the sawing blades. The sawyer, the supervisor of the whole milling process, was responsible for calculating how many board feet of lumber a log would produce and for ensuring that the cut would produce finished lumber that conformed to the size and quality specifications of a particular order and at the same time minimized waste. When the log had passed through the circular saws (or the band saws that superseded them by the late nineteenth century), a number of rough large boards emerged, their width determined by the diameter of the log. These boards might be 5 to 6 feet wide. The edgerman's task was to cut the boards down to narrower widths according to the specific order. The sheets of wood were placed on roller-topped tables and cut with a circular saw. A trimmer then used a circular saw to cut the boards to the requisite length. The processed lumber was next passed down roller-topped tables to be sorted and graded. The carriage pullers, sawyers, edgers, and trimmers were supported by a host of ancillary personnel such as filers, who constantly sharpened the saw blades, engineers, firemen, log pullers, tallymen, blacksmiths, carpenters, cooks, and a large number of common laborers. In the late nineteenth century, the average lumber mill in the redwood region employed about 50 workers.[48]

Working and Living Conditions

Wages in the California redwood lumber industry were among the highest of any lumbering region in North America and far exceeded those paid in the eastern United States and the Canadian Maritime Provinces. In California, wage levels ranged from $26 a month for a common laborer to $150 for a teamster or foreman; in the East, wages for lumber workers varied from $15 to a high of $30 a month.[49] Although a skilled worker might earn upward of $100 a month, most lumber workers earned considerably less. The Dolbeer and Carson Company reportedly paid the highest wages in Humboldt County; in 1887 and 1888, most of the company's workers earned between $40 and $70 a month. In 1887, 169 of 221 were in this wage bracket, and in 1888, 121 of 164. In the same two years, only 7 workers earned $100 a month or more.[50] Humboldt County lumber workers were usually paid in cash on a regular monthly basis. This was unlike many other lumbering regions in the United States where workers were often paid partially in scrip, and sometimes at three-month intervals or in a lump sum at the end of the logging season. The lumber workers' place in the occupational hierarchy was not the only determinant of their wages. Wages fluctuated according to the general state of the industry. During the depressions of the late 1870s and mid-1890s, wages fell by as much as 50 percent for some Humboldt lumber workers. There were also significant differences in wage rates between lumber concerns.[51] Finally, seasonal and market factors influenced the length of the logging season and mill operations and thus affected the workers' total earnings. Typically, a logger and a mill hand worked eight months a year.[52]

During the rainy season, some Humboldt County lumber workers made a living doing odd jobs. Contracting to make shingle bolts was one of the more common pursuits. But only a minority were able to pick up these jobs. Some lumber workers idled away the winter months, the family and better-off men in their own homes, while others flocked to Eureka and eked out an existence at one of the many boardinghouses. A significant proportion of lumber workers left the county for other parts of the state. The majority almost certainly went to San Francisco, the nearest major city, to try to obtain casual labor. The *Humboldt Times* stated that "men working at the several mills and camps are usually retained year after year," and added that "many instances are known in this county where laborers have worked for the same concern 15 to 25 years."[53] The dearth of company records makes this assertion hard to test. Payroll records of the Dolbeer and Carson Company for 1887 and 1888, however, indicate that labor turnover among woodsmen was high. The company employed 302 woodsmen in the two-year period, but only 81 of them worked in both years.[54] But a host of newspaper reports, recollective accounts, and the will of William Carson suggest that many lumber concerns had a core of workers employed by a company for many years. They were likely to be the more skilled workers and to work in the mills.

Until 1890, millmen and woodsmen in Humboldt County worked a twelve-hour day. Mill workers obtained the ten-hour day in 1890, but the twelve-hour day persisted in logging well into the twentieth century. The lumber worker usually began work at 6:00 A.M. and worked until 6:00 P.M., with not much more than a fifteen-minute break for lunch at noon. Dinner was served around 7:00 P.M.[55] For many lumber workers, the only redeeming feature of camp life was the cookhouse. They regarded large quantities of good-quality food almost as their birthright. Psychologically, a hearty meal was some compensation for a gruelling day's work; physiologically, it was essential to workers who often expended 9,000 calories a day. Lumber capitalists were not nutritionists, but common sense and their own experience of the work made them aware of the demands of the occupation. Good food was almost as important as wages in attracting and retaining a crew, and employers could exercise greater control over food quality than general wage levels. The premium on good food was so high that the cook was one of the best-paid workers in camp. By the late nineteenth century, larger companies operated their own vegetable gardens, ranches, slaughterhouses, and dairies.[56]

A lumber worker's food was almost the only feature of his living conditions that was satisfactory. Housing and sanitary conditions at most camps were rudimentary until the 1920s. Between 1850 and 1880, when lumbering operations took place close to Eureka and Arcata, most lumber workers lived in boardinghouses or rented rooms. The dispersion of the Humboldt County lumber industry forced many workers to leave town and live in primitive dwellings in the forest. In the 1880s, the Pacific Lumber Company, located at Scotia, 30 miles southeast of Eureka, led the way in building company housing. The first bunkhouses, constructed in 1884, were about 10 feet square with a hole in the middle of the roof to vent the smoke from the fire in the middle of the cabin floor. By 1887, the company had a boardinghouse

1,000 feet from the mill, measuring 40 by 100 feet, which was de-scribed as having "every convenience for 300 men." There were also 102 houses that were approximately 16 by 20 feet in size. Half were occupied by married men and the remainder by single men, six to a cabin.[57] Until the 1920s, most cabins were without any sanitary fa-cilities except, in some instances, piped water. The cabins were not usually lighted by electricity, and the men provided their own bedding.

Lumber workers had limited recreational time during the work week. After a hard day's work and a large meal, most men retired to their cabins and boardinghouses. Here some of them played cards or chatted and smoked before bedding down to await the 5:00 A.M. whistle. The rudimentary forest camps provided few social amenities until they began to evolve into full-fledged company towns in the early twentieth century. On weekends, many men attempted to make up for their drab weekday existence. By the 1880s, the large lumber companies ran excursion trains to Eureka on Saturday evenings and Sundays. Most lumber workers went to town to enjoy the conveniences afforded by Eureka's red-light district or its saloons. In 1896, there were 77 licensed saloons in the county,[58] most of them in Eureka, and by 1904 there were 63 retail liquor dealers in Eureka (a city of 11,000 residents), or one dealer per 175 people.[59] Undoubtedly, many saloons in Eureka depended on the patronage of visiting lumber workers. Saloons were one of the first social facilities provided by lumber employers as the logging camps developed into company towns. The Pacific Lumber Company built its first saloon in 1888, primarily because it wanted some control over the quantity and quality of liquor consumed by its workers; rarely did the company have to deal with men who were too intoxicated to work the next day.[60] During the early twentieth century, some companies made liquor less accessible, but this was mainly the result of an increasingly militant local temperance movement and the desire of some lumber operators to elevate the moral order of their company towns.

Not all men participated in sexual and alcoholic debauches on weekends; some virtuously tended gardens allotted them by the com-pany. By 1892, most Scotia residents had gardens. Other workers took the train to Eureka and other townships to visit their families. Approxi-mately a third of woodsmen and millmen were married.[61] A few at-tended church or listened to the sermon of an itinerant preacher. Some-times the Women's Christian Temperance Union ventured bravely into the lumber camps and towns, but these missionaries made little impact. As Stewart Holbrook succinctly put it, "what a man wanted came in bottles and corsets."[62] Some companies provided picnicking facilities and occasionally put on a dance. Beginning in 1879, lumber employer John Vance sponsored an annual picnic for employees and Humboldt County schoolchildren. Most lumber concerns closed down for a few days during the Fourth of July celebrations and often provided financial backing for the annual ritual. On July 4, 1896, the Pacific Lumber Company sponsored a picnic that attracted 3,500 people.[63] But, with few exceptions, not until the 1910s did lumber companies make a concerted effort to orchestrate the leisure time of their employees by establishing churches, Sunday schools, libraries, fraternal societies, theaters, movie houses, and baseball teams.

The lives of most redwood lumber workers were unenviable. Their work was physically demanding and dangerous.[64] The Humboldt County voting registers of the 1890s provide graphic testimony to the hazards of working in the lumber industry. A large number of lumber workers on the register are identified as having lost a finger or limb or being seriously maimed. The lumber workers' day was as long as that of most unskilled workers, and their earnings were just as irregular. They also worked in an industry that imposed severe constraints on their social space. The isolated locales in which they lived and worked not only separated them from families and the amenities available in Eureka and Arcata but also subjected their lives outside the workplace to the constant surveillance of employers. The activities of any malcontent were easy to monitor in a logging camp or company town. Even a worker who lived in Eureka or Arcata was hardly invisible in a small town where most employers knew their workers and neighbors by name. Employers in the redwood region could not always agree on price and output schedules, but they cooperated in blacklisting troublemakers. The lumber-dependent economy of northernmost California left most workers with few alternative job opportunities. Agriculture was the other major source of employment in the region, but few lumber workers possessed the necessary combination of land, capital, and expertise to engage in farming.

The company town or single-industry setting gave employers immense power and was a major factor in restraining strikes and trade unionism, in Humboldt County and other lumbering regions across the United States.[65] The first recorded strikes of lumber workers occurred in Pennsylvania in 1872 and in Humboldt County in 1881. Other factors that limited strike activity and the establishment of stable trade unions included a transient labor force, the highly cyclical nature of the lumber market, and the ease with which unskilled lumber workers could be replaced. Logistically, the problems of organizing workers dispersed over a wide area, often in remote locations, were formidable. Although working and living conditions were poor, technological changes in logging and milling did not result in a significant degree of "deskilling." Furthermore, in Humboldt County, wage levels and living conditions were better than lumber workers had experienced in Canada and the northeastern United States. Finally, the paternalism of lumber employers toward their workers and the community, or at least the perception of it, also helped to mitigate conflict.

This is not to say that all lumber workers passively accepted their lot. Small-scale, spontaneous strikes or walkouts were not uncommon in Humboldt County. Two issues, food and foremen, caused most of the stoppages. Lumber workers struck because they wanted a cook or a foreman fired or retained and believed they had prerogatives in these areas. During Humboldt's first strike in 1881, John Vance quickly appeased his workers by firing the cook; lumber employers generally yielded on questions of food and foremen.[66] On these and other issues, lumber workers were more likely to "strike with their feet" by leaving camp in search of better conditions. The success of this tactic, however, depended on the state of the labor market.

By the mid-1880s, lumber workers in Humboldt County and elsewhere in the United States believed that any improvement in wages and working conditions would require the creation of unions, and thousands of lumber workers from Maine to California joined the Knights of Labor. In Humboldt County, however, almost ten years before the Knights emerged to represent them, lumber workers, farmers, artisans, and small businessmen united to express their discontent by supporting a succession of dissident third-party political movements. To the extent that the pioneers of Humboldt and other California counties expected to find a land of boundless opportunity and rough equality in the Golden State, they were to be sorely disappointed. Within a decade of the gold rush, disparities in both economic and political power were as marked as they were in the eastern communities from which they had come.[67] Workers and farmers in Humboldt County and elsewhere in California believed that the cherished American republic was threatened by corruption and a dangerous concentration of economic and political power. A series of events at the local, state, and national levels after the Civil War reinforced this perception and led to the founding of branches of the California Workingmen's party in almost every county during the late 1870s. To many lumber workers, farmers, and artisans there was a close link between the defects in their political system and the widely fluctuating levels of wages and remuneration they received. They turned first to the ballot box to try to remedy these problems.

Chapter 2

The Seeds of Radicalism

The Democratic–Republican Ideology

Humboldt County during the Gilded Age saw the emergence of a vibrant dissenting tradition that shattered the harmony of the pioneer years. In the political arena this discord manifested itself most clearly in support for the California Workingmen's party, the Greenback Labor party, and the Populists, which were representative of a host of independent political parties that sprang up across America. Leon Fink has calculated that in the mid-1880s alone, labor tickets or parties appeared in 189 cities and towns in 34 of 38 states or territories.[1] Yet, with the exception of the Populist movement, these third-party insurgencies have attracted relatively little attention from historians. Workingmen's political parties in the antebellum period, especially the Jacksonian era, have received considerably more attention, with the focus usually on radicalism in a major eastern metropolis seriously affected by the early industrial revolution.[2] Herbert Gutman's seminal work concentrated primarily on working-class culture and social conflict in townships in Gilded Age America and less on the role that workers and small producers played in forging political parties or working within the two-party system.[3] To the extent that dissenting third-party movements have been studied, the focus has tended to be on the Great Upheaval of the mid-1880s and the Populists in the 1890s with comparatively little notice paid to the ideological and organizational antecedents of these movements.[4]

Many studies have shown that in the antebellum period, a democratic–republican tradition dating back to the American Revolution shaped the rhetoric and contours of political debate. In the words of Paul Faler "the American Revolution . . . provided a rich stock of metaphor, language and parallel experiences that all Americans reared in the folklore of the Revolution could easily use and understand."[5] Increasingly, works on the politics of the Gilded Age, especially studies of radical ideology and politics, have shown that the democratic–republican tradition continued to be the central framework of political expression and debate. Yet defining the democratic–republican ideology, and how it evolved, has been the subject of considerable controversy. Eric Foner and Sean Wilentz, in particular, have stressed the elasticity of the democratic–republican concept and how people of very different ideological tendencies invoked it.[6] Its use and evolution in late-nineteenth-century Humboldt County can best be understood in the context of ongoing social and political developments. Nevertheless, it is worthwhile to offer a broad definition of the democratic–republican ideology at the outset, for its radical strains are critical to an understanding of the politics of dissent in Gilded Age Humboldt County. To be sure, the elasticity of the democratic–republican heritage helped mitigate class conflict, as well as being a source of factionalism. But it provided the lens through which Humboldters perceived developments at all levels.

In spite of its remoteness, Humboldt County was not an "island community."[7] Pioneers brought with them an essentially national political culture that drew heavily on the democratic–republican legacy. The bitter sectional conflicts of the 1850s and the Civil War were dominant issues in county politics and helped invigorate and sustain the democratic–republican tradition. In the acrimonious political debates of this era, Unionists repeatedly invoked a central tenet of the democratic–republican ideology: the doctrine of "free labor." Unionists characterized the sectional struggle as one between the noble free laborer of the North and an autocratic "slaveocracy" that had no respect for the rights of labor and the democratic liberties bequeathed to the nation by the Founding Fathers. Speaking to his congregation in December 1863, the Reverend J. S. McDonald of Arcata described the Civil War as a conflict by "honest laborers, who lived by their toil," . . . "about the rights of the laborer" against the South, which "hates to give wages."[8] Humboldt County pioneer, James Beith, was a leading figure in the local Democratic party. In 1856, he had voted for James Buchanan "as the only conservative man in the field."[9] Although critical of the abolitionists and the more extreme Republicans, Beith, like many Humboldt Democrats, rallied to the Union cause as the sectional crisis deepened. In his diary he dwelt on the need to preserve the republic's liberties and on the incongruity of a democratic republic that tolerated a system of slavery. In an apocalyptic mood on the eve of the Civil War, he wrote: "Will the human passion reign and trample under foot all the beautiful furniture of the Temple of Liberty collected with so much assiduity and care by the Founders of the Republic. . . . Will the growth of a century be cut down in an hour? No, I cannot believe it." [10]

The *Humboldt Times*, which was pro-Democratic until shortly before the outbreak of the Civil War, ran editorials, correspondence, and poems eulogizing the "dignity of labor." In February 1858, the *Times* reported that the Reverend D'Estimauville's speech on this subject had received frequent applause.[11] Later the same year, the *Times* expressed outrage at James Henry Hammond's proslavery "mud-sill" speech alleging that free laborers in the North were little more than "white slaves." "The free laborers constitute the real democracy of this county," insisted the *Times*, and whatever might be the case in Hammond's native South Carolina, California was "a State which owes everything to the hardy sons of toil."[12] In January 1860, the *Times* opened the new decade with a rousing front-page homily to the "Workingmen":

> The noblest men I know on earth
> Are men whose hands are brown with toil.
> Who backed by no ancestral graces
> Hew down the woods and till the soil
> And win thereby a prouder fame
> Than follow king or warrior's name.[13]

Embodied in the free-labor ideology was an abiding faith that under a government founded and maintained on true democratic–republican principles, the workingman could rapidly ascend the social ladder. A *Times* editorial entitled the "Poor Man's Country" boasted that "if there is one thing in our government which more than commends it to the people it is the fact that the gate of honor is open to the poor and rich alike."[14] A vital corollary to the ideology of free labor was the labor theory of value. A worker was entitled to the full product of his labor; any government that countenanced a system that denied him this was guilty of supporting "class legislation" and fostering the interests of "monopolies" at the expense of the honest toiler. Although the labor theory of value was critical to the ideology of dissent, it was also a fuzzy concept that could be used to legitimate theories of competitive individualism, corporatism, and, by the 1880s, a proto-socialism embracing the notion of a fundamental antagonism between laborers and capitalists. There was ambiguity as to who constituted the "producing classes" and who was entitled to what proportion of the value of their labor. Despite this lack of clarity, dissenters insisted that government had a duty to safeguard a range of social, political, and economic institutions that would guarantee "equal rights" to all and thus enable people to enjoy the full rewards of their labor. As Beith put it, the ultimate question for all government should be "how to promote best the true social equality." [15] Here again, ambiguity arose: What did "equal rights" and "social equality" actually mean? In general, the equal rights creed did not support the desirability or feasibility of social equality. Instead, it entailed a belief that the political system should provide a structure in which all free laborers had an equal opportunity to succeed—an ideology of "equal libertarianism," as one historian aptly described it.[16] Governed by such principles, a society would exist where, in Beith's words, "none are very rich, none very poor." [17]

The extent to which Humboldters took pride in their republican heritage cannot be exaggerated. At Independence Day celebrations in 1861, one orator spoke of the "immortal Declaration" as the "first formal manifesto of those social and civil institutions which are our birthright inheritance—the first herald of that sublime mission of human society about to be inaugurated on the Western Hemisphere—embodying the universal wrongs of the oppressed, and proclaiming the common rights of all mankind." [18] Twenty years later, Beith, who had joined the ranks of the dissenters, described the Fourth of July as an occasion "which still bids defiance to autocracy" and celebrated the "self-denying virtues of their ancestors who . . . gained the priceless heritage of freedom to bestow it to posterity." He referred to the birth of the American nation as "the establishment of an Empire such as the world has never seen." [19]

Until the end of the Civil War, politics in Humboldt County was dominated by national issues. County conventions and the platforms of the major political parties hardly addressed local issues, and there is little evidence of divisiveness over them. The protracted sectional crisis probably helped subsume tensions, but there were other reasons for the consensus in local politics. Humboldt's pioneers were united by a desire to promote their community to outsiders. Highly conscious of their geographical isolation, they realized the need to attract outside capital and a larger population if the county was to become a viable economic entity. Accordingly, there was a widespread recognition of the need to use county revenues to lay the foundation of a basic economic infrastructure. At the same time, the possibility of discord over appropriations and expenditures was limited by their small scale. In addition, the transience of many early pioneers lessened the chances of a polarization over local issues.

Disillusion and Dissent

In the late 1860s, with the sectional conflict no longer the preeminent issue and the county population growing and becoming more settled, important questions arose concerning county revenues that brought the consensus to an abrupt end. An increasing number of citizens began to feel that the county was going too deeply into debt to fund internal improvements and that the burden of taxation was falling disproportionately on small farmers and workers. A proposal to build a 100-mile road to link Humboldt County with the state road system raised a storm of protest. At a special meeting called in December 1867, dissenters voiced their objections to the $50,000 bond issue to finance the scheme. Leaders at the meeting appointed a Committee of Fifteen to investigate how much money exactly had been raised and spent on road improvements. A letter from "W. J. Sweasey and others" charged the Board of Supervisors with extravagance and incompetence.[20] H. L. Knight, the future secretary of the California Workingmen's party, wrote a series of satirical letters to the *Humboldt Times*, accusing local government officials and special-interest groups of corruption.[21] In 1868, the road bond issue lost by 1,038 to 134 votes.[22]

The county's debt and local tax rates continued to be issues of bitter contention. By 1870, there was strong disagreement as to the extent of the county's indebtedness, since most expenditures had been financed by county warrants, which no longer sold at anything like their par value. The *Humboldt Times* insisted that the warrants should be repaid at par value and that the real amount of the county's debt was only $7,000 and not $24,000, as some alleged.[23] In 1871, a plan to build a railroad from Eureka to the Eel River Valley, entailing a bond issue of $100,000, encountered the same fierce opposition that the road bond had faced. One correspondent, "White Alder," argued that only a small proportion of the county's residents would benefit from the railroad and warned voters to be on their guard "against the rapacious maws of an ever devouring monopoly."[24] The *Times* reluctantly acknowledged the strength of public opposition, and in October the bond issue was defeated by 899 to 143 votes.[25]

The Republican party in Humboldt County retained its ascendancy over the Democrats in the immediate postbellum years, but its image was tainted and its support eroded by a series of charges of corruption. A succession of letters in the *Northern Independent*, from "Taxpayer," alleged that the Republican candidate for the state assembly, J. De Haven, paid almost no local taxes and that the local taxes paid by everyone on the 1869 county Republican ticket amounted to "a mere pittance." [26] At the same time, Knight charged that the vote at the Republican party convention had been blatantly manipulated to secure the renomination of Humboldt County sheriff, W. S. Barnum. He also noted that county records revealed that in the past year Barnum had collected poll taxes from only a third of the county's voters and that Barnum himself had paid no local taxes in spite of his handsome county salary.[27] Barnum's rebuttal to these accusations was not convincing, and several indignant letters from "Union voters" criticized the Republican party leadership for not repudiating Barnum. The *Humboldt Times*, which had staunchly supported the Republican party since the Civil War, did not dispute the charges and endorsed several "independent" candidates in the 1869 elections. At the election, the Republican party's large majority was severely pruned, and Sheriff Barnum was not reelected.

Increasingly, issues of taxation, public indebtedness, corruption, and political cliques became linked in the minds of many Humboldt County residents, a perception that was reinforced by their view of developments in state and national politics. To a growing number of people it seemed that, whether the symptom was a corrupt local sheriff or a national Credit Mobilier railroad scandal, a serious malaise had begun to afflict the American body politic. Numerous instances of actual or alleged corruption at all levels of government in the late 1860s and early 1870s shook people's faith in their political institutions. In Humboldt County, the Republican party had emerged from the Civil War with a large reservoir of moral and political credit that enabled it to buck the trend toward the Democratic party that occurred throughout most of California. But by the early 1870s, many Humboldters felt that the Republicans had exhausted their credit.

In 1871, Louis Tower, who had been an ardent supporter of the Republican party in the 1860s, eloquently expressed the growing sense of foreboding and disenchantment of many Humboldters in a series of articles entitled the "Next Irrepressible Conflict." Tower stated that it was his duty to "call the attention of my fellow laborers—the producers of wealth—to the consideration of our interests as treated in the policies and practices of our government." He asserted that "the tendency of our legislatures both national and state . . . is drifting in favor of capital" and mentioned specifically the growing wealth and power of corporations and railroads; the pervasiveness of corruption in politics; and the "absorption" of the public domain "into the hands of capitalists through Congressional action," which threatened the free laborer with "the fate that has befallen the workers of the older more densely populated countries." Tower spoke of the Republican party in its early days as representing "the rise, progress and culmination of the principle that labor should be free and that the soil, the great bank of labor exchange, should be free also." But, he argued, the conflict between labor and capital was now inevitable, and the "producers of wealth" should form a new party that would elect men of integrity.[28]

The *Humboldt Times* sensed the growing disaffection and entreated the "laboring classes" to retain their loyalty to the Republican party. The newspaper reminded readers that the Democratic party had supported slavery, "the very bane of free labor," had opposed the income tax, and had failed to provide public education in many states; the Republican party, in contrast, had abolished slavery, had thrown open the public lands to settlement, and had established a public educational system in many states.[29] Despite such pleas, disillusionment with the Republicans in Humboldt County mounted. In 1873, when Henry McGowan announced his candidacy for the state assembly as an independent, he expressed many of the same sentiments as Tower. He praised the Republicans for seeing the nation through the ordeal of the Civil War, but, he said, the party "has unfortunately allowed itself to be led by corrupt and designing men into a state of political depravity." In referring to the "great leper spots" that besmirched the party's image, McGowan spoke of "Land and Railroad monopolies, Credit Mobiliers, Back Pay Stealings, and other eruptions of a similar nature."[30]

On August 2, 1873, at a mass meeting at Ryan's Hall in Eureka, a Tax-Payer party was formed. The party's formation paralleled, but apparently had no direct links, with a Tax-Payer Independent party that was beginning to pick up momentum in California under Newton Booth.[31] Booth, the Republican governor of California, had been elected in 1871 with the strong support of the Grange, running on a platform stressing opposition to railroad subsidies. In Humboldt County, many of the leading figures in the new party were former Republicans. The most notable among them was W. J. Sweasey, who had been chairman of the county's Republican party since the Civil War. Sweasey was elected president of the new party, and a full slate of candidates was chosen for the upcoming elections. First among a long list of party resolutions was an expression of strong opposition to "giving lands or money or loaning the National credit to corporations or other persons, for the purposes of creating dangerous monopolies to oppress the people." Another resolution denounced corruption "whether by means of 'Credit Mobilier Frauds' in the East" or "Contract and Finance Companies in California." The Tax-Payer party declared its support for "equality of taxation, so that the burden of maintaining the government shall be borne by the rich in proportion to their wealth." Finally, it endorsed a measure to regulate "the carrying business of the country" by controlling railroad freight rates.[32]

The ensuing campaign was one of the most heated in the county's history. The Tax-Payer party had problems from the outset. The Republican platform, although not quite as populist in tone, was almost indistinguishable from the Tax-Payer program in its planks on taxation, corruption, and monopoly. Several Republican candidates openly acknowledged that corruption and monopoly were serious issues. The Tax-Payer party also had to face the opposition of the county press and repeated allegations that party members were a group of "sore heads and broken down political hacks" who had been shunned by the Republican party, notwithstanding the fact that the Tax-Payer party held its convention before the Republicans.[33]

The Republicans fretted, in particular, about the allegiance of Humboldt's farmers. In 1872 and 1873, there were growing manifestations of their discontent. Farmers in various locales throughout the county began forming Farmers' Protective Unions in 1872 "for the purposes of reflecting the best interests of the farming community of the county and deriving some plan of action for mutual benefit."[34] In 1873, the Humboldt County farmers affiliated with the California Grange.[35] While the Humboldt Grange did not make political endorsements, there can be no doubt that the organization reflected deep-seated discontents. Farmers complained repeatedly to the county press about low prices, and the *Humboldt Times* reported that for "several years" local farmers "have received but indifferent rewards for their labor" and that "in some instances it has taken nearly all . . . to pay commission and expenses of transportation."[36]

The overall performance of the Tax-Payer party was impressive. It succeeded in electing its candidate to the state assembly and lost most of the county contests by narrow margins. The extent of the county farmers' disaffection showed in the strong support the Tax-Payer party received in most rural precincts, equivalent to its showings in Eureka and Arcata.[37] The 1873 election was the first electoral expression of a rising tide of dissent in Humboldt County. Rumblings of discontent had been growing louder since the Civil War and were finally crystallizing into a coherent political movement. Several leading political figures in Humboldt County permanently severed their connections with the Republican and, to a lesser extent, Democratic parties. Sweasey emerged as the leading dissident in the county—a position he occupied for the next decade and that culminated in his nomination for the lieutenant governorship of California on the Greenback Labor party ticket in 1882.

No one else in the county expressed with such lucidity and forcefulness the profound sense of disillusionment felt by many people.

Sweasey was born in London, England, in 1805. At age twenty-one, he captained a sea vessel engaged in trade with the West Indies. In 1837, he left "'perfidious Albion' to set out for the land of the free," and, shortly after arriving in America, he and his family joined Robert Owen's communitarian settlement in New Harmony, Indiana. For several years he was a "near neighbor" and employee of Owen, whom he described as "an old and valued friend." In the 1840s, Sweasey became involved with the Young America movement before taking the overland route to California in 1850. Soon after his arrival, he became a champion of settlers' rights in their battle with the Spanish land-grant holders. He became known as the "Squatter King," and he lived on a ranch near Redwood City until he was evicted. He joined the Democratic party and in 1853 was elected to the California Assembly as a representative from San Francisco. In 1855 he moved to Hydesville, in southern Humboldt County, where he engaged in dairy farming. Within a year, he was chairman of the Humboldt County Democratic party, but shortly after the election of James Buchanan in 1856, he left the party. He helped found the county's Republican party and was its chairman from its inception until 1872.

Sweasey moved with his family to Eureka in 1862 and he established a successful general store there.[38] By 1867, in spite of his prominent position in the county's Republican party, Sweasey had become highly critical of the Republican-dominated county administration. Just before the 1873 elections, he severed his ties with the party. He wrote frequent letters to the local press voicing his profound concern at the direction in which he believed America was heading, the most eloquent of which appeared a few months after the 1873 election:

Look at the corruption and venality exposed in our late national councils. Look at the profligate disposal of our public domain, the noblest inheritance ever bequeathed to a people. Look at our swindling financial system, made and perpetuated to make the rich richer and the poor poorer. Look at the mass of misery and crime in our great cities; near 1,500 homicides in the city of New York alone in one year; thousands thrown houseless, breadless on the street. Why? Are they idle, unwilling to work? Has nature refused her support? Neither. Our harvests were never more bountiful. . . . A century ago honesty and ability guided our national councils. Today can we say so? A few years more of this misrule of the weak minded and where will be the superiority of the condition of our people over the condition of the people of the monarchial governments of Europe? Already our taxes are greater than the taxes of any other people or nation. Our lands are held in quantities larger than German principalities; not by aristocracies of birth, but by aristocracies of wealth, by corporations who have no souls, who never die, who control the weak minded men, who fill our legislative halls, both National and State, while thousands upon thousands are suffering for food, shelter and the commonest necessaries of life.[39]

The depression of the late 1870s reinforced the fears of men like Sweasey and led to a revival of organized dissenting political activity. The dissidents were struck both by the social and political turmoil at the state and national levels and by unprecedented social and economic dislocations in their own community. The destitution caused by the depression hit Humboldt County as early as January 1877. The *Humboldt Times* complained about the "insufferable nuisance" caused by the "professional beggar."[40] A few weeks later, the *Times* stated that "there seems to be a regularly organized band of ruffians in this city. Scarcely a day passes but what we hear of an assault being made upon some of our citizens."[41]

The depression severely affected the Humboldt County lumber industry. The price of redwood lumber plummeted. In 1876, prices stood at an all-time high of $30 per 1,000 board feet for clear lumber; by 1879, the price had slumped to $18 per 1,000 feet.[42] Lumber workers had their wages cut from $5 to $25 a month in February 1877, a move that reportedly gave rise to "considerable complaint."[43] After the July 4 holiday that year, lumber employers closed their mills indefinitely. Hundreds of workers lost their jobs, and there were dire predictions about the repercussions on the local economy.[44] Few mills resumed operations during the remainder of 1877, and poverty and unemployment were widespread. A man who spent five fruitless weeks in Eureka looking for work reported that "every street corner could boast of at least one dozen idlers."[45] The *Humboldt Times* conceded that "several families" in Eureka lived "in very destitute circumstances" and urged the community to be charitable and hold special benefits to raise money for the deserving poor.[46] In the fall of 1877, complaints about tramps recurred in the local press, but several apparent incidents of arson caused much greater alarm.[47] The *Times* reported that a "diabolical attempt was made to burn the city" and called for a special police force to combat the incendiaries.[48]

The local press received a stream of anonymous letters that were indicative of growing social tensions. The *Democratic Standard*, which in 1877 came under the auspices of Greenback Labor party supporter William Ayres, provided a fresh outlet for expressions of discontent. In November 1877, it published a strongly worded letter from "Argonaut," insisting that a man had the right to work and warning that, while people prefer legal remedies, "men cannot be patient when they are hungry." He compared the plight of labor to a turtle "upon which the elephants of capital stand."[49] The *Humboldt Times* received an equally strongly worded communication from "Justice":

Dissensions, like contagions, seem to spread over the country. Even the little Hamlet of Arcata is not an exception. She has a few pioneers who have been fortunate enough to make a little money out of the Indians, the soldiers and the later immigrants, until they have acquired a few town lots and some tenantable housing. Not unlike the railroad kings they are the self-constituted aristocrats who claim the right to extort by law . . . all the blood money possible from the poorer classes.[50]

A widespread suspicion that public land laws were being violated aggrieved many in the county. In a letter to the *Daily Evening Signal*, "Pre-empter" stated that "much complaint is made by the settlers who were trying to file preemption claims in the county." He criticized the long delays of the county surveyor in filing plats and suggested that many people believed that it was a conspiracy to aid the "land grabbers." He inquired whether either of the candidates for the state legislature was interested in these abuses or if they were "in unison with the land grabbing fraternity and monopolists generally."[51] These charges were not without considerable foundation (see Chapter 5). Humboldt County pioneer J. C. Blake recalled that it was common practice for large landholders to circumvent the 160-acre homestead limit by paying another person a fee for filing the initial claim, with the clear understanding that the land title would soon be transferred to the sponsoring landholder.[52]

The findings of a study undertaken by the *Sacramento Daily Record* in 1873, based on data from the State Board of Equalization, revealed that the pattern of land distribution had become very skewed in many California counties, including Humboldt. Forty individuals or businesses owned over 1,000 acres in the county in 1873, and five owned more than 5,000 acres.[53] Joseph Russ, who had come to California in 1850 with a few provisions to engage in merchandising and stock raising, and who had operated a butcher shop in Eureka before becoming a lumber entrepreneur in 1870, owned 23,169 acres in Humboldt County.[54] In evaluating the impact of both land frauds and concentrations, it is important to keep in mind that the state's press gave considerable coverage to these issues and that a large proportion of Humboldt County newspaper space was taken up with extracts from the state and national press. Incidental references indicate that libraries and a significant number of individuals subscribed to a state or even an eastern newspaper, such as the *New York Times*. On the land question, the *San Francisco Chronicle* serialized the findings of the *Sacramento Daily Record* and commented that they revealed a "startling evidence of the existence of a gigantic land monopoly."[55] With undisguised sarcasm, the *Chronicle* referred to Miller and Lux's "little patch in Merced [County]."[56] The *Humboldt Times*, it should be noted, carried the statistics on landholding in Humboldt County. Letters to the county press by the late 1870s on the land question were frequent enough to suggest that sentiment on this issue contributed significantly to the discontent in Humboldt County. Certainly, indignation over land frauds, as much as any other issue, led to the birth of branches of the International Workingmen's Association (IWA) and the Knights of Labor in the mid-1880s.[57]

Land monopoly and fraud received more attention than any other issue in the debates surrounding the election of delegates to the California constitutional convention in 1878.[58] Sweasey wrote several long, impassioned letters on the subject. He asserted that unless reforms were undertaken to ensure a more equitable distribution of land, the result would be "serfdom and slavery or a bloody revolution."[59] He pointed to the turmoil in Ireland as proof of his argument and added that "what was done in Ireland by war and conquest was more successfully done in California by fraud under the pretense of law."[60] Sweasey described in great detail the fraudulent means by which much of California's land was acquired by people shortly after the Mexican-American War. He insisted that similar frauds were being used to obtain land in parts of California not covered by the Spanish land grants and alluded to one scheme to aggrandize "thirty square leagues, north of Cape Mendocino,"[61] an area 30 miles south of Eureka. In another letter, Sweasey spoke of land monopoly as the "greatest evil," and recalled the day he had witnessed 80 families being evicted from their land under the English enclosure laws to make way for a deer park.[62] At the Franklin Society Debating Club in Eureka in 1878, a schoolteacher, George Sarvis, echoed many of Sweasey's arguments. Sarvis spoke in favor of a motion to limit the amount of land an individual or corporation might own on the grounds that "the holding of large and unlimited quantities of land by one individual or an association of individuals disturbs the unalienable right of each citizen and when carried out, destroys popular government."[63]

Humboldt County farmers were not immediately hit by the depression of the late 1870s. Harvests in 1877 and 1878 were bountiful, and prices for most crops held constant, although they began to fall slightly in 1879. Nevertheless, the county's Grange did not hesitate to join other dissidents in calling for far-reaching reforms. The Grange had become a strong force in the social and political life of the county by the late 1870s. There were at least six branches of the Grange in 1877. Complete lists of branches and membership figures are unfortunately hard to obtain, but the fact that the Ferndale Grange boasted a membership of 150 in 1877 (up from 90 in 1874) suggests that the Humboldt County Grange was flourishing.[64] The Grange performed important social and economic functions. The Table Bluff Grange built its own hall,[65] and all the Granges frequently held dances and other events. The Table Bluff Grange (and perhaps others) also established cooperative retail facilities.[66] In the political realm, Humboldt Grangers stressed the need for a stable and expanded money supply based on silver and greenbacks. And, in general, they shared a gloomy prognosis of the American body politic with men like Tower, Sweasey, and Sarvis. In March 1878, the Ferndale Grange passed the following resolution:

Whereas, a people view with alarm the growing tendency (by class legislation) of a bourbon aristocracy, a system of landlordism such as exists in Germany, England and throughout Europe, and which if not checked soon will finally reduce the working classes of America to mere slaves and vassals. . . . The toiling masses of this country are today to the banks and corporations what the peons of Mexico are to the aristocracy of that so called Republic.

Resolved, that we look upon this bourbon element with suspicion and distrust in their efforts to subvert that form of government bequeathed to us by our fathers, and to erect instead a semi-despotic government, controlled by a centralized aristocracy.[67]

The Workingmen's Party

A host of grievances that had been simmering for a decade surfaced in 1877–1878 in the context of the depression and the debate over the need for a new state constitution. Complaints included the cost of state government, inequitable tax laws, corruption in government at all levels, and the political power of the railroads in California and nationwide. This conjuncture of events and discontents led to the formation of a California Workingmen's party in Humboldt and 39 other California counties.[68] Humboldt voters expressed their growing disquiet in September 1877 when a statewide referendum was held on whether to call a convention to rewrite the 1849 California Constitution. In general, Californians content with the status quo were opposed to a convention. Humboldt County voted in favor of a convention by a margin of 10 to 1 (2,552 to 258 votes);[69] voters statewide approved the measure by less than a 2 to 1 majority (73,400 to 44,200 votes).[70]

In San Francisco, another issue gained prominence at this time. Anti-Chinese sentiment reached new heights during the depression of the late 1870s, a fact that historians have viewed as the most important element in the birth of the Workingmen's party there. The Chinese population of Humboldt County increased from 38 in 1870 to 242 in 1880,[71] and by the late 1870s Eureka possessed a Chinatown of sorts.[72] The local press commented occasionally on the alleged existence of opium dens and brothels in Eureka's Chinatown, and several attacks on Chinese people, usually by Eureka youths, took place. Notwithstanding this, and the fact that in 1885 Eureka achieved the dubious distinction of being one of the first western communities to expel its Chinese population, Sinophobia was not a major issue in county politics for a number of reasons.[73] First, by 1880, the Chinese constituted only 1.5 percent of the county's population, whereas in San Francisco they made up 16.3 percent of the inhabitants and 8.7 percent of the state population. Moreover, Humboldt's Chinese population was relatively dispersed. In 1880, Eureka, with its so-called Chinatown, contained only 101 Chinese people out of a total population of 2,700. Second, while competition from Chinese labor may have aroused some animosity, few Chinese were employed in the county's two principal industries, lumber and agriculture. Most worked as miners (66), laborers (62), cooks (37), and in the laundry business (23). Only 6 of the 228 Chinese employed in the county worked in the lumber industry.[74] Thus, the Chinese in Humboldt County did not threaten white labor as directly as they did in San Francisco and other parts of California. Significantly, when lumber employers tried to make more extensive use of Chinese labor in the early 1880s, anti-Chinese sentiment rose dramatically. Undoubtedly, most Humboldters favored Chinese exclusion by the late 1870s, but a host of other grievances were far more important in the formation of the California Workingmen's party.

The Humboldt County Workingmen's party originated in May 1878 to contest elections to select delegates to the California constitutional convention. Sweasey, the party's first chairman, was the candidate for the county delegate seat. James Barton, a farmer from Ferndale, received the senatorial nomination for the 27th District. The party's convention passed a string of resolutions: Public officers convicted of bribery should be liable to a twenty-year jail sentence; taxes should be levied only "to meet the expenses of government"; and "taxation should be equal, so that the burden of maintaining government be borne by the rich in proportion to their wealth." Also, railroads should be taxed in relation to their "actual cash value," while the large land-holdings of corporations and wealthy individuals should be taxed at the same rate per acre as small landholders. All legal means should be used to halt the immigration of the Chinese "and other inferior races who cannot amalgamate with us."[75] A few days after the convention, the party founded a newspaper, the *Workingman*, which was edited by Sweasey and Barton.

The county Democratic and Republican organizations joined forces to elect delegates to the constitutional convention. County Judge C. C. Stafford applauded this cooperation, for "as matters now stand it is possible for the Communists to get control of the Convention."[76] The fusion plan aroused the ire of the Workingmen's party. The *Democratic Standard* asserted that "the managers of the two parties, under the direction of the monopolists, have joined hands . . . against the 'common enemy,' that is, the workingman."[77]

At the June 19 election, the Humboldt County Workingmen's party triumphed over the "nonpartisan" party. Both Sweasey and Barton were elected delegates to the constitutional convention. On the whole, the votes for the two men were remarkably evenly distributed over the county, with both candidates picking up approximately the same levels of support in Eureka as they did in the rural precincts. In Eureka, which accounted for a third of the county's total vote, Sweasey and Barton won 56 percent and 60 percent of the vote, respectively. Outside Eureka, Sweasey's share of the vote in all precincts combined was slightly lower (50 percent) and Barton's somewhat higher (67 percent). The consistency of the two men's performance throughout the county's 23 precincts indicates the breadth of support for the Workingmen's party.[78]

Barton proved an especially effective spokesman at the constitutional convention. He spoke with particular stridency on the issue of "land grabbing," calling for a state investigation and the repossession of fraudulently acquired lands. But he declared that he was pledged to no "agrarian measures" and that he was not at the convention "to disturb the rights of property." He advocated "equal taxation" as the best means to stop land grabbing. To this end, he introduced several resolutions calling for amendments to the state's tax system, including the adoption of a state income tax. He also spoke in favor of a retrenchment in state expenditures and a reduction in the salaries of state officials.[79]

The Humboldt Workingmen's party was pleased with the outcome of the constitutional convention and, unlike the San Francisco branch of the party, did not split on the question of ratification. Within two weeks of the convention, the party launched a vigorous campaign to ratify the new constitution, which promised strict regulation of railroads and other public utilities, a more equitable system of taxation, an eight-hour day on all public works projects, and a series of anti-Chinese provisions. The *Democratic Standard* was the only newspaper in the county to endorse ratification unequivocally. It denounced the California Democratic party for opposing ratification and accused the party of betraying "the true principles taught us by a Jefferson and a Jackson," and called on its readers to "remember General Jackson and his war upon the privileged classes."[80] In the ratification referendum on May 7, 1879, California voters endorsed the new constitution by a relatively small margin of 77,959 to 67,134 votes; but in Humboldt County the ratification majority was much more decisive, with 1,714 votes in favor and 1,051 against.[81]

The Humboldt Workingmen's party perceived the ratification as a triumph for the workingman, and the party's success encouraged the belief that the time was ripe for a basic realignment of political forces to regenerate a corrupt and decadent America. With remarkable frequency, letters to local newspapers harkened back nostalgically to the days of Jefferson and Jackson when the American republic supposedly had true Democrats at the helm. As one writer, "Jeffersonian," put it: "We are upon the eve of a reorganization of political forces. The two old parties have had their day." The Democratic party represented democracy in name only and had "drifted far from its moorings," while the Republican party was dominated by corporations and pro-Chinese sentiment. He concluded that the Workingmen's party was the only true standard-bearer of pure democratic principles.[82]

The profound concern expressed about the peril to American democracy cannot be dismissed as partisan political rhetoric. "Is this a Republic?" asked the *Democratic Standard* at the head of its editorial column immediately after the ratification election. It recounted how, just before the election, workers at one lumber mill had found a ticket under their dinner plates marked "Against the Constitution." The *Standard* commented: "When the daily laborer can be intimidated and forced to vote against his judgement what is he but a slave," and the editorial concluded that "if we are to be a republic let it be so in fact. Our sires laid down their lives to establish one. We should be prepared to maintain it, if needs be with our lives."[83] A month later, the *Standard* reported that some employers in the county had dismissed workers who had voted for the new constitution.[84] Events at the local, state, and national levels produced profound disquiet on the part of many Humboldters, who saw themselves as defending a sacred democratic–republican legacy. Not surprisingly, they invoked the figureheads, symbols, and rhetoric of a supposedly golden age.

The Humboldt Workingmen's party began taking steps in the spring of 1879 to consolidate its organization to contest the forthcoming statewide and county elections. In March 1879, a convention was held to elect delegates to a state convention of the Workingmen's party and to encourage the establishment of workingmen's clubs. By June 1879, clubs were mushrooming throughout the county.[85] In the same month, a convention nominated candidates and drew up a platform. The platform extolled the new constitution stressing, in particular, how it would reduce the burden of taxation. But it reiterated that the resolute implementation of the new constitution depended on electing "faithful friends" to all branches of government.[86]

Who were the "faithful friends" nominated by the Workingmen's party?[87] Most of the candidates were in their forties or early fifties and had come to California in the 1850s. Almost all had resided in Humboldt County for at least ten years. A majority were natives of the New England and Middle Atlantic regions and came from relatively humble origins. Very few had held public office before, and only one had done so in Humboldt County. Two farmers, both Grangers, were on the ticket; one owned a "small farm" and the other a "comfortable farm." Thomas Cutler, the candidate for sheriff, was the only merchant on the ticket. He was, allegedly, one of only two merchants in Eureka who supported the Workingmen's party "against all the threats of the San Francisco wholesale merchants and railroad carriers." Two of the men on the ticket ran livery stables. One was Pierce Ryan, the senatorial candidate for the state's 27th District; the other, John Carr, had spent most of his life as a miner and blacksmith. The nominee for county clerk was a carpenter, and the candidate for county treasurer had worked in the lumber mills for six years. Three professional people—two lawyers and a schoolteacher—rounded out the ticket. Their prospective offices of district attorney, superior court judge, and school administrator demanded at least a modicum of professional training and experience.

The Workingmen's party conducted a spirited campaign against the Republicans and Democrats in the county. Leaders of the new party berated the old-line forces for opposing ratification of the state constitution and portrayed themselves as the true standard-bearers of the American democratic tradition. J. D. H. Chamberlin, the Workingmen's party candidate for superior county judge, opened a speech at Ferndale by quoting at length from the Declaration of Independence.[88] The *Democratic Standard* warned that there were "vital principles involved in the election of the most unimportant officer. . . . The tory spirit has revived after 100 years of rest and today opposes the honest yeomanry of our country with all the oppressive bitterness that persecuted the heroes of American freedom."[89] On the evening before election day, the Workingmen's party staged a torchlight parade in Eureka that drew supporters from all over the county. The *Standard* described the procession as "composed entirely of farmers, laborers and mechanics."[90]

Although the Workingmen's party did not achieve the sweeping success it had in electing delegates to the constitutional convention, its performance was impressive. Every candidate for statewide office on the Workingmen's ticket got a majority of the vote in Humboldt County. Party candidates for the state senate and legislature were elected, and the party won half the county's executive positions, losing the remainder by only a few votes to the fusionist opposition. Precinct returns again indicated that the Workingmen's party received consistent support throughout the county, performing best in the burgeoning agricultural townships of Ferndale and Table Bluff. In most other rural precincts the party performed no better, and sometimes worse, than in Eureka, where the party fell only a few votes short of a majority in almost all county and state contests. Statewide, the Workingmen elected the chief justice of the state supreme court, 5 of 6 associate justices, and 16 assemblymen and 11 state senators. This result was not unimpressive, but it failed to give the party a majority in the state legislature and was somewhat disappointing in view of its strong showing in the 1878 constitutional convention elections.

The ineffectual performance of many party representatives at state and local levels and persistent factionalism in the San Francisco branch led to a rapid decline of the party after the 1879 state elections. The gathering political momentum of the National Greenback Labor party encouraged some members of the Workingmen's party, including Denis Kearney, leader of the San Francisco branch, to join the Greenbacks. In addition, the success of the Workingmen's party encouraged California's Republican and Democratic parties (especially the latter) to become more responsive to the demands of the Workingmen's party on such issues as Chinese exclusion, land monopoly, and stricter regulation of railroads. Many Workingmen's representatives aligned with one of the two major parties, usually the Democrats, in a process that Alexander Saxton has dubbed "the institutionalization of labor politics."[91]

The Workingmen's party's decline in Humboldt County reflected the demise of the party statewide. Its supporters were discouraged by the overall performance of the party in the 1879 state elections and in municipal elections in Humboldt and other counties in early 1880. Throughout the 1879 campaign, party leaders stressed that the new constitution was a dead letter unless the party obtained a majority in the state legislature. Thus, the Humboldt County Workingmen's party virtually turned the election into a referendum on the future of the party. Immediately after the election, the *Democratic Standard* declared that the new constitution had been "practically nullified." It lamented the well-publicized factionalism of the San Francisco branch and the fact that a considerable number of Workingmen's party representatives were moving into the old parties.[92] Humboldters who retained their faith in the new party after the elections soon became disillusioned with the performance of some representatives. In April 1880, the *Standard* reported "much talk of dissatisfaction among the workingmen of Eureka about the policy which some of the county officers elected on the Workingmen's ticket have chosen to pursue."[93] George Shaw, who had been elected county assessor on the party ticket, incurred the wrath of many people when he added an office clerk to his staff at a salary of $135 per month and selected a long-time enemy of the Workingmen's party as his main adviser.[94] By April 1880, Shaw was so unpopular that he required a bodyguard.[95] Disillusionment with the Workingmen's party can be gauged from the following communication of one disgruntled Humboldter:

Mr Editor, I am mad, desperately mad. . . . In the first place we adopted the New Constitution. Of course I expected it would be the means of lightening our burden of taxation by lopping off the County Court, reducing expenses in Grand Jury matters, reducing the length of the sessions of the Legislature, etc. I should not have voted for that instrument had I not believed that it would help us. . . . O, how gloriously we have been bilked. But it is the fault of the people themselves, by electing men to the Legislature and the Board of Supervisors, who were hostile to the New Constitution.[96]

Growing interest in the Greenback Labor party hastened the dissolution of the Humboldt County Workingmen's party. Greenback clubs sprang up throughout the county between 1878 and 1880. In fact, remnants of the Workingmen's party reconstituted themselves as the Humboldt Greenback Labor party. The Greenbackers' panaceas had a much stronger appeal in Humboldt County than they did in San Francisco and many other California counties.

By the late 1870s, a coherent dissenting tradition had emerged in Humboldt County. The evolution of this tradition owed much to the persistence of values associated with an antebellum democratic–republican ideology that stressed the superiority of the American political system. Chauvinistic and almost millennial assumptions engendered a profound set of beliefs and expectations about the nature of the American political economy. In particular, the free-labor tenet and its corollary, the labor theory of value, stressing as they did the immense contribution of the free laborer to America's progress, heightened expectations about the future, reinforced the workingman's sense of his moral worth, and endowed him with a civic responsibility to scrutinize the destiny of the republic. Between 1866 and 1880, developments at the local, state, and national levels convinced many Humboldters that pernicious economic and political events threatened the sanctity and purity of America and seriously threatened the free laborers' advancement.

Undeniably, contradictions and ambiguities existed in the democratic–republican legacy. Two contradictions, in particular, are worth noting. Both derived from a marked discrepancy between the dissenters' penetrating political analysis and their often superficial prescriptions. For example, on the crucial question of land monopoly, Sweasey took a radical stance in advocating a statutory limitation on the amount of land a person might own. Barton and the Ferndale Grange, for all their deeply felt anxieties about the concentration of land ownership and land fraud, could not countenance so direct an interference with the rights of private property.[97] Paradoxically, many dissenters railed against what they perceived as the dangers of unfettered capitalism but could not bring themselves to advocate far-reaching controls (with the possible exception of the railroad regulation) over private property rights. This disparity between a keen perception of fundamental problems and a naive faith in piecemeal solutions that ignored underlying structural problems stands out in the dissenters' faith that all could be rectified if only good, honest men were elected. Even a man as disenchanted as Sweasey could in one breath speak of dangerous social and economic trends and the threat they posed to the republic and in the next proclaim his belief in the ability of the "best men" to rectify the situation.

Notwithstanding its ambiguous features, the democratic–republican tradition provided Humboldt's dissenters with an arsenal of ideas. Increasingly, they would jettison many (but not all) of the contradictory strands of the tradition and embrace reforms that entailed at least a measure of state control over private property. The Humboldt Workingmen's party bequeathed to the county a dissenting ideological legacy that the Greenback Labor party, the International Workingmen's Association, and the Knights of Labor were to draw on in the 1880s, and the Humboldt Populists relied on heavily in the 1890s. Many leaders of the Humboldt Workingmen's party played important roles in these movements. In 1886, the *Arcata Union* commented with alarm and derision on the growing strength of the People's party, the political arm of the Humboldt Knights of Labor, describing its leadership as "in the main the same old political fossils . . . that have monopolized every reform movement from the days of Kearney."[98]

Chapter 3

The Greenbackers

A National Political Culture

The political culture of Humboldt County was to a surprising degree
national in its orientation. Local and state issues concerned Humboldters of course, but they were keenly and increasingly aware of
national developments. The cosmopolitan origins of the early settlers
was undoubtedly a factor, and as Michael Katz and his associates have
argued, "High rates of transiency may have worked against a local
sense of community but nationally had the opposite effect—it created
a sense of national identification."[1] In addition, a shared democratic–
republican heritage reinforced by sectional crisis and the Civil War
heightened Humboldters' sense of their national identity. Moreover, as
Robert Sharkey has observed, the 1860s was a decade of nationaliza-
tion in many phases of economic life.[2] The national banking system,
the income tax and conscription (for part of the Civil War), a high protective tariff, the Homestead Act, and various land-grant acts became
law.

In no area of public policy did the scope of federal government
activity and power increase more than in the sphere of national monetary policy. Certainly the banking system had been a contentious issue from the founding of the nation. But the financial exigencies of
the Civil War, the printing of almost $500 million greenbacks, and a
vast increase in the national debt embroiled the federal government
in monetary policy on an unprecedented scale.[3] Decisions about how
to fund the national debt and how much to expand or contract the
money supply had direct and far-reaching impacts on people's lives.
Furthermore, as Sharkey, Irwin Unger, and David Montgomery have
demonstrated, these were not issues that concerned only the moguls
of finance. People from all classes perceived an intimate relationship

between their economic well-being, that of the nation, and national monetary policy. During 1866 and 1867, currency reform became an issue of paramount interest to the American labor movement. In 1868, William Sylvis, president of the National Labor Union, proclaimed that "when a just monetary system has been established there will no longer exist a necessity for Trade Unions."[4] Sharkey, Unger, and Montgomery, while suggesting the importance of the monetary question at the community level, arrive at this conclusion largely by inference. Most of their evidence comes from statements by national politicians, businessmen, currency theorists, and labor leaders.[5]

The saga of the Humboldt County Greenback Labor party indicates the extent to which disquiet over national monetary policy percolated down to the local level. By 1880, the panaceas of Greenback theorists found a receptive audience in Humboldt County partly because they entailed a comprehensive critique of the American economy and the nation's ailments since the Civil War, and partly because the county was hit by the severest agricultural depression of the Gilded Age. The prescriptions of the Greenback Labor party suffused Humboldt County's dissident political culture with an even more cosmopolitan perspective, one that envisaged a greater role for the state.

The Dissenters Regroup

Two Greenback clubs were founded in 1878, at Rohnerville and Iaqua in rural southern Humboldt County,[6] but this was the only manifestation of support for the Greenback movement before 1880. In the early summer of 1880, the *Democratic Standard*, which had been giving increasing publicity to the Greenback Labor party, urged reform-minded citizens to establish Greenback clubs. By late summer, hardly a township in the county did not have a club.[7] On July 17, 1880, the remaining members of the Humboldt Workingmen's party assembled at the Eureka Greenback Club to dissolve their organization, one hour before the founding convention of the Humboldt County Greenback Labor party. Many leading lights of the defunct Workingmen's party were elected to high offices in the new party: W. J. Sweasey was elected vice-president; J. N. Barton became head of the committee on resolutions. The convention endorsed both the ticket and platform of the national Greenback Labor party. M. E. Morse delivered a rousing keynote speech in which he asserted that "the robbers and traitors, made robbers and traitors by the vicious system of land monopoly, usury and financial jugglery borrowed from the old world, have disinherited, defrauded and pauperized the wealth producers, the toiling hard working millions, of our country."[8]

The years 1879 and 1880 proved especially hard for Humboldt County farmers. In the summer of 1879, unseasonably heavy rainfall destroyed most of the potato crop, reducing production from 19,608 tons in the year ending July 1, 1879, to 4,714 tons in 1880 and to only 2,907 tons by 1882.[9] An unusually cold winter in 1879–1880 inflicted heavy losses on the county's sheep farmers.[10] Wool production declined from 696,844 pounds in 1879 to 352,980 pounds in 1880 and to only 400 pounds the following year.[11] In the summer of 1880, a plague of grasshoppers devastated fields and orchards in many parts of the county.[12] Falling prices compounded the farmers' woes and led to a decline in the production of cereal crops. From 1880 to 1882, annual wheat production declined from 86,600 bushels to 39,079; the production of barley went from 55,418 to 11,593 bushels; and the number of cattle raised fell from 27,815 to 19,393.[13] William Ayres embarked on a tour through the county in the fall of 1879. He reported that in southern Humboldt County, in the fertile Eel River Valley, "the cry of hard times is universal."[14] Writing from the region, "Win Too" reported that "migration and depopulation is one of our most sad occurrences. I observe some of our most striving and industrious people passing by, going to seek homes and fortunes in northern counties."[15] In September 1881, the *Humboldt Times* noted the drastic decline of cereal farming in the county.[16] The *Times*, however, was unsympathetic. It blamed farmers for relying too much on the potato crop "and a few head of scrawny cattle" and added that "it is just this type of man who is attracted by the panaceas of the workingmen's party or the greenback party."[17]

One such farmer was Charles Ferdinand Keller, who in the early 1880s was to succeed Sweasey as the county's leading dissident and sow the seeds of a trade union movement. Keller, who was born in Germany in 1846, emigrated with his parents to Pennsylvania, and over the strong opposition of his father, enlisted in the Union army in 1864. He came to California in 1867 and attempted to establish a brewery in San Bernardino. Then he took up a land claim with some other settlers in the vicinity of San Buena Ventura. The land, however, was part of a disputed Spanish land grant, and after two years of expensive legal battles, Keller and his cohorts were evicted.[18] In the mid-1870s, Keller moved to Centerville, 15 miles south of Eureka, filed a homestead claim, and commenced farming. In May 1880, he began writing a series of impassioned and embittered letters to the *Democratic Standard*:

Men are no longer equal. There is an aristocracy exempt from taxation that feeds upon the vitals of the nation. . . . They have the money hence they control the labor; for if you shut off the supply of money labor cannot exist. This being the case they have the power to declare what a day's or month's labor shall be worth. . . . Labor is subservient to capital. We have lost our individuality, and are a nonentity as regards the affairs of the nation.[19]

Keller's polemic provides an important clue as to why the nation's monetary system and the size of the money supply were issues of profound concern to Gilded Age radicals. The answer lies in the perceived connection between the democratic–republican tradition, the labor theory of value, and the money supply. To the dissenters, money represented the *exchange value* of different commodities. If the value of people's labor was to be rewarded properly, there had to be a sufficient quantity of money in circulation to reflect the labor value of the producing classes. In the view of many Gilded Age radicals, for at least a decade before the Populists appeared on the scene, the money supply simply did not represent the collective value of the labor of the producing classes. Moreover, contraction, or lack of expansion, of the money supply hurt the producing classes and benefited the nonproducing, moneylending class. As the nation's money supply decreased, the value of the dollar rose; as a result, the value of loans and the interest on them became increasingly burdensome on the producing classes, who were dependent on the loans.[20] In an editorial, the *Democratic Standard* expressed this view succinctly. It characterized the Greenback Labor party as the party "opposed to a bondocracy" and asserted that "it is the game of bankers to reduce the money circulation per capita to so small a figure that the laborer is virtually a slave in their hands."[21]

The Humboldt County Greenbackers insisted that the people, and indeed Congress, had no control over the nation's money supply. The Eureka Greenback Club, meeting in March 1881 in the context of congressional debates to consider the terms on which the national debt was to be refunded, declared that "the actions of the banks prove . . . that the power to control, to expand or contract the currency of the nation must not be delegated to any corporation, but must be restored to the national Government where it belongs."[22] William Ayres summarized the Greenbacker position in a lengthy article in which he stated that "we Greenbackers believe in a trinity of money, gold, silver and paper, all interchangeable, and that each should have equality . . . that all should be issued direct from the government" and that "a careful limitation shall be placed by constitutional amendment . . . determined by a careful analysis of the needs and requirements of commerce and exhange, and a faithful comparison of this volume of the money medium now in use by the most successful and prosperous commercial nations of the world." Ayres said that the amount of money in circulation in America was much smaller per capita than in Europe, and he produced a battery of statistics purporting to prove it. He concluded that "by having a sufficient amount of money issued by the government gauged per capita to fully accommodate the business of the country, and not subject to the control and contraction of 2,300 banking corporations . . . we should to a great extent destroy the robbery of the industrial classes that has been going on for so long."[23]

In early September 1880, the newly formed Humboldt Greenback Labor party met to adopt a platform and nominate a ticket for the upcoming elections. With the notable exception of the Eureka delegation, the majority of Greenback delegates were farmers.[24] The party nominated Campbell Berry as their candidate for Congress in the 3rd District. Berry was a native of Jackson County, Alabama, who had migrated to California and had become a farmer in Sutter County.[25] He was the Democratic party incumbent, and received the nomination of the Humboldt Democratic party as well. Nevertheless, the Greenbackers were convinced that he was loyal to their principles. Chosen as candidate for the state assembly was Gilman Mudgett, who had held offices in several states before coming to California. He had been a "messmate" of General Weaver during the Civil War and an "independent" since 1870.[26]

The *Humboldt Times*, alarmed by the challenge of the Greenbackers, lamented that "many former Republicans . . . have got off the old track, and . . . have accepted the fallacious doctrines of the Greenback party."[27] The *Times* published a series of articles entitled "The ABC of Finance." But the principal weapon employed by the *Times* to discredit the Greenbackers was ridicule. The Greenback program was derided as the work of hopelessly naive and utopian cranks "demanding an unlimited and ceaseless flow of paper 'money,' whose only value is the color of the ink in which the word 'dollar' is printed."[28] The *Times* also tried to convince Greenback voters that Berry and Mudgett were working in the interests of the Democratic party and had no real commitment to Greenback principles. Yet reports in most of the county press, both pro- and anti-Greenback, indicate that Berry's position was totally consistent with the Greenback platform throughout the campaign.

The Humboldt County Greenback Labor party performed impressively at the 1880 elections. Humboldt voters gave James Weaver, the Greenback Labor presidential candidate, 25 percent of the vote (725 of 2,880 votes cast); Democrat Winfield Hancock also received 25 percent of the vote, and Republican James Garfield garnered a 50 percent share. The vote for Weaver in Humboldt County contrasted with the mere 2.1 percent of the vote he received in California and the 3.3 percent he obtained nationally. It is more difficult to gauge the strength of the Greenback vote in Humboldt County from the other results because the Democrats also endorsed Berry and did not nominate anyone for the state assembly seat. Mudgett beat his Republican opponent for that seat, however. Berry was narrowly outvoted by his Republican rival in Humboldt County, but secured enough votes from other counties to be reelected. Precinct returns reveal that the Greenback Labor party replicated the performance of the Humboldt County Workingmen's party in 1878 and 1879.[29] Weaver performed best in the agricultural townships of Ferndale and Table Bluff; although he did not do as well in Eureka, he still secured a creditable 26.3 percent of the vote in the county's metropolis. This was a higher proportion of the vote than he obtained in well over half the rural precincts. The Greenback Labor party, like the Workingmen's party, made its poorest showing in small rural precincts in the most remote sections of the county. The solidity of Greenback support in Eureka and its comparative weakness in many rural precincts indicate that it would be wrong to describe the party as simply one of disgruntled Humboldt farmers.

Factionalism and Political Opportunism

The Greenback Labor party was the focal point of oppositional political activity in Humboldt County for the next two years. By the 1882 election, however, support for the party had waned considerably. The Greenback candidate for governor of California, Thomas J. McQuiddy, received only 10 percent of the vote, although this compared favorably with the meager 3 percent he got statewide. Even Humboldt County's favorite son, W. J. Sweasey, running as the Greenback candidate for lieutenant governor, obtained only 14 percent of the vote in Humboldt County. Thomas Devlin, the Greenback candidate for the state assembly, received a respectable 20 percent of the vote. But the Greenback candidates for most county offices fared poorly, rarely getting more than 15 percent of the vote.[30] Richard Sweasey (W. J. Sweasey's son) and Stanford Turner were the Greenbackers' only successful candidates in county contests. After the 1882 elections, the Humboldt County Greenback Labor party expired as an effective political organization and resorted to endorsing the nominations of the "best men," who were usually Democrats.

In 1882, the county's agricultural economy was still in a severe depression, and so it is hard to attribute the decline of the Humboldt Greenback Labor party to any amelioration in the farmers' condition. A complex array of factors, largely unrelated to the economy, account for its demise. The close relationship between the fate of Greenbackers at the local, state, and national levels cannot be overestimated. Any momentum that the Humboldt Greenbackers might have gained from their creditable performances in the 1880 election was offset by the party's poor performance at the state and national levels. Dedicated grass-roots support could not sustain indefinitely a local party that addressed itself primarily to national issues. The local press gloated over the weak showing of the Greenback Labor party nationally after 1880. Thus, following Weaver's poor performance in his home state of Iowa in the 1881 election, the *Humboldt Times* commented that "the fiat craze has seen its balmy days, and some other ism must be hunted up around which the faithful can rally."[31]

Factionalism within the California Greenback Labor party also helped to undermine the movement's coherence and credibility. The *Democratic Standard* repeatedly noted the internecine struggles among San Francisco Greenbackers, and Humboldt Greenbackers were frequently at odds with the dominant element in the state party. For example, in 1882, Humboldt Greenbackers and the state party nominated different candidates to contest the 3rd congressional district. Part of the reason for the division was that by the 1882 elections, the California Greenback Labor party had to confront a rejuvenated Democratic party bent on attracting the workingman's vote. The strength of the Greenback party in Humboldt County emboldened the local Democratic party to adopt an even more brazen copy of the Greenback program than that of the California Democratic party. The Humboldt Democratic platform spoke of "labor as the basis of all capital" and stated that the "paramount living issue of the day" was whether the people will "submit to be ruled by the ever-grasping and never satisfied corporations." The platform expressed firm opposition to any increase in the bonded debt at the local, state, or national levels; another resolution demanded "honesty and strict economy in all departments of public service." The "great curse of land monopoly" was to be discouraged "by all legitimate means."[32] The Greenback platform on this issue was a little more specific. It demanded that many of the land grants to the railroads be revoked and that these lands revert to the public domain at a minimum price to bona fide settlers.[33] Humboldt Democrats did not propose to "substitute legal tender paper for national bank issues," as the Greenbackers advocated, but they were in favor of the "unrestricted coinage of silver and gold" and laws to restrict the economic and political influence of the banks.[34]

The platform of the Democratic party at the local and state levels revived the sagging fortunes of Humboldt Democrats. At the 1882 elections, they shared the spoils with the Republican party in county contests and garnered almost as many votes as the Republicans in statewide races. The local and state Democratic party's shift to a more populist stance not only preempted the Greenbackers on many issues but also led to a split among Humboldt Greenbackers between those wanting fusion with the Democrats and those determined to adhere to the third-party route.[35] Humboldt Democrats cunningly refrained from making nominations at their convention, to encourage fusionist sentiment among the Greenbackers. After a bitter struggle, led by Keller and the Ferndale Greenbackers, the antifusionists got their way. Leading Greenback fusionists, however, including Ayres, continued to plot fusion after the convention.[36]

Local factors also led to the demise of the Humboldt Greenback Labor party. The party's stance on the Chinese question and temperance proved a political liability, and injudicious nominations sealed the Greenbackers' fate. In 1880, relations between the county's white and Chinese residents began to deteriorate. The small township of Garberville, located in the southern extremity of the county, expelled all Chinese people in March of that year. A brief newspaper account gave no reason for the expulsion.[37] During 1880, the Eureka press commented with increasing frequency and disapproval on the existence of opium dens and prostitution rings in the city's Chinatown. More important, some lumber employers seriously contemplated the extensive employment of Chinese labor. "The impending crisis has arrived," announced the *Democratic Standard*. The *Standard* warned that "some of our millowners threaten the poor white man who is eking out a miserable existence at a mere pittance" by employing Chinese workers in the mills and cautioned that "such a course would be suicidal on the part of the millowners."[38] By the early 1880s, employers were making more extensive use of Chinese labor in railroad work, in the fishing canneries on the Eel River, and in agriculture. In 1884, the *Standard* declared, with reference to harvesting the potato crop, that "instead of the Indian who has done that kind of work the abominable 'Heathen Chinee' are swarming in herds to dig the potatoes and take the wages out of the country."[39] In the lumber industry, most employers retreated from their threat to employ Chinese labor. The only recorded attempt was thwarted in March 1882 when 21 white men went on strike at Fay's Shingle Mill at Fairhaven after 22 Chinese workers were hired.[40]

George Speed, who was to become an important figure in the Humboldt County Knights of Labor and a nationally prominent leader in the IWW, took the initiative. He rallied his fellow workers and marched to the mill. The Chinese workers were removed and placed on the next boat leaving the county. When Speed's employer, George Fay, asked him by what authority he acted, Speed replied, "By the force of public sentiment which is higher than any written law."[41]

The growing sense of unease about the presence of Chinese in Humboldt County manifested itself on March 9, 1882, when in the context of pending federal legislation to restrict Chinese immigration, a mass meeting in support of the legislation took place in Eureka.[42] The passage of the Chinese Exclusion Act may have mollified some fears, but not all. Anti-Chinese sentiment would culminate in the expulsion of the Chinese from Eureka in 1885 and from the whole county in 1886. The platform of the Humboldt County Greenback Labor party in 1882, however, did not contain an anti-Chinese plank. By contrast, the Humboldt Democratic party adopted a very strong anti-Chinese plank that echoed the wording of the state Democratic party. The failure of the Humboldt Greenbackers to pander to anti-Chinese sentiment almost certainly cost it support.

The Humboldt Greenbackers' sudden support for temperance reform also proved costly to its fortunes. Temperance organizations in the county, such as the Sons of Temperance and the International Order of Good Templars, had enjoyed a good membership since the first lodges were founded in the early 1850s. But in 1880, a wave of temperance revivalism swept the county. In a two-week visit, the Reverend D. I. K. Rine induced over 800 people in Eureka and Arcata alone to sign a pledge of total abstinence.[43] No political party in Humboldt County endorsed temperance reform in 1880, but by 1882 the *Democratic Standard* was calling for vigorous enforcement of a "Sunday Law" prohibiting drinking alcohol on the Sabbath. The 1882 election platform of the Humboldt Greenbackers not only called for "strict" enforcement of this law but also advocated an amendment to the state and national constitutions that would prohibit "the manufacture, sale or use of all intoxicating beverages."[44] The Humboldt Democratic and Republican platforms did not address the issue. Whether the Greenbacker support for prohibition was born of political expediency or conviction is a matter of conjecture. Regardless of their motives, their stance on temperance backfired politically. Numerous letters to the press revealed that people did not think that temperance laws could be effective and expressed concern that a large and expensive police force might have to be recruited to enforce prohibition. At the same time, saloon license fees provided the county with an important source of revenue. Finally, many people did not believe that legislating temperance should be the province of government. Robert Gunther asked what right government had "to dictate what they [the people] shall eat, what they shall drink, and how they should spend their time?"[45]

Injudicious nominations hurt the Greenback Labor party as much as they had the Workingmen's party. In several instances, both parties nominated people who betrayed the cause, either by ignoring the party platform when elected or by reverting to their former party affiliation shortly afterward. Pierce Ryan, elected to the state senate on the Workingmen's ticket in 1879, returned to the Humboldt Democratic party in 1880.[46] A number of others elected on the Workingmen's ticket followed suit. Most damaging to the Greenbackers' cause in 1882 was the record of Gilman Mudgett, whom they had elected to the state assembly in 1880. Humboldt Greenbackers were stunned when Mudgett, a month after assuming his seat, voted against repeal of the highly controversial and unpopular Debris Bill, passed by the California legislature in 1880. This bill had set up drainage districts to cope with the devastation hydraulic mining was causing California farmland. One of the critical dams constructed to deal with the problem failed. Half a million dollars had been wasted, and there were strong suspicions of fraud.[47] Humboldt County was not directly affected by the disaster or the hydraulic mining controversy, but this was an issue about which Humboldt Greenbackers felt strongly. They hastened to repudiate Mudgett, and Greenbackers at Ferndale and Petrolia circulated petitions calling for Mudgett's resignation.[48]

Both the Workingmen's and Greenback Labor parties were naive victims of political opportunism. In fairness, though, given the short history of the parties in the county, it was difficult to ascertain the sincerity and loyalty of aspiring third-party candidates. It was also tempting to nominate someone of established political stature in the county who would lend a new party credibility and respectability. Furthermore, even dissidents expected some political experience from men who would represent them in the state legislature, and many county offices required a modicum of professional training and experience.

The Humboldt Greenback Labor party's existence was as short-lived as that of the Workingmen's party, but it would be wrong to conclude that there was something ephemeral about the dissenting culture that gave rise to them. The short history of the Greenback Labor party indicates that the discontent of the late 1870s reflected more than a desire to reform the state constitution. There was a deep-seated discontent with Gilded Age capitalism that continued to express itself in the mid-1880s when the IWA and the Knights of Labor appeared on the scene and in the 1890s when the Populists became a strong force in county politics. The Humboldters' disquiet about the political economy of Gilded Age America was reinforced by the monetary policies of the federal government in the 1870s and early 1880s. Among Humboldt radicals, interest in the financial panaceas of the Greenback Labor party accentuated the cosmopolitan orientation of a dissenting ideology that was anything but parochial by 1880. The increasing scope of federal involvement in national economic policy militated against a localist orientation and convinced dissenters of the need for national regulation of the banking system and controls on corporations, especially railroads.

Chapter 4

An Emergent Labor Movement

For almost two decades after the Civil War, dissent in Humboldt County took solely political forms. No organization appeared that could be described as a trade union in either actual or incipient form. In this respect, Humboldt County differed little from other population centers along the Pacific Coast. Before the 1880s, only San Francisco possessed a labor movement of significant proportions, although a few trade unions formed and disbanded in Sacramento, San Jose, Stockton, Oakland, and Portland.[1] The post–Civil War years from 1865 to 1880 were also lean ones for the American labor movement as a whole. Many cities and towns, especially in the West, lacked a sufficiently large artisan workforce to sustain trade unions. The industrialization of the West did not commence in earnest until the last two decades of the nineteenth century.[2] And the labor movement in San Francisco lacked the resources and the inclination to reach out to the remote hinterlands of California and spread the gospel of unionism. To some extent also, an abiding faith in the efficacy of political action inhibited the emergence of a trade union movement in many western communities.

The mid-1880s witnessed the development of the modern-day American labor movement under the auspices of the Knights of Labor and the American Federation of Labor. Throughout the nation, workers flocked to join unions. Many communities in the Far West, including Humboldt County, followed suit. This chapter examines the complex interplay of factors leading to the founding of the Humboldt County labor movement.

Expansion and Fraud in the Lumber Industry

Following the depression of the late 1870s, the Humboldt County lumber industry underwent a period of rapid expansion. The booming market for lumber in the San Francisco Bay Area and rapidly developing southern California transformed the lumber industry. Between 1882 and 1887, the output of the county's mills doubled, from 64 million feet to at least 120 million feet—one estimate put the figure at 190 million feet. The number of lumber workers employed in Humboldt County increased to 2,000 by the mid-1880s. Although a considerable amount of the capital to finance this expansion came from outside the county, local entrepreneurs continued to own and manage the majority of lumbering concerns. In 1883, however, Humboldt County and San Francisco businessmen, at the instigation of a group of Scottish capitalists, embarked on a scheme to reorganize the Humboldt County lumber industry on a scale that would have transformed it beyond all recognition, from a multibusiness community of small to medium-size lumbering concerns to one dominated by a colossus controlled almost entirely by outside capitalists. Both the means and ends employed by this conglomerate, which incorporated itself as the California Redwood Company in 1883, provoked the outrage of Humboldt County radicals and sowed the seeds of the county's first labor movement.

The saga of the California Redwood Company must be set against the background of dubious land-acquisition practices that had been going on since at least the 1870s. Reports from the U.S. Commissioner of the General Land Office and the California Surveyor General indicate that during the 1870s and 1880s, Humboldt County lumber companies acquired vast tracts of redwood lands by fraudulent means.[3] The confessions of S. A. D. Puter are most revealing. In 1908, after being prosecuted by the federal government for land fraud, Puter recounted his involvement in a book entitled *Looters of the Public Domain*.[4] In 1875, while employed as an axman by the deputy U.S. surveyor in Humboldt County, Puter gained valuable information about the most desirable land claims. He proceeded to line up people to file "dummy" homestead entries; when the claims were confirmed eight to ten months later, he acquired ownership of them and sold the best lands to "Eureka capitalists" for a handsome profit. Because the "dummy" entry system required the collaboration of a number of individuals, many Humboldters were aware of it. A Ferndale farmer, Richard Johnston, declared in 1882 that it was "a well known fact" that vast tracts of redwood timber were "gobbled up by speculators, to my mind, in a rather questionable way," and he went on to describe at length how the dummy entry system worked.[5]

In the fall of 1882, a group of entrepreneurs from Humboldt County and San Francisco, acting at the behest of the Scottish capitalists who were to form the California Redwood Company, began using the "dummy" entry system to perpetrate one of the largest timberland frauds in American history.[6] David Evans, one of the county's most eminent lumbermen, and C. H. King of San Francisco hired people to locate and survey desirable lands. They then employed agents to engage a large number of entrymen. The agents made little effort to conceal their mission, operating brazenly from a saloon three blocks away from the U.S. Land Office in Eureka. According to a congressional report, "a large number of prominent citizens of Eureka" were aware of what was going on. The agents were so zealous in the performance of their duties that "farmers were stopped on their way home [and] merchants were called from their counters and persuaded to allow their names to be used to obtain land."[7] In addition, sailors living in Coffee Jack's boardinghouse filed their first citizen papers so that their names might be used for dummy entries. Four hundred dummy entrymen filed timber claims, and after agreeing to transfer the land deeds later, received from $5 to $50 for their efforts. This scheme involved 57,000 acres of what the secretary of the interior called "perhaps the most valuable tract of timberland in the United States."[8] The secretary's estimate of the amount of land was on the conservative side. In his 1886 report, the commissioner of the General Land Office stated that a special agent sent to Humboldt County to investigate the fraud estimated that "not less than 100,000 acres" was involved,[9] and a story in the *New York Times* in April 1886 put the figure at 96,000 acres.[10]

The fraudulent land acquisitions and the prospect of a massive consolidation of the county's lumber industry caused consternation among Humboldt radicals. Suddenly they were confronted, on their very doorstep, with a glaring example of a heinous evil they had railed against for almost twenty years. Louis Tower, who had been active in the Greenback Labor party, stressed the parallel between developments at the local, state, and national levels. In a searing letter to the *Democratic Standard*, he denounced "our money kings," who have "so exploited labor—have so circumvented and controlled the industries of the nation" that the people had been reduced to a level not much above a "bare subsistence." He lambasted the Vanderbilts, the Goulds, and the Spreckels and then, turning to developments in his own county, accused "lumbermen and others" of land fraud "thus shutting honest labor from the benefits of the public domain." He added that "the natural law of labor is that it shall gather its own fruits" and that "if this law is constantly interfered with . . . the people, like a mighty river, obstructed at every assailable point, will rise in their might and sweep away every obstruction." [11]

But Tower's fellow Greenbacker, Charles Keller, played the main role in trying to mobilize the community against the depredations of the California Redwood Company. In late March and April 1883, Keller wrote a series of letters to the *Democratic Standard*. He stated that he had "no notion that this community will be surprised by this statement," but he implored, "Can nothing be done to stop these land thieves and this nefarious practice?" He proposed that the Central Committee of the Greenback Labor party "take the matter in hand." [12] Confronted with a mixture of hostility and indifference, Keller's indignation was kept alive by continuing reports of land frauds, supplied to him by patrons of his butcher shop. "The stealing was so gross," he recalled, "that I induced various of my informants to make affidavits before a notary public stating that these reports were correct." [13] Keller forwarded the affidavits to the Land Office in Washington.

Undoubtedly, some residents were as outraged as Keller and Tower, but they made up a minority of the community. It is likely that a considerable number of people had simply become inured to the spectacle of land fraud. Indeed, a not insignificant number may have violated federal land laws, albeit on a small scale, to acquire more than the 160 acres that the Homestead Act allowed. There was, though, a more fundamental reason people were prepared to condone or overlook large-scale land fraud involving the Humboldt County lumber industry. The federal land laws in the early Gilded Age imposed legal constraints on the land-acquisition practices of lumber companies that were not altogether conducive to the effective and rational operation of a lumber concern. Homestead and preemption laws applied to lands suitable for agriculture, not to timberlands. Thus, a large number of claims encompassing timberlands were fraudulent, since the lands were not suited or intended for agricultural use after they were cleared. The Timber and Stones Act of 1878 made it legally possible to acquire timberlands in California, Nevada, Oregon, and Washington Territory. Under the act, 160 acres of government-surveyed timberland could be sold to any person or association of persons at a minimum price of $2.50 per acre. The applicant had to swear that he was not acquiring the land for speculative purposes, that he had not contracted to sell the patent to someone else, and that the land was unsuitable for cultivation. [14]

One of the principal concerns of a lumber entrepreneur was to ensure that, over the long term, his mill would have an adequate and accessible supply of timber. There would have been little point in undertaking heavy capital investments in equipment and transportation facilities if a sufficient supply of lumber could not be guaranteed over the lifetime of the investment. By the 1880s, few Humboldt County lumber companies owned less than 1,500 acres. The Pacific Lumber Company commenced operations in the mid-1880s, having acquired a land base of 12,000 acres of redwood timber. By the late 1880s, the Dolbeer and Carson Company owned over 20,000 acres of timberland.

In the context of the activities of the California Redwood Company, the county press harped on the contradictions and limitations of federal land laws as they pertained to timberlands. No newspaper put the case more forcefully than the *Democratic Standard*, which, still under the editorship of William Ayres, performed a dramatic *volte-face* on the land-monopoly question. Three weeks before it published Keller's tirade, exposing the massive land frauds taking place, the *Standard* commented that lands were being acquired in the county by means that would "shame a Louisiana Returning Board."[15] At the very same time that it was publishing Keller's letters, however, the *Standard* took issue with him. When Keller cited the Timber and Stones Act chapter and verse, the *Standard* responded by saying that the law could not have been so impractical as to limit each man or association of individuals to 160 acres of timberland.[16] In another article, the *Standard* argued that "so far as the redwoods are concerned, it takes large capital to generate them in the manufacture of lumber." Moreover, the *Standard* attempted to turn the arguments of Keller and Tower on their head when it asserted that "poor men cannot work them" [the redwoods], and "if they can locate them, it is to secure what benefit may arise from a sale" as this was "the only way a poor man can realize any benefit from his timber right."[17]

Ayres had other reasons for defending the California Redwood Company. He was among the approximately 200 people who had filed a dummy land claim while the company was active in the county. And, like almost all other participants, he eventually had his land claim invalidated by the federal government.[18] Ayres's involvement in the affair and his persistent attempts to discredit investigations by the federal government were to haunt him for the rest of his public life.

It would be a mistake, however, to view the support for the California Redwood Company in a totally cynical light. Many people—with memory of the depression of the late 1870s still vivid—believed that infusions of outside capital would bolster and stabilize the county's lumber industry. The *Democratic Standard* was not the only paper to make this argument. On May 5, 1883, the *Times-Telephone* (a name temporarily assumed by the *Humboldt Times*) confirmed rumors that a syndicate was trying to buy most of the county's timberlands and noted with satisfaction that "the taxable property would be greatly increased" and that "a new life would be given to the manufacture of lumber."[19] The *Ferndale Enterprise* assured its readers that this "movement" would not "work any injury to our people . . . enough mill property will always remain in the hands of private parties to protect themselves, and create a lively competition in the lumber industry."[20]

Herbert Gutman has argued that, in many Gilded Age communities, a broad coalition of labor and small businessmen resisted the encroachment of outside capitalists.[21] To the extent that this was true, it was less true of single-industry communities. The dependency of a community on one industry inclined many people, including workers, to perceive a mutuality between their interests and those of the community's dominant industry. In addition, it is hard to overestimate the scope for repression and victimization in single-industry communities. Thus, a boycott of Keller's butcher shop contributed to driving him from the county;[22] and the blacklisting of several of the county's early labor leaders, including George Speed, forced them to leave Humboldt. The lengths to which some of the California Redwood Company officials were prepared to go to stifle a federal investigation indicates how ruthless some individuals in the lumber industry could be. Not only were investigating agents offered bribes, but also, according to the *General Land Office Report* for 1886, "Witnesses were spirited out of the county; others were threatened and intimidated; spies were employed to watch and follow the [land] agent and report the names of all persons who conversed with him; and on one occasion two persons who were about to enter the agent's room . . . were knocked down and dragged away."[23] Finally, an attempt was made to poison one of the investigating agents.[24]

The International Workingmen's Association

By the summer of 1883, Keller had decided that battling the California Redwood Company would take more than indignant letters to the press and forwarding affidavits to the Land Office in Washington. "If ever there was a time in Humboldt County for an intelligent organization of wage workers that time is now," he wrote in early August 1883.[25] He informed the *Democratic Standard* that on a recent visit to San

Francisco he had joined the International Workingmen's Association (IWA) and intended to form branches of the organization in Humboldt County. The IWA, founded by Burnette Haskell in San Francisco in 1882, had established a significant following in parts of California and several western and Rocky Mountain states. Haskell, a lawyer, began his career in radical politics and the San Francisco labor movement in January 1882 when he started publication of a weekly newspaper called *Truth*, which for a time became the official organ of the San Francisco Trades Assembly. The object of Haskell's IWA was "to assist and aid the organization of labor, the various trade unions, Farmers' Alliances and all other forms of organization in which the producers have organized or may organize themselves." The IWA leadership adopted a cell system, patterned after many secret revolutionary societies, whereby each person in the cell was supposed to form a group of nine without divulging the names of his recruits to his cell.[26]

Keller stressed that the new organization was "for educational purposes, to aid the organization of the laboring classes" and that it was "not a political measure, neither can it be used by political party tricksters; it is a social move for the amelioriation of the condition of all laborers and for the betterment of society."[27] But, to Keller, the IWA amounted to much more than a string of workingmen's debating clubs. Indeed, he believed that the IWA should become a trade union in its own right in Humboldt County. In letters to the San Francisco Executive of the IWA, he wrote of the need for an emergency fund financed by quarterly dues as being essential "to resist monopoly."[28] Keller lost no time in launching the Humboldt County IWA. By September 1883, he reported that at least three groups of the IWA had been founded, and in a letter to the *Democratic Standard* he claimed that the organization had more than 60 members in Humboldt County.[29] In late September and October, Keller forwarded a steady stream of membership applications to IWA headquarters in San Francisco. He also requested more copies of *Truth*, Henry George's *Progress and Poverty*, and *Underground Russia*, which, he said, were "doing good work."[30]

It was not only the fraudulent land activities of the California Redwood Company that agitated Keller and other IWA members. In August 1883, Keller wrote to *Truth* complaining that the lumber companies were attempting to flood the labor market in Humboldt County: "Every steamer brings a new invoice of labor here to an already overstocked labor market. These poor men are enticed here by capitalist lies." Within a few weeks, Keller said, there would be 500 men idle in Eureka.[31]

Amelia Jones, who along with her husband, Samuel Jones, a shoemaker, was an IWA member, wrote to Haskell echoing Keller's complaint. She charged that the lumber companies were engaged in a deliberate campaign to slash wage rates. To this end, she said, the companies discharged loggers and were now advertising for 500 men. "The people here are alive to the issue," she reported, and they "feel like throttling the double headed monster." The "International" was doing all it could "under the circumstances," but she stressed that the local press "are doing all they can in favor of Monopoly, and bow in humble submission to the Golden Calf." She reported a concerted effort by the IWA to sell *Truth* throughout the county, for "there are hundredths [*sic*] of people here that are willing and ready to hear the truth." [32]

On October 9, 1883, Keller wrote to Haskell and Charles Burgman of the IWA Executive Division stating that the newspapers "have shut down on me" and that the Humboldt IWA had decided to buy a small press. In the meantime, Keller asked them to print a thousand copies of an address he had drafted "To the Laboring Men of Humboldt County." [33] The three-page pamphlet accused the lumber companies of "a systematized plan . . . to bring wages down to starvation figures" by flooding the labor market and related how the California Redwood Company had acquired most of its land. The address then turned to the question of impending wage reductions of from $10 to $20 a month and urged workers to resist the cuts. A special appeal was aimed at "our resident merchants," who were "in the same boat with labor as regards this campaign." Within a few years, said Keller, the syndicate would establish its own stores and warehouses:

There is but one preventative—unite with hard handed labor so that you can resist every unjust demand by the lumber syndicate. . . . The remedy consists in thorough organization: such an organization is now taking place in your very midst. . . . We have already sixty active organizations in the county with a membership of nearly three hundred. Any sober, industrious man or woman can become a member of the Association. [34]

Interested parties were directed to visit Keller, secretary of the Humboldt Branch of the Pacific Division of the IWA, at his market in Eureka. The address ended by guaranteeing all members that "the company" would not discover their names and affirmed:

We have associated ourselves for protection only; we have no wish to interfere with the actions of any man or his business, so long as he or they do not trample on our joint rights, among which we count, freedom of speech . . . and honest and sufficient wages for an honest days work. We understand well the truth, that labor creates wealth, and we have determined that the man who produces, shall enjoy more fully the wealth his labor creates. [35]

Ira Cross is probably right in saying that the IWA's claim of 60 organizations and 300 members in Humboldt County was an exaggeration, although there is no evidence to disprove Keller's assertion. Cross estimates that the IWA had at least 19 groups in San Francisco, 10 in Humboldt County, 2 in Oakland, and 1 apiece in a scattering of locations in California. Undoubtedly, Humboldt had by far the largest IWA membership in California outside San Francisco and one larger than estimated by Cross.[36]

What kind of people joined the Humboldt IWA? Using the patchy records left by Haskell, one can obtain the names of 44 people who were definitely members. Not included in this figure are the names of people in the county who subscribed to *Truth* and had personal contact with Haskell and who were almost certainly IWA members. The occupations of 24 members can be determined from Haskell's papers and the 1884 register of Humboldt County voters. There were five lumber workers, five laborers, three gunsmiths, three shoemakers, two farmers, one cook, one harnessmaker, one butcher, one journalist, one photographer, and one engineer. All but five of these members lived in Eureka. This is obviously a very small sample on which to generalize about the composition of the IWA in Humboldt County, but it does suggest that the majority of members were urban wage laborers.[37]

Notwithstanding the support for the IWA in Humboldt County, one must ask why the organization failed to attract a mass following. First, there was an enormous leap entailed in moving from third-party political activity to joining a secret and self-professed revolutionary organization. Second, it cannot be reiterated too strongly that in joining such an organization in a community dominated by a single industry, an individual jeopardized his livelihood. Third, the dispersed nature of the population outside Eureka and poor intracounty transportation facilities militated against a cohesive countywide organization. Moreover, the county press chose virtually to ignore the IWA, let alone give it any support.

Finally, there were contradictory and self-limiting features to the IWA's philosophy and *modus operandi* that circumscribed its ability to develop a broader base. The IWA's organizational structure, with its small, secretive groups operating in self-imposed isolation from one another, was not conducive to building a grass-roots organization that could effectively protect the rights of labor. Membership data reveal that a number of IWA members were related, and Keller's correspondence indicates that he was very cautious about admitting people to the organization. It was also difficult for the IWA to operate as a labor organization when members were not bound by workplace ties or even the same occupational backgrounds. There was, indeed, an ambiguity of purpose about the IWA, particularly in its early months. Was it a trade union, or was it essentially a working-class organization dedicated to radicalizing the people-at-large through the dissemination of propaganda?

Thus, structural and ideological contradictions weakened the IWA. From the outset, Keller, with his usual perspicacity, saw the need to cement the structure of the organization in Humboldt County. In a letter to Haskell on October 9, 1883, he brought up the question of establishing an emergency fund. "At present a great many do not know what to make of our organization, because we have no Constitution, no general law to govern and hold together." He argued that an emergency fund would "give the men an opportunity of holding out in case of a reduction in wages next spring" and that the establishment of such a fund would reinforce the bonds holding the IWA together, for "where a man's money is there is his heart also."[38] It is perhaps significant that the IWA leadership in San Francisco did not respond to Keller's suggestion.

But for all its contradictions and limitations, the IWA in Humboldt County marked an important turning point in the history of radicalism in the community. It signified that a solid core of dissidents no longer retained an abiding faith in the ability of political action to address the nation's evils. This realization was a necessary condition for the foundation of a labor movement, and it grew, at least in part, from disappointment with the Workingmen's and Greenback Labor parties' performances. An increasing number of radicals believed by the mid-1880s that the road to salvation lay not exclusively in the political arena but also in the organization of the working class as a self-conscious, extrapolitical entity. In 1880, when he embraced the Greenback cause, Keller asserted that "the greatest fault of the people is the neglect of the duty toward the state. It is this neglect that makes them servants where they should be masters." The Greenback Labor party should elect "honest men" and eliminate "the power of the machine politicians."[39] In 1884, in a lengthy article in *Truth*, Keller stated:

A change in political parties . . . will never bring about the reforms desired by the laboring class of our population. . . . Any real change in the condition of the workers must be brought about by the workers themselves; it must be home-made; it must be fashioned by men who are themselves toilers, who know and can appreciate all the hardships labor is heir to, and not a kind of gloved gentry who can boast a Henry Ward Beecher in their ranks. . . . Laborers can obtain ALL they desire without taking political action, without riot and revolution. The remedy lies with them and them only.[40]

Keller advocated an "inter-State Labor Union" that would encompass all labor organizations and wield such power that it would control "the entire labor market" and be "independent of and superior to the Government."[41] Keller wrote this piece from the San Francisco Bay Area. In early January 1884, demoralized by the boycott of his butcher shop and the refusal of the press to publish his letters, Keller left Humboldt County with his family.[42] He continued to be active in the IWA, founding a branch in Traver, California. He also became, with Haskell, a founding member of the Kaweah Cooperative Colony in Tulare County, California.[43]

The Humboldt IWA did not expire as an active organization after the departure of Keller. In January 1884, *Truth* reported that the Humboldt IWA had put out two issues of a newspaper called *International*.[44] The Humboldt IWA continued to induct members until at least April 1885.[45] Haskell visited Humboldt County in January 1885, and his diary entries indicate that the organization was far from defunct. Haskell addressed a number of IWA meetings, including one at the small township of Freshwater that was attended by 50 people. "A lot of good material there," he noted in his diary. He also spoke at Axe Hall in Eureka on January 6, but his presence went unreported in the Humboldt press.[46]

The Lumbermen's Union

The Humboldt IWA exploited the mounting resentment against the California Redwood Company, which was about to start operations in 1884 with 700 men, in spite of an ongoing investigation by a federal grand jury. Before the season commenced, however, the company provoked a serious confrontation with the lumber workers. In February 1884, the company issued a terse notice stating that henceforth the sum of 50 cents would be deducted from each employee's wages in order to finance a hospital plan for workers. Under the plan, the company would provide a hospital facility staffed by two doctors. Married men could be treated at home, and their families were eligible for treatment at half price.[47]

The hospital plan was not well received by the lumber workers. A special meeting was set "for the purpose of considering the feasibility of forming a WORKINGMEN'S PROTECTIVE ASSOCIATION" at Russ Hall in Eureka.[48] Daniel Cronin, one of the leading figures in the Humboldt IWA, called the meeting to order, and W. J. Sweasey chaired it. Patrick Dunn was elected secretary. Cronin expressed strong opposition to the mandatory nature of the hospital plan. He added that the men were insulted at not having any say in the plan's formulation and that they were suspicious of the company's motives and the competence of its doctors. Cronin alleged that the California Redwood Company was trying to coerce its workers into accepting an automatic 50-cent deduction to pay for the plan. Robert Gunther, a farmer, spoke up on behalf of the lumber workers, objecting to the compulsory nature of the plan and insisting that the 50-cent premium would more than cover costs, a point reiterated by Sweasey. David Evans, the spokesman of the California Redwood Company, claimed that the men had asked for the plan and denied any pressure was being exerted to make men subscribe to it. The meeting polarized into pro- and antihospital factions, with the latter in the distinct majority. As the meeting was about to adjourn, Cronin urged workers to join the Humboldt Workers' Protective Association, and 126 men responded to the call.[49] George Speed recalled vividly the factors that brought about the first organization of Humboldt County lumber workers: "changes being attempted by a big lumber pool" intent on reducing wages and imposing a hospital plan "without giving us any say in the management."[50]

The Humboldt Lumbermen's Union, as the organization was renamed, was officially launched on February 16, 1884, at Buhne Hall in Eureka. The hall was filled to capacity, and 228 more men joined the union. M. H. Grant, a photographer and IWA member, was elected president; Charles Baldwin, a clerk, became secretary; and W. J. Sweasey was chosen as treasurer.[51] The constitution and the proceedings of the Lumbermen's Union were secret, but in May 1884, Cronin reported that meetings had been held at Eureka, Arcata, and Blue Lake, and a total of 80 new members had enrolled. He stated that the union sought to assist its members in periods of illness and injury and give "a respectful burial to our dead," and he proudly related how he had just dispensed $56 in benefits to a union member. Cronin made it clear that the union was more than a benevolent association: "We propose to protect labor from any unjust demand. Organization begets organization. Capital is organized, why not labor?"[52] Cronin's optimism concerning the Lumbermen's Union is corroborated by Millard Gardner, who shortly became the official organizer of the Knights of Labor in Humboldt County. He recalled that within a few months, the union had 600 members and a treasury of about $900.[53] The *Times-Telephone* put the membership at 700 by August 1884.[54] In the face of the strength of the Lumbermen's Union, the California Redwood Company dropped its hospital plan.

During the summer of 1884, the Lumbermen's Union decided to

invite a Knights of Labor organizer to Humboldt County. James Johnson, a leading light in both the IWA and the Knights of Labor in San Francisco, went to Humboldt County in July 1884.[55] On July 22, Johnson organized a local assembly with approximately 70 members.[56] In its August issue, *Truth* confirmed the founding of L.A. 3337, or the "Humboldt Assembly," as it soon became known.[57] In mid-August, the Lumbermen's Union decided by "mutual consent" to dissolve itself because it was believed that the Knights of Labor was "better adapted to the requirements of the members, and that such of the Lumbermen's Union as are not ineligible by reason of their occupations joined, or may join, the Knights of Labor."[58] According to Gardner's recollections, "every member" of the Lumbermen's Union joined the Humboldt assembly. Daniel Cronin was elected Master Workman, and another IWA member, James Timmons, was elected secretary.[59]

Keller and his fellow IWA members played a critical role in laying the groundwork for the Knights. They skillfully exploited the resentment against the California Redwood Company and built a cohesive and well-directed movement. The machinations of the company impelled Humboldt dissenters to take a stand in their own backyard against one of the more sinister manifestations of the corruption of the American republic. An increasing number of radicals despaired, by the mid-1880s, of redressing such evils by the electoral process alone and emphasized the self-organization of the working class. It is surely significant that at least five of Humboldt County's most prominent radical figures—W. J. Sweasey, Daniel Cronin, George Speed, Charles Keller, and Alfred Cridge—were, at one time or another, members of "utopian communities." These men, like many other Gilded Age radicals, sought to establish a society on transcendent and truly cooperative social values.[60]

Chapter 5

The Rise and Fall of the Knights

Between 1869 and 1896, 15,000 assemblies of the Knights of Labor were established, and at least 2 million people joined the Order. The appearance of the Knights in Humboldt County in the mid-1880s coincided with their emergence as a full-fledged national labor organization that, at its zenith in 1886, had 800,000 members. In Humboldt, as in many other areas of the country, the Knights constituted the first mass organization of workers. In Humboldt, the IWA played a vanguard role in politicizing people's discontents and laying the foundation for the Knights. The Knights tapped a long-standing dissenting tradition revitalized by local events and developments at the state and national levels. While they drew inspiration and sustenance from the radical strands of the democratic–republican tradition, some of the ambiguities of this legacy led to the formation of an Order that was ideologically diverse and institutionally inclusive. The bitter factionalism that resulted circumscribed the ability of the Humboldt Knights to act as an effective trade union on behalf of their working-class constituency. This was a major reason why, after establishing a strong presence in the county, the Knights ultimately proved to be as transitory an organization in Humboldt County as they were nationally.[1]

The Knights Arise

In Humboldt County, 10 assemblies of the Knights of Labor formed between August 1884 and the summer of 1886. At their peak, in 1886, the Knights boasted 2,000 members,[2] and almost all the county's towns had assemblies. In addition to three assemblies in Eureka, there were assemblies at Arcata, Blue Lake, Bayside, Freshwater, Port Kenyon, Rio Dell, and Rohnerville. Eight assemblies were "mixed," which generally meant that members came from a variety of occupations. For example, the Bayside assembly contained lumber workers and farmers, but the Freshwater assembly had only lumber workers. The original Humboldt assembly, although designated as mixed, was composed primarily of lumber workers.

The growth of the Knights of Labor in Humboldt County occurred during a depression that rivaled the one of the late 1870s in its severity, particularly in its impact on the lumber industry. Its effects shook the moral legitimacy of the lumber owners, especially the California Redwood Company. Many who had been unconcerned about the activities of the company began to view it in a different light.

In July 1884, the Humboldt Lumber Association ordered a 25 percent cut in production and laid off many lumber workers.[3] Within six months the price of clear redwood lumber plummeted from $32 to $22 per 1,000 feet.[4] During 1885, the depression deepened; most lumber companies did not commence operations in the spring of 1885. The California Redwood Company, which in June 1884 had employed 1,000 men, employed only 50 in April 1885.[5] Unemployment in the county reached record levels. The *Times-Telephone* spoke of "hundreds" of unemployed men in Eureka alone.[6] A correspondent for the *San Francisco Chronicle* reported that "never . . . was so much want known to exist" in Humboldt County, and spoke of "hundreds of laborers . . . bereft of the bare necessaries of life in a state of semi-starvation," sleeping in the woods and living on shellfish.[7]

By April 1885, the unemployed began to show signs of discontent and rudimentary organization. After a *Times-Telephone* editorial stating that the majority of the unemployed were not interested in finding work "unless they can dictate wages," an indignant letter appeared in the *Humboldt Standard*, signed by John Larson and "350 others," protesting the "scurrillous language published in the *Times-Telephone* against the workmen." It called the letter an affront to "every honest workman now out of employment."[8] On May 4, 1885, a mass meeting of unemployed workers took place in Axe Hall in Eureka. A series of resolutions denounced the California Redwood Company for its massive land frauds and for luring large numbers of workers to the county when there was little prospect of employment. The final resolution asked honest businessmen and citizens to put pressure on the "infernal syndicate" to start work or abandon its claims, and threatened to present evidence to the General Land Office in Washington.[9]

Large meetings of unemployed workers took place almost daily.

On May 10, 1885, unemployed workers and some of the county's leading businessmen met in Eureka. Many speakers dwelt on the fact that
"worthy families in our midst" were living in a state of destitution.
A committee was appointed to ask the Eureka City Council if street
work could be provided for the unemployed, and David Evans and
Joseph Russ were delegated to approach the California Redwood Company to ascertain when work might be resumed. Finally, a committee
was chosen containing two of the county's most respected lumber entrepreneurs, William Carson and Timothy Brosnan, to raise funds for
the poor.[10] Although there were several incidents of alleged arson in
the latter part of May, the overall effect of the meeting was to defuse
a volatile situation. No further demonstrations occurred, in spite of
the fact that the California Redwood Company, and most of the other
lumber companies in the county, did not resume operations, and the
Eureka City Council did not provide work for the unemployed.

Leading members of the Knights and the IWA played major roles in
organizing the unemployed and politicizing their discontents. Both the
chairman and the secretary of the May 10 meeting were IWA members.
At least two of the four men (including Alfred Cridge, the editor of the
Western Watchman, the organ of the Humboldt Knights)[11] delegated
to approach the Eureka City Council about jobs were members of the
Knights. In addition, two of the five men chosen to see the County
Board of Supervisors were IWA members.

The depression overlapped with the ongoing saga of the California
Redwood Company and was an important factor in the birth of the
Knights in Humboldt County. But the emergence of the Knights also
owed much to the fact that they were able to draw on long-standing
discontents over developments at the state and national levels. The
diary of James Beith vividly conveys this. Beith, consumed with disappointment and indignation that both the state and national Democratic
parties had failed to bring about any significant reform, especially to
control the power of the railroads, drew heavily on ideas associated
with the radical strands of the democratic–republican tradition:

Labor is to society and humanity what the right arm is to the body. It is the
grand conservative force which develops every form of civilization . . . it is
the instrument by which we gather all our wealth. If this self-evident fact is
conceded, why is its claims to distinguished attention, legislative action and
supervision, methodical adjustment of profits, and remuneration and complete
fraternisation with Capital been so long delayed?[12]

A year later, in 1886, Beith echoed these sentiments in an even more
strident tone. He insisted that the "labor question" must be resolved "or

else we are on the eve of revolution," and he castigated "the ingenious methods by which Capital and aggregated Capital—Monopoly—distort the proper distribution of the gains and bring about inadequate compensation for service—or toil. We are dropping into the old system of Master and Serf." Beith berated the "upper class" for losing sight of that "Jeffersonian maxim that all men are born free and equal." [13]

The correspondence of many Humboldt Knights evidenced the same profound concern. A self-confessed Knight and lumber worker, Robert Smith, insisted that the laborer had the right to organize "to give him a fair share of the wealth created by his labor." He complained that employers, nationally and locally, had arrived "at a concert of action" to keep wages low. Why, he asked, "should not laboring men organize for their own protection," at a time when "great monopolies" were "cornering lands, coal and many of the necessaries of life?" [14] Another Knight refuted the charge that the Knights represented a violent and destructive philosophy and invoked the radical democratic–republican tradition in melodramatic rhetoric:

Is the builder likely to destroy the structure that he himself has erected by his blood, sweat, and labor, when it is the most beautiful the world has ever seen? . . . Oh, America. May God in his mercy never let you see the day that you are afraid of your workingmen, for then, indeed will your glory be departed. Again when bloody treason hurled her black flag of rebellion and slavery at that home and government we had established, who was the first to offer up themselves for the government? Was it not what was styled greasy mechanics from freedom loving Massachusetts? History says yes. . . . Yet because we take and claim the same right as Americans to meet together and consult for our benefit in our lodges, neither interfering with any persons or their property but attending to our own duties . . . do you then call us socialists? Oh, ye of little faith. Be not afraid. We, sons of toil, fight your battles, create your wealth, establish your government, keep you clothed in purple and fine linen . . . therefore why ye stand in fear and trembling? Have you robbed the laborer of just compensation for his labor? [15]

Several Knights declared forthrightly that they were socialists. They denied advocating violent revolution and the expropriation of all private property. Socialism represented something different to them. One Knight described it as a system under which labor would receive "just and fair remuneration" and in which the government would own all the land and the means of transportation and communication "in trust for the whole people." [16] Another Knight asserted that Horace Greeley, Thomas Jefferson, Tom Paine, Patrick Henry, and George Washington were all socialists, and stated that he was "in love with both the men and their leadership and I should always reverence the teachings and noble deeds of those old patriotic sires that have passed on to the Social Kingdom where rent, interest and profit do not exist."[17] A recurrent millennial theme appeared in the writings of H. M. Burnett, an IWA member and gunsmith who became Master Workman of local assembly 5312 in Eureka. Burnett espoused socialism and looked forward to a "peaceful Revolution from the damnable cut-throat competition of the present day, to a 'Cooperative Commonwealth' where all men would be equal and would have the right to 'life, liberty and the pursuit of happiness,' pivoted in the Declaration of Independence, but never embodied in constitutions and laws."[18] Franz Weyrich, a Ferndale carpenter, who became District Master Workman of the Humboldt Knights, was unperturbed when one of his townsman accused him of being a socialist. "Socialism is the science of re-constructing society on an entirely new basis, by substituting the principle of association for that of competition in every branch of human industry," he stated boldly.[19]

Evidentiary limitations make it difficult to assess the social composition of the Knights of Labor in Humboldt County, but enough evidence can be gleaned from various sources to venture some informed generalizations.[20] Undoubtedly, lumber workers joined the Knights in large numbers. As noted, the Freshwater assembly and part of the Bayside assembly were composed of lumber workers while the Humboldt assembly was the direct descendant of the Lumbermen's Union. Indeed, its first two officers, Dan Cronin and James Timmons, were lumber workers. Lumber workers elsewhere in the county joined the Knights, but in assemblies outside Eureka agricultural workers and farmers made up a significant proportion of the membership. Most of the officers in the outlying assemblies were farmers, including James Barton from Ferndale. In January 1885, only a week after his visit, Haskell reported to the *Labor Enquirer* that in Humboldt County "the Grangers are reorganizing as the Knights of Labor."[21]

Leaders of the Eureka Knights were people of relatively humble occupational standing. Aside from Cronin and Timmons, the occupations of six other leaders could be traced. There were two laborers, two clerks, one carpenter, and one gunsmith. The two men who served as official organizers of the Knights in Humboldt County also came from modest backgrounds. Millard Gardner was listed as a laborer on the voting register. Pliny Earl Davis, Gardner's successor, arrived in Humboldt County in 1882. For several years, he ran a small stationery store, and on Saturdays worked as an auctioneer. His business was not very successful, and by the time he joined the Knights, he had sizable debts.[22]

A Trade Union or a Moral Order?

The Humboldt Knights, like the Order in many other regions, attracted people who had never belonged to a labor organization but who believed that the producing classes must organize to halt the erosion of their fundamental social, economic, and political rights. It was one thing, however, for people to agree on the necessity for self-organization and the fact that the American republic was afflicted by a serious malaise and quite another for dissenters to concur on specific strategies. The problem was that the democratic–republican tradition was based on a cluster of general political beliefs and verities. Although some of its elements—notably the labor theory of value—enabled dissenters to formulate a penetrating critique of the ills of Gilded Age capitalism, the ambiguous legacy of the tradition attracted dissenters of different stripes. Conflicts emerged when they were forced to confront specific questions that hitherto they had consigned to the realm of general abstraction. This was especially true when it came to the "labor question." Dissenters who shared a deep-seated concern that something was profoundly wrong with the American political economy could still adhere to anything from a mutualistic to a highly antagonistic conception of class relations.

Tensions and contradictions were reflected in many branches of the Knights of Labor, including the Humboldt County assemblies. At the risk of oversimplification, it is useful to distinguish between two tendencies within the Knights. On the one hand, the Knights embraced people who viewed the Order as a trade union that would look after their bread-and-butter interests at the workplace and that would, in the political realm, redeem America's corrupt and corporate-dominated institutions. Knights of this ideological persuasion invoked not only the Order's formal declaration of principles[23] but also pointed to the important role that the Knights had played in strikes and political campaigns, especially during the mid-1880s.

At the other extreme were Knights who perceived the Order primarily as a fraternal organization dedicated to the moral and educational enlightenment of its members. Knights of this persuasion agreed that America was afflicted by serious social and economic problems, but usually did not regard conflict between labor and capital as inevitable. They believed that relations between the two could and should be harmonious and viewed the strike weapon, as the Knights' leader Terence V. Powderly once put it, as a "relic of barbarism." Instead, the emphasis should be placed on the individual's capacity for self-improvement through education and temperance. Collectively, Knights could form cooperatives to avoid entrapment in the sprawling tentacles of Gilded Age capitalism, but it was not the task of the Knights to constrain or circumscribe the logic of capitalism. Rather, the Knights should recapture the respect for the dignity of labor and reform the system by dint of their worthy example. Knights of this ideological persuasion also drew on the formal principles of the Order for inspiration and support, and on the well-publicized pronouncements of Powderly favoring these more moderate goals.[24] To characterize the division within the Knights in this fashion oversimplifies matters to some extent. Most important, there were many radical Knights, who while seeing the Order principally as a trade union, also viewed it as an agency of moral and educational enlightenment.

The confusion about what the Knights of Labor represented was reflected in a letter of Mrs. W. S. Johnson of Eureka to Powderly. She reported that she and her husband had many friends who belonged to the Knights and were urging them to join. She had tried in vain to obtain a copy of the Order's bylaws "so as to know what I was joining." The picture was all the more confusing, she said, because in the two Eureka assemblies, "there is some that belong to the Order that are not much credit to the Order," although she insisted that she was "no Mrs. Prisy body" and that she and her husband "are with the working class heart and hand." She closed by asking Powderly for his advice and more information about the principles of the Knights.[25]

Internal dissensions were sharpest among local assemblies in Eureka. Occupational diversity contributed to profound political differences, which were accentuated by the presence of a hard core of radical IWA members. The primary locus of dissension was Humboldt assembly 3337. Although the majority of its members were lumber workers, its mixed assembly designation and its rapid growth resulted in the inclusion of a considerable number of businessmen. According to George Speed, "it checked our work as they endeavored to use the organization for political purposes."[26] A bitter conflict ensued between IWA members and sympathizers and other elements in the assembly who, led principally by businessmen, attempted to wrest control from what they saw as the pernicious influence of socialists and anarchists. Charles Devlin, a Eureka shoe manufacturer and member of the Humboldt assembly, wrote to Powderly complaining that when Haskell visited Humboldt County in January 1885, he had described the Knights as only a "primary school" of the IWA and that "ever since we have had trouble and discord in our ranks."[27] Devlin appealed to Powderly to throw his weight against the IWA. Another account of the factional struggle came from a Eureka IWA member in a letter to the *Labor*

Enquirer. He asserted that many members of the Humboldt assembly who sympathized with the IWA had been blacklisted and that the anti-IWA faction had "by pouring poison in the ears of the most susceptible . . . succeeded in splitting our ranks causing many to withdraw, others to quietly drop out and deny they were members and creating the impression that those who were standing by the ship were nothing more or less than incendiaries, dynamiters, etc."[28] On one occasion, a vigilante mob forced some members to leave town, and George Speed recalled that Dan Cronin "was one of the first to feel the blacklist."[29]

As the IWA correspondent to the *Labor Enquirer* observed, the Humboldt County press delighted in exacerbating and highlighting tensions within the assemblies of the Knights. The press made constant references to the alleged presence of incendiaries, dynamiters, and socialists in the Eureka assemblies, while lending moral support and encouragement to the more conservative Knights. An editorial in the *Arcata Union*, published in September 1886, stated that the Eureka assemblies contained "some of the best citizens of Eureka; men who are foremost in the education of children, first in elevating the morals of the community, true and loyal to the Government and its laws." Nevertheless, there were "quite a number of men" among the Eureka Knights who are "just as thorough Anarchists as any of the seven now under sentence of death in Chicago." The editorial berated those Knights who had given moral and financial support to striking sailors and urged the Order to expel the "dynamite element" from their ranks.[30]

There is no evidence that radical Knights advocated violent revolution. James Beith was present at one of the largest unemployment demonstrations in May 1885 when the radical Dan Cronin addressed the crowd. Cronin did talk of a "Coming Revolution," but he did so, in Beith's words, "with a singular degree of placidity" and argued that the revolution would not be achieved with "guns and bayonets but with intelligence and a consciousness of power to direct the force of the storm." Beith found "the attitude of the Knights is of the most commendable and laudable character—to educate the heart and head of the members; to familiarize them to all discussion of all problems of social science, the distribution of Capital and Wages; the equitable control of Corporations."[31]

The Knights endeavored to rectify their negative image in the local press by writing frequent letters to the press and holding special social events to clarify their purpose to the general public. On February 13, 1886, for example, the Knights held an "Invitation Social" in Eureka, which was attended by 200 people. There was an evening program of music and dancing, and at 11 o'clock *Western Watchman* editor Alfred Cridge made a speech explaining the goals of the Knights to try and dispel some myths about the Order. The *Humboldt Standard* reported that while many "had expected to see horns, cloven feet, etc., among those classed as cranks, socialists, incendiaries, etc," the occasion had reflected very creditably on the Knights.[32]

The radical Knights, however, continued to be vilified by the press and subjected to blacklisting and physical intimidation. The radicals stubbornly stood their ground, but factional fights between them and the more conservative Knights limited the Order's ability to function effectively as a trade union. Crucially, attacks on the radical Knights began to take their toll in the summer of 1886, just when growing discontent on the part of lumber workers and sailors called for an aggressive trade union strategy. The more conservative Knights increasingly assumed the role of managing, and ultimately defusing, rank-and-file militancy. Reflective of this trend was the fact that the *Watchman* fell under the editorial auspices of William Ayres in September 1886 and became the mouthpiece of the moderate Knights. This shift, especially in the context of a growing militancy among rank-and-file Knights, exposed a glaring disparity between the lofty rhetoric of the Knights and their ability to make concrete improvements in the working conditions of their members.

In the summer of 1886, the Humboldt Knights received an influx of new members who were eager to strike. A disconcerted Millard Gardner, the official county organizer, complained to Powderly that many new members did not understand the true principles of the Order, and that while "we have meny [sic] good men here that we no [sic] would not do us any harm Our Boys or a good many of them only think about striking."[33] The issue that most agitated the Knights was the ten-hour day. By the summer of 1886, the redwood lumber industry was one of the few major lumber regions in the United States that still operated on a twelve-hour day. The Knights had helped Michigan lumber workers obtain the ten-hour day after a protracted struggle in 1885 and 1886. More important, many lumber enterprises on the Puget Sound had peacefully conceded the ten-hour day in the summer of 1886. The *Watchman* went out of its way to deny newspaper reports that Humboldt lumber workers belonging to the Knights planned a general strike for the ten-hour day the following spring.[34] At the same time, the *Watchman* urged restraint on the part of the Knights, insisting that Humboldt County's lumber employers were as enlightened as their counterparts in the Puget Sound area and that under no circumstances should the Knights resort to striking.[35]

Lumber workers renewed their agitation for a ten-hour day in March 1887. The *Watchman* offered moral support, saying that "the twelve hour day gives no time for rest, study and self improvement . . . it brutalizes the laborer instead of civilizing and elevating him." Many more mill operatives would "attend lectures and other means of education," said the *Watchman*, if they did not have to get up at 5:00 A.M. and go to bed shortly after dinner.[36] Throughout the spring and summer of 1887, leaders of the Knights discouraged militant action on the part of the lumber workers. For instance, when executive members of the District Assembly learned that employees of the Elk River Mill Lumber Company planned to strike on June 1, they dispatched a committee to dissuade them.[37] Two weeks later, the Port Kenyon Knights passed a motion in favor of the ten-hour day, "could it be brought about by the harmonious action of the employers and employees."[38] At about the same time, "Cid" wrote a letter to the *Watchman* strongly favoring the ten-hour day. He noted approvingly, however, that although there had been talk of a general strike, "thanks to the Knights of Labor and kindred organizations workingmen have learned that there are more effectual ways of redressing their wrongs."[39]

Rather than sanction a strike, leaders of the Knights appointed a special committee to look into the ten-hour-day question. This committee approached most of the lumber operators in Humboldt County.[40] Lumber employers claimed not to be opposed to the shorter day in principle. Their main objection was that it would put them at a competitive disadvantage with their counterparts in Mendocino, where the twelve-hour day was firmly in effect.[41] Prompted largely by this response, the Humboldt Knights launched an organizing drive in Mendocino in June 1887. P. E. Davis, District Master Workman of all Humboldt County assemblies, went to Mendocino to spearhead the endeavor. Davis soon encountered difficulties "on account of the manufacturers owning whole towns and all the surrounding to their mills, and denying him the opportunity of a public meeting."[42] Before long, however, both the *Watchman* and Davis were trumpeting the success of the organizing drive in Mendocino. In fact, their claims were exaggerated; notwithstanding a prolonged and costly campaign, Davis organized only one assembly in Mendocino County.[43]

The Humboldt lumber employers, no doubt unimpressed with the results of the organizing campaign in Mendocino County, showed little inclination to concede the ten-hour day. During the summer of 1887, at a conference that apparently most Knights were unaware of until it was reported in the *Watchman* on October 1, Davis once again met with the Humboldt lumber employers. He confessed in his report on the meeting to the District Assembly that he had received little encouragement from the lumber manufacturers, although they did promise a formal response to the ten-hour-day request.[44] In the wake of Davis's report, the *Watchman* criticized the lumber employers for not responding to the request. But although the *Watchman* lamented the "bad faith" of the employers, it concurred with the decision of the Knights' leadership not to call a strike. Indeed, the *Watchman* praised the "better counsels of the Knights" for prevailing in the face of a "determination to strike arbitrarily."[45]

The reluctance of leaders of the Knights to sanction a strike may have stemmed in part from their belief that strikes were doomed to failure. The *Watchman* repeatedly argued that strikes rarely succeeded. Moreover, as the moderate resolution of the Port Kenyon Knights on the ten-hour question suggests, rural assemblies would probably not have supported a strike over this issue. It is unlikely that Humboldt County farmers, who worked from dawn to dusk for most months of the year, would have been prepared to support strike action to help lumber workers obtain a ten-hour day.

But, in the last analysis, the determination of the Knights' leadership to avert a strike rested not so much on an assessment of the outcome of such action as on their preference for a nonconfrontational course of action. Throughout the struggle over the ten-hour day, leaders of the Humboldt Knights placed a naive faith in the beneficence of the lumber employers. Confronted with resistance, they meekly accepted the argument that the Humboldt County lumber industry could not be competitive if it reduced working hours. (In fact, as we will see in the next chapter, Humboldt County lumber employers took such a step three years later without seriously affecting their competitive position vis-à-vis Mendocino's lumber industry.)

As an alternative to a strike, the *Watchman* urged the Humboldt Knights to redouble their efforts to elevate the moral and intellectual condition of their members. At the end of the 1886 logging season, and in the context of the first strike rumors over the ten-hour issue, the *Watchman* offered the following homily:

Organization and education is the great power which the Knights of Labor propose as a remedial agent. With intelligence arises a sense of individuality in each worker, which begets self-respect, and commands the respect of others. First organize and educate then an intelligent presentation of your case will command attention and acquiescence, for then you will have become the superior force in the social economy.[46]

In March 1887, when sentiment for a strike resurfaced, the *Watchman* reiterated its message: "A thorough understanding of the principles and theory of the Order is worth more than all strikes for when this is acquired there will be no necessity or occasion for a strike, for they will then have acquired the power to ask and enforce whatever is right."[47]

The *Watchman* suggested a number of means by which the Humboldt Knights might bring about the lumber workers' moral regeneration. Seasonally unemployed loggers were urged to attend classes at the Eureka Academy and Business College, instead of making "the usual run of the town during winter."[48] In January 1887, the Knights sponsored a series of free lectures open to the general public, beginning with a well-attended lecture on astronomy.[49] And within the confines of their own assemblies, the Knights discussed a wide range of social and political issues. Important anniversaries often served as occasions for a special celebration. The Humboldt assembly began making preparations to celebrate George Washington's birthday in January 1887. There was to be a dramatic performance followed by a light meal and liberal servings of hot coffee.[50] Several times, the *Watchman* urged lumber workers to band together and establish a cooperative sawmill or shingle mill[51]—a somewhat fanciful suggestion in view of the fact that, as the *Watchman* admitted, such a venture required a minimum capital investment of $10,000.[52]

The *Watchman* stressed repeatedly that temperance was an absolute prerequisite if the worker was to elevate his moral and social standing.[53] Lumber workers were urged not to waste their hard-earned savings in saloons during the winter. The *Watchman* boasted that the Knights could take credit for having done "more to lessen intemperance and foolish squandery of money than any one other organization."[54] Evidently, their work was far from complete; a February 1887 report stated that "almost nightly there are bloody frays." The Humboldt assembly responded by announcing its determination to "take a hand in suppressing low whiskey dens and dance houses."[55] Accordingly, it carried out a threat to have the names of all persons who signed a petition for a liquor license published in the *Watchman*.[56] At the same time, the *Watchman* strongly endorsed the crusade of a newly formed branch of the Women's Christian Temperance Union in Eureka.

Clerks and Seamen Join the Struggle

The Knights of Labor was not the only representative of organized labor in Humboldt County in the mid-1880s. In 1886, three occupational groups organized in Eureka for the first time: a branch of the Coast Seaman's Union (CSU), which was founded in San Francisco in 1885;

a branch of the International Typographical Union (ITU), while the Eureka clerks formed a union to reduce their hours. There was a considerable amount of cooperation between the Knights and these new labor organizations.

The clerks had an even longer day than the lumber workers, usually, beginning work at 7:00 A.M. and working until 9:00 or 10:00 P.M. The newly formed Clerks' Union proposed that from May 1 to October 1, merchants should close their stores at 7:00 P.M. and for the remainder of the year, at 8:00 P.M. Union members drew up a petition and tried to secure pledges from Eureka merchants to observe the shorter hours. Confronted with the recalcitrance of a few of the city's merchants, the union sent circulars to the Knights of Labor, the CSU, and the general citizenry, appealing for their cooperation in enforcing the new closing hours.[57] The CSU responded by ordering its members to boycott all merchants not abiding by the shorter hours. The Knights also supported the clerks; pressure from the Knights in Ferndale resulted in all merchants there adopting shorter hours,[58] while in Eureka the clerks founded a trade assembly of the Knights in July 1887.[59]

The Clerks' Union obtained considerable public support, but the community and the county press did not take such a benign view of the sailors' and longshoremen's organizational activities. The reason for this was that the nature of the shipping industry dictated that militant tactics would have to be employed to establish a stable and effective union. The unskilled nature of most seafaring work, and the highly centralized hiring procedures developed by the shipowners, meant that a union's efficacy, if not its survival, depended on its ability to control hiring and, ideally, to impose a union shop. This issue was at the root of repeated conflicts between West Coast sailors and shipowners during the late nineteenth and early twentieth centuries. Sailors were also among the most exploited workers in America. Wages were often as low as $20 a month and subject to sudden fluctuations. Sailors were at the mercy of boardinghouse keepers who served as employment agents for shipowners and captains. Once at sea, a ship's captain possessed autocratic powers. He could even order corporal punishment. In the words of Hyman Weintraub, the sailor's life was "a purgatory of unending hell."[60]

At the ports of Eureka and Arcata in Humboldt County, sailors and longshoremen attempted with varying degrees of success to impose a union shop even before a CSU branch was established. Between 1885 and 1887, in a desperate effort to establish a secure foothold for the CSU in Humboldt County, prounion sailors attacked nonunion sailors for strike-breaking and for violating union wage scales. In November

1885, Louis Smith complained that he was beaten by four union sailors for not joining the union and for agreeing to sail for $20 a month, instead of the union scale of $30.[61] There were numerous such incidents. One of the most dramatic occurred during a general strike by West Coast sailors and longshoremen in September 1886. Twenty members of the Humboldt CSU were arrested for rioting after they boarded a schooner in Arcata harbor and allegedly intimidated a nonunion sailor.[62] Inevitably, these tactics incurred the opprobrium of most of the community. The CSU leadership in San Francisco did not condone such methods; indeed, they endeavored to restrain their zealous Humboldt County members.

Notwithstanding the lack of public support, the CSU succeeded in organizing most of the sailors and longshoremen in Humboldt County. By 1887, the CSU branch in Eureka had 113 members; only one man was not a union member. Ship captains were recruiting through union headquarters instead of through boardinghouses.[63] A deeply felt sense of grievance plus the comparatively homogenous makeup of the workforce facilitated the CSU's growth. Scandinavian-born sailors made up a high proportion of the labor force and played a vital role in founding the union. Many officials of the international union, including Andrew Furuseth, who served as president from 1887 to 1938, were also of Scandinavian descent. The role of the Scandinavians was especially important in Humboldt County. In 1880, when they constituted less than 3 percent of the county's population, 36 percent of the sailors were Scandinavian by birth.[64] During the 1880s, as Scandinavian emigration to Humboldt County swelled, they played an even more important role in the county's seafaring trade. Charles Peterson, who spent much of his life working in the Humboldt lumber industry, recalled that during the 1890s, "the lumber fleet" was known as the "Scandinavian Navy."[65]

The Eureka Knights lent the CSU considerable support in the first precarious months of its existence in Humboldt County, especially during the general strike on the West Coast in September 1886. The *Watchman* carried several articles vividly depicting the plight of the sailor. George Speed, chairman of the Executive Board of the Humboldt County Knights, called out all members of the Knights employed in ancillary occupations, such as longshoring and catering.[66] An official notice appeared in the *Watchman* warning Knights not to "assist or aid in any way vessels which are connected with present difficulty."[67] At least one assembly levied an assessment to support the strikers.[68] H. M. Burnett stated that "no sailor can truthfully say that the comrades of Eureka let one of their members go hungry or without shelter."[69]

The radical wing of the Knights was responsible for mobilizing support for the sailors and longshoremen, but the radicals paid a heavy price. Whenever union sailors were alleged to have been involved in a violent incident, the press held the "dynamite element" of the Knights responsible. The *Arcata Union* used the mass arrest of sailors in September 1886 as an occasion to call on moderate Knights to purge extremists from their ranks.[70] Burnett repudiated the sailors' use of violence and asserted that the incident that led to the arrest of 20 union sailors had cost the strike and the labor movement considerable public support.[71] The hostile climate of community opinion aroused by the radicals' support for the sailors exposed them to the vindictiveness of their enemies. Many Knights who had actively supported the sailors were discharged from their jobs and blacklisted, including radical leader George Speed.[72] This was a blow from which the radical Knights never recovered, and it paved the way for the ascendancy of the moderate and conservative Knights.

In the aftermath of the sailors' strike of 1886, the Humboldt Knights' support of the CSU became more qualified. Xavier Leder, local agent of the CSU, reported in June 1887 that after talking with Eureka Knights, he learned that "the former proceedings of the Eureka branch of the CSU are looked upon with slight disapproval on account of the rash and apparently reckless action taken by members of our organization on certain occasions in days gone by."[73]

The Knights and Politics

The participation of the Humboldt Knights in local politics corresponded with the period of greatest nationwide political activity by the Knights. Before 1886, the Knights of Labor played a relatively minor role in electoral politics, preferring to concentrate on lobbying efforts to influence congressional legislation. The Knights' disastrous defeat in the strike against the Gould railroad empire in the Southwest and the rapid expansion of the Order in 1886 encouraged Knights to play a more active role in local politics. The Humboldt Knights did not participate in local politics until 1886. The sorry saga of the Greenback Labor party in Humboldt County produced cynicism and apathy among potential third-party supporters, and many Knights believed that political activity would be diversionary and divisive. Alfred Cridge was a strong political abstentionist. He insisted that people had to be "energetically educated" to dismiss the "bogus ballot delusion," which was like "the old man of the sea squatting on the shoulders of the labor movement."[74]

Cridge's departure from Humboldt County, an influx of new members during the summer of 1886, and the success of the Knights' political ventures elsewhere prompted the Humboldt Knights to reevaluate their antipolitical stance. The Eureka Knights were the main force behind the launching of a Citizen's party to contest local Eureka elections in June 1886. The party's platform was moderate in tone and content. It promised a "just, honest and economical administration of our municipal government" and the enforcement of all state laws and local liquor laws. The final plank of the platform stated: "We believe that dance houses and all other places of iniquity are demoralizing in their tendencies, degrading in their morals and are not legitimate elements of honest industry, and we therefore demand their immediate abatement."[75]

The Knights' venture into local politics was a success. The mayor, a majority of the City Council, and the police chief were Knights. The successful candidates reflected the Knights' diverse social composition and included the perennially elected city assessor, who became mayor, a merchant, two blacksmiths, and a harnessmaker. The significance of the victory should not be exaggerated. The Knights maintained a low profile throughout the campaign, viewing themselves not so much as the political arm of an organization articulating a program of radical social transformation but as part of a broad, nonpartisan citizens' coalition to rationalize city government and legislate the moral edification of the citizenry. As the *Arcata Union* commented, although the election was "carried principally by the Knights of Labor, it must be remembered that the ticket had the support of the religious and temperance element, and that there was no politics connected with it."[76]

The Knights played a more conspicuous role in county and state elections in the fall of 1886. They were the leading force behind the establishment of a People's party in August and constituted at least one-third of the delegates at the founding convention, which adopted a 13-point platform highly reminiscent of that of the Greenback Labor party. The platform called for the establishment of a national monetary system that would ensure an adequate supply of money and demanded recognition of the "national issue" as full legal tender in the payment of all debts. The government was not to establish or recognize any banking corporations. Another plank advocated government ownership of all telegraph and telephone services, railroads, and other vital means of transportation. Additional planks included a demand for a graduated income tax, a law "to secure both sexes equal pay for equal work," immigration laws to exclude the Chinese permanently, legislation to make all public offices elective, and the holding of a referendum on the "regulation of the liquor traffic." [77]

Having resuscitated the Greenback Labor party's platform, the People's party proceeded to repeat many of the mistakes of its predecessor. Most notably, the party demonstrated poor judgment in selecting its nominees. Many people on the ticket had recently held office under Republican or Democratic party labels and were, as the *Arcata Union* snidely put it, "recent converts to the Workingman's cause." [78] In fairness to the People's party, two of its nominees had been Greenback Labor party candidates in 1882, and the most important nomination went to P. E. Davis, who was selected to contest a seat in the state assembly. Davis appears to have had the full confidence of the Humboldt Knights, for in the summer of 1886, Powderly received several letters from assemblies in the county urging that Davis be appointed official organizer.[79] Davis also succeeded Cridge as editor of the *Watchman* until his candidacy in the fall elections forced him to relinquish the position in September 1886. But Davis's nomination proved disastrous. Within three weeks of accepting the nomination, Davis attended the Democratic party convention where he also received the nomination for a seat in the state assembly. Davis's move took everyone by surprise. He was ridiculed and denounced by most of the county press as an opportunist and a hypocrite. The press recalled the many occasions on which Davis had pilloried the Democratic party. One wag commented that Davis was "now the People's party–Democratic party–Greenback party–Knights of Labor–Independent nominee for the assembly." [80] Davis protested that he had always been loyal to the Democratic party, only to have it revealed that in 1884 he had signed the local Blaine–Logan roll and supported the Republican party.[81]

As the elections drew closer, the *Watchman* exhorted the Knights to support the People's party ticket and described those Knights still opposed to getting involved in politics as "tools" of the old parties. The People's party, however, did not perform well in the elections. Davis lost to his Republican opponent by a substantial margin (1,314 to 919 votes), and the only People's party candidates elected were two men who had recently held offices under the Democrats and Republicans.

Disappointed at the outcome of their venture into state and county politics, the Knights consoled themselves with the fact that they controlled the Eureka City Council. It was soon evident that the platform of the Citizen's party was not a smokescreen for a program of radical social transformation by the Eureka Knights. Between 1886 and 1888, the Eureka City Council embarked enthusiastically on a program of civic improvement that presaged many Progressive era reforms. The council had a comprehensive survey of the city undertaken by an eminent municipal engineer from Oakland. Extensive improvements were made to the city's sidewalks and sewer system, and steps taken to improve the quality of the city's paved roads—accomplishments proudly recalled by Millard Gardner almost thirty years later. After the council had been in power for only six months, the *Watchman* boasted that the City Council had been transformed "from a sort of neighborly affair" that did most of its business on the "mutual admiration plan" to a council run on sound and efficient principles.[82] During the 1888 election campaign, the *Watchman* drew voters' attention to the "marvellous change in the general appearance of our streets and sidewalks" that had taken place under the new council and noted that, in spite of the civic improvements, the municipal tax rate had fallen from $1 to 65 cents per $100 of assessed valuation.[83]

The Eureka City Council also endeavored to elevate the moral fiber of the citizenry. Knight and council member W. L. Mercer introduced several resolutions calling for stricter enforcement of the liquor and red-light ordinances. Accordingly, liquor license fees were raised substantially. This measure did not attract universal support in Eureka. From the late evening of July 3 until the early morning of July 4, 1887, Mercer's house was pelted "with a fusillade of bombs and other missiles" by a mob that the *Watchman* described as "the lower order of saloon men."[84] Incensed that two officers called to the scene simply stood on the sidewalk laughing, the *Watchman* accused one of the officers of being a ringleader.

The Citizen's party was defeated decisively at the 1888 Eureka municipal elections. A lumber magnate, John Vance, was elected mayor, crushing his opponent, Josiah Bell, by 657 votes to 313. Strong anti-temperance sentiment undoubtedly contributed to the party's defeat. Shortly before the election, the *Watchman* heartily endorsed a local-option law that would have instituted prohibition in Eureka and effectively tried to turn the election into a referendum on the issue. The *Watchman* attributed the defeat of the Citizen's party to the efforts of the "whiskey ticket" and the general organizational collapse of the Eureka Knights.[85]

The Demise of the Knights

In fact, the Knights had expired as an effective organization in the county well before the June 1888 election. References to the Knights of Labor in the local press, including the *Watchman*, are conspicuous by their absence during 1888. The Knights held a Thanksgiving Ball in 1887, but this is the last mention of any kind of social, industrial, or political activity on their part. Symbolically, in the following month several well-known Humboldt radicals departed to join the Puget Sound Cooperative Colony, and the *Watchman* offered free pamphlets to its readers on the new utopian colony.[86] In 1890, assemblies were established in Eureka, Freshwater, and the Eel River Valley, and the *Watchman* claimed the Knights were experiencing a renaissance in the county.[87] However, reports of the rebirth were greatly exaggerated. The born-again Knights attracted a minimal following, and none of the assemblies survived the year.

The Humboldt Knights thus vanished from the stage as abruptly as they had appeared. Their demise resulted from a complex mix of factors, some within and some beyond their control. In evaluating the reasons for their eclipse, it must be borne in mind that the fortunes of the Knights nationally began to wane at the same time as they did in Humboldt County. In the late 1880s, the influence of the labor movement receded in small communities across America, and in many cases disappeared altogether. Until the early years of the twentieth century, unionism was confined mainly to skilled workers usually affiliated with the American Federation of Labor and residing in the larger American cities. Lumber workers, who had been virtually unorganized before the advent of the Knights, helped establish at least 84 assemblies in 24 states.[88] After the disintegration of the Knights in the late 1880s, almost all lumber workers were without union representation for twenty years.

Many of the factors that made it hard to sustain an organized labor movement in Humboldt County pertained elsewhere, particularly in small to medium-size, single-industry communities in which employers had immense power and could keep workers under virtual round-the-clock surveillance. In a small city such as Eureka, let alone a logging camp or full-fledged company lumber town, it was impossible for agitators like Dan Cronin and George Speed to melt into the anonymity of a metropolis, as many of their counterparts could. In the extractive industries, such as lumber, the regional predominance of an industry greatly facilitated the organization and coordination of employer resistance to unionism.

The lumber workers' vulnerability to repression was accentuated by the fact that many of their skills could be acquired within a relatively short time by an unskilled worker. Relatedly, the lumber worker's position was weakened still further by the evolution of a national labor market in the 1880s. By this time, lumber capitalists operated on a scale that enabled them to bear the costs of advertising for men and transporting them nationally, and to take advantage of the nation's integrated railroad network. From 1883 onward, there were recurrent complaints about the Humboldt lumber employers' practice of advertising for labor as far afield as the Midwest and Atlantic states, and the flooding of the labor market at the beginning of the logging season. The Humboldt Knights posted warnings in labor papers throughout the nation, telling workers that the northern California labor market was being saturated.

Finally, the lumber industry and many other extractive industries were highly sensitive to cyclical fluctuations in the economy, which was not conducive to the establishment and maintenance of stable unions. It made a highly mobile workforce even more transient. Thus, during the depression of 1885, the Knights experienced a very high turnover rate. In the four established assemblies, a total of 413 people joined in 1885, but 325 left, leaving a total membership of 196 at year's end. Humboldt assembly 3337, composed principally of lumber workers, accounted for nearly three-quarters of this turnover.[89] Undoubtedly, other factors entered into the high turnover, but the unstable economic climate was the primary one. Many lumber workers had to migrate in search of work during hard times, and a majority of them left an area at the end of a regular logging season.

Yet the demise of the Humboldt Knights cannot be explained by these factors alone. The ideological and organizational nature of the Knights and the resultant contradictions also played a major role. The Knights were heirs to a vibrant democratic–republican tradition that provided the basis for a penetrating critique of the Gilded Age political economy. The economic and social turbulence of the mid-1880s reinforced the dissenters' disquiet. To Humboldt County dissidents, developments in their own county, notably the saga of the California Redwood Company and the destitution of 1885, were a microcosm of events occurring across the nation. By the mid-1880s, they believed that the redemption and regeneration of America would have to be achieved through the self-organization of the producing classes, whose fundamental rights were being abrogated by rapacious monopolists in league with corrupt politicians. Such a sweeping analysis enabled dissenters to share a broad consensus but, at the same time, it masked important differences among dissenters, especially when it came to prescribing concrete action. Rant as they did about the greed, power, and selfishness of monopoly in the abstract, one wing of the dissenters could accept that the interests of labor and capital might be antagonistic; this was particularly true when it came to confronting capitalism in their own backyard. It was one thing to denounce the Vanderbilts and the Goulds, and another to castigate lumber capitalists such as William Carson and John Vance, who had risen from rags to riches and whose enterprises were critical to the community's prosperity.

Paradoxically, although elements of the democratic–republican tradition—the labor theory of value and the belief that a rough state of socioeconomic reward and opportunity should prevail—pointed the way to a class analysis, many dissenters refused to believe that things had reached such an impasse. They attributed the nation's malaise to a spirit of rampant acquisitive individualism and believed in founding a more equitable and cooperative social order, but they could not repudiate all the individualistic strands of the democratic–republican tradition. They viewed the ills of Gilded Age America as an aberration deriving from a few malfunctions and, especially, from the machinations of a few wicked men. If these men could be removed and a few reforms enacted, the sum total of individual endeavors would lead to a Cooperative Commonwealth and the reaffirmation of the superiority of the American form of government. Dissenters of this ideological tendency were unwilling or incapable of seeing the Knights principally as an agency for extracting concessions from capitalism. Instead, these Knights hoped to purify the existing system and convince everyone of labor's worthy place in the sun.

This wing of the Knights coalesced uneasily with the radical faction. Generally more proletarian in their occupational backgrounds, the latter asserted a proto-Marxian concept of the social order that accepted a fundamental antagonism between labor and capital. They saw the Knights as a trade union to represent the day-to-day interests of workers and as an agency of radical social transformation. "They are instituted to meet the traffic of every day life as it occurs between labor and capital," stated a correspondent to the *Watchman*, attempting to characterize the difference between Knights of a trade-unionist orientation and Knights who saw their "mission . . . as a training school to educate a future purpose; not for present action; save as present benefit may incidentally grow out of it."[90]

This ideological cleavage was to produce bitter factionalism among the Humboldt Knights that was heightened by the presence of a hard core of IWA members, on the one hand, and a significant complement of businessmen and farmers, on the other. In an *ante mortem* on the fate of the Humboldt Knights, Beith vividly described the disarray, confusion, and division:

Frequently a blend of the orders—the trade unions and kindred of that ilk, held session in the same hall with the same body—making a perfect Babel of confusion and misunderstanding. Men who were probably capable of understanding a single order were confused by this multiplicity—and in the propaganda of these measures brought the order into contempt. Anarchists, Socialists and Red Internationalists found a cordial footing on the floor and discussed their measures and modes until the poor bewildered Knight was unable to distinguish to what category he belonged. . . . Is it to be wondered that the end soon came?[91]

Ideological splits among the Humboldt Knights did not follow neat lines or correspond precisely to the social class of members, but, assuming the Humboldt Knights were representative, it would be misleading to view the Knights as a unified ideological entity. Such an interpretation evades serious questions about the Knights' limited efficacy as a trade union and political organization, not to mention their ephemeral presence in Humboldt and many other regions of the country. In the light of the above contradictions, it is not surprising that, in 1889, the Eureka correspondent of the *Coast Seamen's Journal* wrote that the Humboldt Knights had expired "without having accomplished anything whatever by way of bettering the condition of the labor classes."[92]

Chapter 6

Paternalism and Community

After the demise of the Knights of Labor, the organized labor movement failed to resuscitate itself in the following decade. The weakness of the county's labor movement in the 1890s paralleled a decline in the fortunes of the movement at the state and national levels. In Humboldt County, only longshoremen, sailors, carpenters, and printers preserved their organizations. For most of the 1890s, their presence was little more than vestigial, owing much to their affiliation with well-established national and regional labor organizations. The depression of the mid-1890s was an important factor in undermining the strength of existing unions and preventing the revival of others. But the weakness of the labor movement was not simply a result of a depressed economic climate. In many cases, especially among lumber workers, the fragility of the union movement was apparent before the depression hit the county.

Factors working against the organization of stable trade unionism among lumber workers were formidable, but this does not provide a full explanation of the ephemeral and episodic nature of lumber unionism in the late nineteenth and early twentieth centuries. Any account of labor relations in this period must weigh the considerable influence of paternalism and mutualism.[1]

The Roots of Reciprocity

Several elements fostered the ideal of a fundamental harmony and reciprocity between labor and capital among a significant segment of the Humboldt community. The fact that many of the county's lumber entrepreneurs had risen from humble origins in Humboldt County lent credence to the ideology of social mobility so integral to the democratic–republican ideal. The county's increasing reliance on the lumber industry also encouraged an interdependent relationship between employers, workers, and community. In addition, the small and often intimate setting of both workplace and community social relations sustained a distinctly personal quality to human contact between all classes. Finally, the scope of the social and economic power of lumber employers militated to some extent against an antagonistic perception of the social order. In the face of this power, it was tempting for workers to cling to notions of reciprocity and obtain whatever concessions they could within this framework. In their turn, lumber employers, conscious of their power and moral legitimacy, strove to foster a paternalistic and deferential ethos among their workers.

An early example of an attempt to create a benevolent image occurred in 1882 when pioneer Joseph Russ opened his mill. The *Humboldt Times* pronounced it to be a "model mill," especially with respect to the "generous and liberal concessions allowed to the men."[2] Russ's mill had a large, well-equipped cookhouse, and each man had a room and comfortable bedding. The main living quarters had a large reading room, which was kept supplied with newspapers from around the country. At a special dinner for his workers, shortly after the mill opened, Russ dwelt at length on the improvements he had made: "I try always to measure such things as I would have them measured out to me . . . your physical and mental powers are your capital, and I have endeavored by these changes to so protect that capital." Russ's speech reveals that his benevolence was not motivated solely by altruism but that he was also acutely sensitive to the precariousness of the relationship between labor and capital and the fact that a well-treated worker might be a more productive one:

At present it seems to be the sole aim of employers to obtain the greatest amount of work at the least possible cost, while those employed too often take no further interest in their work than to put in the alloted hours. . . . I am convinced that labor adjusted on this basis has a constant and almost inevitable tendency to engender and precipitate strikes and the other harsh and desperate remedies for supposed and actual grievances. The remedy for this is a community of interest between employer and employee.[3]

Over a quarter of a century later, Noah Falk, one of Humboldt County's few surviving pioneer lumbermen, echoed Russ's views. The actions of "self-interested persons" caused "friction and ill-feeling" between labor and capital, and could be avoided if labor was "treated with justice." Falk insisted that "the capitalist is the friend of his men, or should be," and he added, "I sincerely believe that the workingmen of this county will bear me out when I say that never in the long years I have been here, have I been unwilling to give them their due."[4] The fact that a year earlier (1907), the Elk River Mill and Lumber Company, owned by Falk, had not been touched by a strike that closed down most of the Humboldt County lumber industry suggests Falk's benevolence was more than rhetoric.

Dan Newell, who operated the largest independent logging operation in the county during the late nineteenth century and who had migrated directly from the woods of Maine to the redwoods of Humboldt County in the late 1850s, was renowned for his managerial ability and the generosity with which he treated his employees. In an interview with the *Western Watchman* in 1896, Newell spoke candidly of the reasons why he treated his workers so well: "A man has got to know what he is about in the first place; and so far as I'm concerned I hire good men and pay good wages; you can't log worth a cent with cheap men; get good men, pay 'em good wages, and you do good work; at least that's been my experience."[5]

The decision of Humboldt County lumber owners to grant the ten-hour day to all mill workers illustrates the complex motives underlying their paternalism and provides good evidence that a significant number of lumber workers had deferential attitudes toward their employers. The length of the working day had been a recurrent issue in Humboldt County since the mid-1880s. In the late 1880s, after the demise of the Knights, the carpenters' and clerks' unions kept it alive. Against this background, in late August 1890, William Carson announced that he was instituting a ten-hour day for mill workers without any reduction in wages.[6] Within a few days, all the major lumber operators in Humboldt County followed suit. Their action was hailed in the county press as a deed of supreme benevolence.

Undoubtedly, Carson and the other employers did not reduce hours in the face of direct and immediate pressure on the part of the mill hands. John Haist, the Eureka agent of the Coast Seamen's Union, stated bluntly that "this concession cannot be called a labor victory, for it came to them unexpected, unsolicited and perhaps undeserved."[7] Several factors account for the sudden reduction in hours. First, by 1890, the lumber market had recovered fully from the slump that had beset it in the mid-1880s, thus making the reduction in hours more economically palatable. Second, since lumber employers were often closely involved in the day-to-day supervision of operations, some may have desired a shorter working day themselves and been acutely aware of the hardship that a twelve-hour day imposed on workers. George Speed recalls that his boss at the Flanigan and Brosnan logging camp was strongly in favor of the ten-hour day, as it would allow him more time with his family; and Speed's employer even offered to donate money to support the organizing drive in Mendocino to bring about a ten-hour day in the redwood lumber industry.[8] More important, with the ten-hour day established in the Great Lakes and Pacific Northwest lumbering regions, the twelve-hour day in the redwood region threatened to become something of an anachronism and to undermine the employers' reputation for benevolence. In a retrospective analysis two years later, the *Western Watchman* offered this as the primary reason for the concession.[9] Finally and relatedly, although not confronted with an immediate groundswell of discontent over the working day, the lumber employers were motivated in part by a desire to preempt future agitation on the issue. The concession in 1890 occurred during the peak of a campaign for shorter hours by clerks, carpenters, painters, and masons. Three days before Carson's announcement, a letter appeared in the *Humboldt Standard*, signed by 91 men from the building trades, declaring that after September 1, they would work only a nine-hour day.[10] At this time also, the Knights were showing fleeting signs of making a comeback in Humboldt County. In terms of defusing a resurgent labor movement, it was rational for lumber employers to grant the ten-hour day and portray it as an act of benevolence, rather than appear to be succumbing to another round of pressure by lumber workers on the issue at some future point.

Most of the mill hands employed in the Humboldt Bay region were surprised and elated by the concession. The news broke on Saturday, August 30, and as rumors spread that the other lumber operators were going to follow the lead of Carson, mill workers decided that some kind of demonstration of gratitude was in order. Shortly after 8:00 P.M., hundreds of mill workers began assembling in front of City Hall. A procession led by two bands then marched to the house of lumber employer David Evans. By the time the parade reached Evans's residence, there were at least 1,000 people present. Evans threw open the doors and windows of his house as the bands serenaded him. George Murray then made a formal statement of thanks to Evans on behalf of the mill workers. In his response, Evans claimed that during his life he had occupied almost every position in the mill, and insisted that he still considered himself "a laborer." For many years, he said, he had felt that a reduction in the millmen's working day was overdue. The procession then marched to the residences of William Carson and John Vance, where almost identical scenes followed.[11]

Not everyone regarded the ten-hour concession as a supreme act of benevolence. In a long and scathing letter published in the *Western Watchman*, W. Bolonies of Eureka chided the mill workers for their passivity over the issue and for participating in a charade "in which the laborer is made to play the role of recipient of this or that man's bounty." He was especially cynical about the motives of Eureka Mayor John Vance: "The idea he sought to convey is, that, employers are dispensers of bounty to those they employ and consequently laborers should regard them as benefactors." [12] Bolonies asked lumber workers to consider who really produced the wealth and concluded by urging millmen and woodsmen to form unions.

The spontaneous outburst of jubilation and the lavish expressions of gratitude that followed the news of the ten-hour day indicate that many mill workers perceived the concession as a supreme act of benevolence. It is also significant, as the *Western Watchman* noted critically,[13] that the mill workers did not choose a spokesman from among their own ranks to thank the mill owners; instead, they selected a prominent figure in the community to speak for them. The anniversary of the ten-hour day was celebrated for several years, especially by William Carson's employees. On the first anniversary, a letter of gratitude from "All Employees of the Bay Mill" appeared in the local press:

When we read of the existing troubles between employers and employed in various sections of this and other countries . . . we are most impressed with the fortunate circumstances of our situation. . . . While it is a source of regret that differences between capital and labor in other places should lead to misunderstandings, loss, and bitter contentions, it yet contributes to our pleasure that our hours of labor were lessened without loss of wages and without any request by us. We sincerely hope that each recurring anniversary of this event will turn the thoughts of every mill laborer toward the person to whom we are all indebted for the reduction. Finally, we hope that you may recall our appreciation of your act each year and never have occasion to regret . . . that the step was taken.[14]

Lumbermen, Paternalism, and Republicanism

The integral role played by many lumber employers in the social and political life of the community reflected and reinforced the esteem in which they were held by both lumber workers and the community at large. In the realm of politics, four prominent lumbermen—John Vance, David Evans, C. C. Stafford, and D. J. Flanigan—served as mayors of Eureka between 1888 and 1901. William Carson served several terms on the Eureka City Council. He was a Republican presidential elector in 1896 and ran unsuccessfully for mayor against David Evans in 1899. Joseph Russ was twice elected to the California state assembly on the Republican ticket. This is not to argue that lumber entrepreneurs dominated the political life of the community. With the possible exception of tax assessments and internal improvements, lumbermen could do relatively little to foster their business interests at the local (especially municipal) level. Lumbermen were far more concerned with political developments at the state and national levels, which had a greater impact on their fortunes. The political role of the lumbermen at the local level was primarily a function of the fact that they were highly esteemed members of the community and, like the "best men" in many communities, believed it was their civic duty to run for office.

The role of lumber operators in local politics mirrored the important social role they played in the life of the community. The Gilded Age was an age of voluntarism, and many social institutions depended on the generosity of local businessmen. Lumbermen in Humboldt County gave important financial support to such institutions as churches, charities, educational institutions, and the free public library. They frequently sponsored communitywide events, such as the annual Fourth of July celebrations, the Admission Day anniversary, and a midsummer fair. In 1879, John Vance began organizing an annual picnic for the schoolchildren of Humboldt County, which often drew as many as 2,000 people.

In evaluating paternalism in late-nineteenth-century Humboldt County, it is important to appreciate that, even in the "metropolis" of Eureka, Humboldters lived essentially in a face-to-face setting where interpersonal relations were such that many members of the community were on a first-name basis. This is conveyed most vividly in some of the recollective accounts. J. C. Blake nostalgically recalled the "fraternity" that existed among the old pioneers: "Everyone knew everyone else, including his peculiarities and many were the tales told around the big open fireplace in the evening when one would stop at a neighbor's, and we were all neighbors, even if we lived many miles apart."[15] As a child, Blake was well acquainted with lumber operators Isaac Minor, William Carson, and John Vance. He remembered how kind and friendly these men were to children, and recalled specific occasions when he was approached by them to be asked what type of hogs he was caring for or how he was progressing in school.[16]

This web of relationships was reinforced outside the workplace by such institutions as the churches, schools, charitable institutions, and a plethora of fraternal orders. Fraternal orders played a central role in the life of the community from the 1850s until well into the twentieth century.[17] The Humboldt County press repeatedly boasted that Eureka had more fraternal societies than any other city of its size in the United States.[18] In 1889, the *Times* reported that the Odd Fellows' membership was over 500 in Eureka alone,[19] and in 1919 the Odd Fellows retained 10 lodges countywide, comprising 1,426 members, in addition to 9 sister Rebekah lodges with 1,213 members.[20] The Masons, the Native Sons and Daughters of the Golden West, the Knights of Columbus, and the Woodmen of the World, to name but a few, all had large memberships. At a grand celebration in 1899, the Woodmen of the World, a fraternal order founded in Colorado in 1890, drew over 2,000 participants.[21] The small community of Blue Lake, with a population of not more than 800 people, possessed 11 different fraternal orders in 1907.[22]

The size of these fraternal orders indicates that they were hardly exclusive domains restricted to the elite members of the community. Obituaries of lumber workers in the local press reveal quite often that they belonged to a fraternal order. At a jubilee celebration of the Odd Fellows in 1899, one of the keynote speakers insisted that the order encompassed men from all classes: "It is not confined to those of any occupation or avocation. We find the laborer and the professional men, the merchant and the mechanic, all engaged in the noble work. And it is right that it should be so for the benefit of the community in general."[23]

Communitywide events such as the New Year's ball and Sunday picnics fostered the spirit of fraternity. Sunday picnics were especially important social occasions. Whether sponsored by the Odd Fellows, the Farmers' Association, The Blue Noses (people of Canadian origin), the Union Sunday school, or in honor of (California) Admission Day, Sunday picnics often attracted 2,000 people. The annual Fourth of July celebrations invariably drew the largest crowds. Mill and woods operations usually ceased at this time for a few days. At the Independence Day festivities, besides the patriotic orations and the reading of the Declaration of Independence, there were elaborate parades, gun salutes, sports programs with prizes for the winners, literary renditions, band music, pie-eating contests, a free barbecue, horseraces, and bike races. The day was usually capped off by a Grand Ball. Retired lumber worker Ralph Frost recalled the "good old days" in the 1880s when people from all over the county flocked to Eureka for a "three day carnival on the streets, side shows, fireman's hose contests, lots of firecrackers and fireworks."[24]

The Independence Day ritual was not simply a convivial occasion that helped foster a sense of social harmony in the community by drawing people from diverse class, religious, and national backgrounds to a common meeting place. It also provided the perfect setting for people of different political persuasions to venerate the shared and cherished republican principles on which the nation was founded.[25] Occasionally, dissenters attempted to use the July Fourth ritual to popularize the more radical precepts of the democratic–republican tradition. For example, in 1880, when the Greenback Labor party was gathering momentum, Keller stated at the Independence Day celebration in the small township of Centerville that he and his fellow Greenbackers would "on that day declare anew the principles that all men are equal before the law," and they would examine "the duties that devolve upon us in order that we may hand over to our posterity the privileges that were conferred upon us by our forefathers."[26] Such instances were rare, however. Invariably, Independence Day was one on which conservative political elements invoked the individualistic, corporatist, and chauvinist strains of the democratic–republican tradition to try and dispel the notion that a class system had evolved in America. The *Humboldt Times* called for a spectacular Fourth of July celebration in 1881 in rhetoric typical of that accompanying Independence Day festivities:

We have one of the best countries in the world. It is a common country and belongs to John Smith, just as much as it does to Dick Jones and Tom Brown. We are granted privileges alike, and one receives shelter or protection to the same extent as another. There is no such thing as an aristocracy, codfish or otherwise, and such ideas are only advanced by the narrow minded, bigoted, sordid, sour disappointed individuals. There is no such thing as caste.[27]

Such eulogies were not confined to Republican organs like the *Humboldt Times*. The *Western Watchman*, one of northern California's most established and outspoken dissident newspapers in the late nineteenth century, wrapped the memory of the sacred day in almost identical rhetoric in 1889: "The Fourth of July is a national day on which all hearts may throb in unison to a common aspiration of patriotic sentiment."[28] The following year, the *Watchman* described the Declaration of Independence as "one of the greatest advances made in human liberty, civilization and government."[29] The invocation of a shared and unique republican heritage on July Fourth, and indeed on other occasions, engendered a sense of local and national community that helped transcend underlying actual or potential social conflicts.

It is worth noting that as early as 1874, 3,000 people attended Independence Day celebrations in Ferndale with the Grangers contributing a significant complement.[30] In 1898, the Sailors' Union, the successor to the Coast Seamen's Union and still a militant union, played a prominent role in the Fourth of July parade.[31] Independence Day celebrations continued to attract several thousand people throughout the first two decades of the twentieth century. Only at the height of their power in the early twentieth century did the labor movement and the Socialist party attempt to organize rival festivities.

One aspect of the editorial in the *Humboldt Times*, quoted above, is especially important in understanding how the ritual could be used as a forum for the moral legitimation of the existing social order. This was the strong emphasis on the link between republicanism and the ideology of social mobility: the notion that America provided an arena in which all had an equal chance to compete and succeed. This assertion had considerable plausibility in a community where many of the lumber capitalists came from humble origins—a fact that David Evans and John Vance stressed when they responded to the mill workers' effusions of gratitude at being granted the ten-hour day. But the county press did not dwell on Horatio Alger stories solely in the context of Independence Day. They harped on the theme repeatedly, often during times of social and political dissension within the community. In 1888, the *Arcata Union*, fearful that the newly formed Union Labor party might attract significant support in the county, vigorously denied that the country's laws had produced a rigid class system. Malcontents who made such assertions were accused of ignoring the fact that:

Ninety percent of the wealthy men of Humboldt County started in life poor, some of them without a dollar, and that it was by pluck, strict economy and indomitable industry by which they accumulated money to help themselves, and that not one single one of them has made his fortune at banking. Is there any other country on earth where this state of things can be found? It seems to us that a country cannot be wholly misgoverned where the way is thus open for a poor man to get to the front.[32]

When William Carson ran for mayor of Eureka in 1899, the *Humboldt Standard* reminded citizens that, forty years ago, Carson had come to Humboldt County as a "poor man and worked as a common laborer in the woods," who by dint of hard work and frugality had "laid the foundation for his present ample fortune."[33] Not only did such stories lend credence to the ideology of social mobility, but they also heightened the deference and respect with which the self-made lumber entrepreneurs were viewed by their workers and the community at large and inclined people to regard their benevolence as acts of altruism inspired by empathy for the lot of the common man.

Although a substantial element of calculation inspired the benevolence of many lumbermen, it would be mistaken to view the Humboldt County lumber patrician in a totally cynical light. As Eugene Genovese has argued with respect to American slavery, paternalism could be born out of a genuine human concern and empathy as well as a shrewd sense of self-interest.[34] That many lumber operators had come from humble origins, that they often had worked in a wide range of logging and milling occupations, and that even after they had become entrepreneurs, they were involved in the day-to-day supervision of the work process and knew almost all their workers on a first-name basis were facts that made it hard for lumber operators not to feel some sympathy and responsibility for their workers.

The closest approximation to a bona fide altruistic paternalist was William Carson. No one in the county's history has been more revered for his beneficence. A newspaper tribute to him in 1899 presaged eulogies that would be bestowed on him after his death in 1912:

There are hundreds of poor people in Humboldt County who have been aided by him and did not know from whom the assistance came. . . . No man has ever gone to William Carson for help in a good cause and gone away empty-handed. No man has gone to him on behalf of the widow or the orphan, the sick or the needy and been refused assistance. During the hard times of the past few years his hand was always open to assist the worthy poor, and many a person has been clothed and warmed and fed by his generosity.[35]

Carson's reputation was not simply the mythical creation of the local press. Carson gave generously to many philanthropic causes, in and outside Humboldt County, including churches, orphanages, a meeting hall for Civil War veterans, and to victims of an Italian earthquake in 1908. He also mailed checks semiannually, ranging from $50 to $250, to people (usually women) who lived in New Brunswick and Maine.[36] Some of the recipients might have been relatives, but none bore Carson's name, and there was never an accompanying letter to indicate that this was the case.

Carson's benevolence extended to the welfare of his employees. He had a firm policy by the late nineteenth century of hiring only Humboldt County residents, as job seekers from all parts of California and the nation were cordially informed. Carson paid men incapacitated by injury or illness anywhere from half to the full amount of their wages for the duration of their affliction.[37] At Christmas, he customarily gave his employees a bonus. A few days before Christmas in 1904, he gave his married employees a $5 gold piece and the unmarried employees $2.50 in silver.[38] Upper-echelon employees got more generous amounts. On Christmas Eve, 1903, Carson wrote to his director of railroad operations enclosing a check for $250 "as an expression of my appreciation of your faithful and efficient service . . . and the loyalty you have always shown to the interests of the company."[39]

Carson's correspondence indicates clearly that he sometimes felt very genuine bonds of affection and concern for an employee. In 1904, he was compelled to fire his woods foreman, Fred Christie, because he had become an alcoholic. For many years, Carson and his son Milton showed great concern and interest in the fate of Christie and his wife. In 1909, Carson wrote to his San Francisco agent informing him that Christie was in the city and that, should he need any funds, he was to be provided with them.[40] In 1911, when Christie applied for a job in the Oregon lumber industry, Milton Carson wrote a glowing letter of recommendation stating that he would make an excellent foreman if "he had mastered that habit."[41] Periodic newspaper descriptions of the Dolbeer and Carson operations, and Carson's obituaries, noted that many employees had served with the company from twenty to forty years. "Workers were a big family at Carson's," stated one obituary.[42] When Carson died in 1912, he bequeathed sums that ranged between $1,000 and $15,000 to 33 of his employees, almost all of whom had worked for him for ten to forty years.[43]

In evaluating the overall impact of paternalism in shaping the nature of labor relations in late-nineteenth- and early-twentieth-century Humboldt County, it is important to note that its extent varied among employers. Even within the same enterprise, there were significant differences in how workers were treated. The archetypical patrician, William Carson, did not exhibit the same concern for the welfare of an unskilled and unmarried woodsman as he did for his foreman or one of his highly skilled employees who had worked for him for over a decade. Evidence suggests that it was the skilled worker of long standing who was invariably the recipient of acts of benevolence when misfortune struck. As a general rule, the pioneer lumbermen who could trace their roots in the county to the 1850s and 1860s were the greatest bestowers of beneficence. Significantly, one of the first mills founded by outside capital had the reputation for being the harshest regime in Humboldt County. J. C. Blake, who recalled men like Carson and Vance with reverence, remembered the cruelty with which Colonel Bauer of the Humboldt Lumber Mill Company, founded in 1883 by the Korbel brothers, treated his workers. Blake described Bauer as a "perfect gentleman" in social matters "but in the management of the Company he was more of a tyrant." The company employed many men from Bohemia. Bauer, a "Bohemian gentleman," viewed the workers as "serfs."

Not uncommonly, he used his walking cane to chastise workers from his native country. Not all workers were as submissive. One day, Bauer crept up on a worker who was illicitly smoking a pipe and brought his cane down heavily on the offender's posterior. The smoker pivoted and delivered a "haymaker" that sent Bauer sprawling. On learning that the man was Irish, Bauer decreed that, in future, no Irishmen would be employed.[44]

It is difficult to gauge the extent of the benevolence of the lumber employers. To draw attention to the deeds of a man like Carson, and indeed those of other lumbermen, is not to suggest that most felt a boundless sense of social responsibility toward their employees and the community at large. If one assumes that, in general, lumber employers were as willing to trumpet their acts of benevolence as they were after the ten-hour-day concession, and that most of the county press was willing to serve as their publicity agents, then grandiose acts of munificence were comparatively rare. Charity was usually dispensed selectively by the lumbermen: to their own church, their pet local institution, and ordinarily to employees of long standing and then only in exceptional cases of hardship. The poverty during the depressions of the late 1870s, the mid-1880s, and mid-1890s, and the inability of local charitable institutions to cope with it, points to distinct limits to the lumbermen's benevolence. Their refusal to concede the ten-hour day in 1887 and their unwillingness to extend this concession to woodsmen in 1890 also indicate the boundaries of this benevolence. Moreover, notwithstanding the glowing descriptions of Russ's mill, recollective accounts and the early reports of the California Commission of Immigration and Housing indicate that living conditions in almost all lumber camps remained very spartan until at least World War I.

Regardless of the limits and motives underlying their benevolence, lumber employers were successful, to some degree, in instilling feelings of gratitude among a significant proportion of their workforce. The scenes that followed the ten-hour-day concession are evidence of this. Further evidence can be offered. In 1896, William Carson posted a notice in the mill, under a picture of William McKinley, promising employees a pay raise if McKinley was elected.[45] When Carson honored his promise, over a year later, his employees decorated the picture of McKinley with white roses and yellow ribbons.[46] It was not without significance that John Vance was known by his employees and throughout the community as "Uncle John." The funerals of pioneer lumbermen such as Vance and Carson were very well attended by lumber workers and people from the community. Even the funeral of Mrs. Carson in 1904 witnessed a "general outpouring of rich and poor alike that lined the streets in front of the house," including over 200 lumber workers.[47] But perhaps the best evidence that paternalism paid off in Humboldt County was the failure of the International Brotherhood of Woodsmen and Sawmill Workers (founded in the county during the early twentieth century) to organize many of the lumber workers employed by the surviving pioneer operators. It was in the large mills established or taken over by capitalists from outside the county that the union attracted most of its following.

The ability of the lumber entrepreneurs to foster paternalism and mutualism was greatly enhanced by the fact that, by the late nineteenth century, the fate of the local economy was inextricably tied to the fortunes of the lumber industry. The lumbermen did not have to broadcast the interdependence of the community, the workers, and the lumber industry. It was self-evident, and other businessmen and the county press reminded the community of this on repeated occasions. This interdependency partially helps explain the effusions of gratitude with which workers greeted the ten-hour day. A more widespread and revealing manifestation of the degree to which workers perceived a link between their well-being and that of the community occurred in 1892 after a federal River and Harbor Bill, appropriating $1.7 million for harbor improvements, became law. A parade took place on the Saturday after the news was received that the *Western Watchman* described as the "largest and most enthusiastic ever" in the county's history. Every union in the county—including the carpenters, the printers, and the sailors—took part, and all the mills were represented by a large contingent of workers with a lumber employer at their head. Woodsmen from Flanigan, Brosnan carried a banner that read *Humboldt Will Go Ahead.* Dolbeer and Carson's mill crew carried a placard stating *Deep Water Brings Railroads. We'll Get Them You Bet.* [48]

To recognize the role played by paternalism in mitigating tensions between labor and capital is not to argue that labor becomes so totally subservient to capital that it abrogates all notion of its rights. As Genovese and other historians of the subject have argued, paternalism almost inherently entails an element of reciprocity between the subordinate and the superordinate. Labor relations in the Humboldt County lumber industry, particularly during the 1890s, illustrate this point.

The ten-hour day, while it was not an immediate or direct outgrowth of pressure from the mill workers, was not one that they were willing to relinquish easily. Two weeks after the announcement was made, a "laborer" from the lumber town of Scotia wrote to the local press admitting that while the news had taken the mill hands by surprise, "we got there and we mean to stay there."[49] The clearest manifestation of the mill workers' determination to preserve the ten-hour day occurred in 1892 during a protracted struggle by their counterparts in Mendocino County to obtain a similar concession and the attempt by one Humboldt County lumber operator to extend the working day. In April 1892, Isaac Minor threatened to increase the workday in his Glendale mill to eleven and a half hours. Minor later claimed that this was a temporary expedient to meet a backlog of orders and that he had obtained the consent of his employees. The accounts are conflicting; nevertheless the vast majority of Minor's millmen walked out and closed down the mill.[50] "Not since the ecision [*sic*] of the foul cancer of Chinese labor, which formerly knawed [*sic*] at the vitals of Humboldt's progress has such excitement prevailed," wrote a "Ten Hour Adherent."[51] In the face of such resolute opposition, Minor abandoned his attempt to lengthen the working day.

The Millmen's Union and the Limits of Paternalism

The events at Minor's mill sparked a mass meeting of mill workers in the Humboldt Bay area. In early May 1892, representatives from nine mills met to consider a course of action.[52] The mill workers were alarmed, not only by what had transpired at Glendale, but by the continued and bitter opposition of the Mendocino lumber owners to the establishment of the ten-hour day. They feared that the obstinacy of the Mendocino lumbermen might cause the Humboldt lumber manufacturers to retract their concession.[53] Many mill workers believed that the situation called for some kind of organization. The *Western Watchman* urged the mill workers to join the Knights, who were spearheading a struggle for the ten-hour day in the Mendocino mills.[54] The mill hands, however, spurned the advice of the *Watchman* and formed an independent Millmen's Union. The preamble of the new union's constitution noted the "happy experience in this county of the ten hour system" and stressed the mill workers' determination to maintain the ten-hour day.[55]

Several features of the founding meeting of the Millmen's Union and the nature of the union are of note. To begin with, many of the major lumber employers in Humboldt County were present at the founding meeting. The mill owners participated in the proceedings for three main reasons. First, while they stressed the competitive disadvantage they were operating under vis-à-vis their Mendocino rivals, they were at pains to assuage fears that the ten-hour concession was about to be abrogated. Second, they were keen to support an organization that might lend valuable assistance to the ten-hour-day struggle in Mendocino. Finally, they were anxious to exert as much control as possible over the new union.

The Millmen's Union, while born of a determination to preserve the ten-hour day, demonstrated the limits of "militancy" among the lumber workers in the 1890s. The mill workers allowed their employers to attend their founding meeting and refused to consider seriously affiliating with the Knights or any other regional or national labor organization. This was in stark contrast to the mid-1880s when lumber workers readily joined the Knights and when lumber employers were excluded from the Order. At the founding meeting of the Millmen's Union, the *Western Watchman* observed that "the rank and file of the working men did not show up very prominently in the discussion."[56] The *Watchman* accused the mill owners of playing a major role in the establishment of the union and of deliberately diverting the mill workers from forming "a sound labor organization, upon true economic principles." The *Watchman* admitted that the union might do some good, but warned that it "will return no strength for continued effort in labor's cause for reason that the *prompting influence* will be withdrawn."[57] The Eureka correspondent to the *Coast Seamen's Journal* concurred. Although he thought that there were many "earnest" men in the new organization, he lamented the fact that "the promoters of the new organization are all men who hold responsible positions in the various mills, and the men to whom the millowners would look to for the carrying out of their plans."[58] Indeed, many of the officers of the Millmen's Union were upper-echelon mill employees.

In January 1893, leaders of the Millmen's Union wrote a long and melodramatic letter appealing to the Mendocino mill owners to grant the ten-hour day. The letter began by reminding the Mendocino lumbermen of an old axiom: "The better the boss the better the hand." It also drew attention to the fact that employers in many industries had recently reduced the hours of labor and insisted that the ten-hour concession in Humboldt County had not reduced the workers' daily output. "The establishment of the ten hour day will relieve you from the stigma of selfishness, and give you a place in the column of progress that is now marching over the land."[59] The Mendocino mill owners, however, ignored the appeals. The Millmen's Union never attained more than a few hundred members, and by 1894 it had vanished. In spite of its short-lived existence and its fundamentally conservative nature, the fact remains that, notwithstanding the stubbornness of their Mendocino competitors and the severe depression of the mid-1890s, the Humboldt County lumber employers adhered to the ten-hour day.

Assessing the precise extent to which paternalism affected labor relations in Humboldt County is complex. Even more complex is the question of the degree to which deferential attitudes at the workplace and in the community at large affected political values and voting behavior. The deference and respect accorded the lumber owner may not have been manifested in the polling booth. Nor can the success of lumbermen in local politics necessarily be regarded as evidence of their political hegemony. It is worth repeating that local elections in the late nineteenth century were almost always of a nonpartisan character between the "best men," and only rarely were there serious divisions over substantive local issues. The defeat of William Carson by rival lumberman David Evans in the Eureka mayoral election of 1899 also indicates that lumbermen were not a monolithic entity in the local political arena and that the man with the best paternalist credentials did not necessarily win. Moreover, the scope of local government power and activity in a small community was relatively limited in the late nineteenth century. Only in the Progressive era was municipal government in a rapidly growing city like Eureka forced to expand its scope as it confronted problems largely attendant on growth, such as maintaining streets and providing public transportation and efficient and low-cost public utilities. Local politics became at once more contentious and partisan; the "best men," especially lumber owners, ceased to play a conspicuous role.

It is possible that in state and national electoral contests, Humboldt County lumber employers may have had an important influence from the pioneer days. Almost without exception, they were Republicans. Is it purely coincidental that in every election in the Gilded Age and the Progressive era, the Republican presidential nominee obtained a majority in Humboldt County, in spite of the fact that, statewide, the California Democratic party established itself as a viable alternative party within a decade of the end of the Civil War? In 1890, F. A. Cutler, the chairman of the Humboldt Democratic party, expressed hope in a letter to California Democratic Congressman Stephen White that the fortunes of the Humboldt Democratic party were about to take a turn for the better, asserting that his voice had "reached deep into the laboring classes of our county, the majority of whom hitherto have been controlled by our mill owners and the redwood kings."[60]

Notwithstanding Cutler's judgment, electoral mechanics, and Carson's interest in the outcome of the 1896 presidential election, it would be a mistake to overemphasize the political influence of the lumber owners. Carson and the others did not play the conspicuous role in state and national elections that they had in 1896. Moreover, impressive third-party performances by the Workingmen's party, the Greenbackers, and the Populists indicate the parameters of their political hegemony.

In the sphere of social relations, however, the evidence indicates that notions of reciprocity, deference, and paternalism played a significant role in mitigating social conflict, even though it remains hard to determine precisely the extent of paternalism and the degree to which workers internalized a mutualistic ethos. In single-industry and company towns dotted across the American landscape of the nineteenth and early twentieth centuries, the power of employers alone fostered a spirit of accommodation among some workers. Powerlessness need not have this effect, but as John Gaventa has noted with respect to Appalachian coal mining communities: "Powerlessness may affect the consciousness of potential challenges about grievances strategies, or the possibilities of change. Participation denied over time may lead to the acceptance of the role of non-participation."[61]

Paradoxically, while some elements of the democratic-republican tradition provided the foundations for a radical critique of Gilded Age America, others provided the basis for a reciprocal conception of class relations. The democratic–republican tradition contained a mix of individualistic and corporatist ideas that could be invoked to extol a harmonious model of the social order. In particular, an important strand of the tradition glorified the ideology of social mobility while stressing that there was nothing incompatible between the sum total of individual endeavors and the greater good of society. Although the contradictions of this logic became increasingly apparent to dissenters, in a community setting such as Humboldt, this mutualistic view of social relations still had considerable appeal to certain segments of the community.

Chapter 7

The Dissenters' Last Crusade: Populism in Humboldt County

After the poor showing of the Knights of Labor in the 1886 county and state elections, dissenting third-party political activity lapsed for several years in Humboldt County. The *Western Watchman* beseeched voters to support the Union Labor party in 1888 but, as the *Watchman* noted, the party was poorly organized in California, and in Humboldt County fielded only a few candidates. Notwithstanding their tactical errors and ideological contradictions, the Workingmen's and Green-back Labor parties, and the Knights had popularized a set of ideas and platforms that would support the local Populist movement in the 1890s. Not surprisingly, then, Humboldt became one of the banner counties of a vigorous California Populist movement in the 1890s.[1]

The Alliance Takes Hold

Prior to the emergence of the Populists, the founding of a Bellamy Nationalist Club in Eureka in January 1890 evidenced the profound disquiet that some Humboldters felt about the destiny of the repub-lic.[2] The *Arcata Union* referred disparagingly to a "Bellamy craze" in Eureka, while the *Watchman* and the *Coast Seamen's Journal* welcomed the development.[3] "Social evolution, the investigation of socialistic problems, are just now taking a very interesting phase," reported the *Watchman*.[4] The Eureka correspondent of the *Coast Seamen's Journal* noted approvingly the considerable interest and involvement of the

local trade union movement in the Nationalist Club.[5] The Nationalist movement, however, proved to be as much a fad in Eureka as it
was nationwide. For several months, regular meetings earnestly discussed the works of writers such as Edward Bellamy, Henry George,
and Laurence Gronlund, but by the summer of 1890 the movement
evaporated. Nevertheless, the Nationalist movement was testimony to
the continuing vitality of a dissenting tradition in Humboldt County
and contributed several prominent figures to the local Populist movement. Expressions of disquiet echoed throughout Eureka as the 1890s
opened. The address of graduate Paul Follenius at the Eureka Academy
Commencement Exercises, for instance, began by decrying the pursuit
of wealth for its own sake, then added:

> It has been clearly demonstrated by eminent writers that in no country in
> the world is the concentration of wealth going on as rapidly as in ours; in no
> other country is there a class that can compare with the wealthiest class of
> Americans. It may not be a pleasant truth, but it is truth nevertheless, that in
> our country the middle class is fast disappearing; that the masses of people are
> becoming more dependent on the few. Independent tradesman are becoming
> servants in gigantic monopolies and are ruled over by the lords of trade.[6]

At the very time that the Nationalist movement was waning in
California, the Farmers' Alliance was taking root in Santa Barbara in
the spring of 1890. By November, 173 suballiances had been founded
and the Alliance held its first state convention. The *Watchman* carried
a full report of the proceedings and admonished the farmers of Humboldt County for not jumping on the Alliance bandwagon.[7] In early
January 1891, the *Watchman* issued another clarion call for the formation of suballiances in the county.[8] Goaded by the *Watchman* and
encouraged by a visit from a state Alliance organizer, J. W. Hines (a former Humboldt County resident), the farmers of Humboldt responded.
By February 1891, ten suballiances and a county Alliance had been
founded.[9] William Ayres was elected secretary of both the Eureka and
Humboldt County Farmers' Alliance. Charles Devlin, a former Knight,
became president of the Eureka suballiance, while a sheep farmer,
H. C. Hanson, presided over the county Alliance. Fourteen suballiances, embracing almost 1,000 members, were in existence by the
spring of 1892.[10]

The Humboldt County Alliance's strong following cannot be explained in terms of the economic hardship of the county's farmers.
While the embattled wheat farmers of Tulare and San Luis Obispo
counties may have joined the California Alliance in the hope of improving their condition, the Alliance flourished in Humboldt County

where the agricultural economy was not depressed. In the period from 1880–1889, the average amount of mortgage debt on each acre of Humboldt County farmland was $5.40. This was nearly half the average for all California counties ($9.84), and of the state's 53 counties, only 8 had a lower level of mortgage indebtedness on their farms than Humboldt during the decade.[11] In 1890, the average annual mortgage on Humboldt County farms was $2,404, significantly below the statewide average of $3,406, and 30 California counties had higher average levels of mortgage indebtedness on their farms.[12] In 1891 and 1894, William Ayres embarked on extensive travels through the county, but the lengthy accounts of his travels, which he dutifully sent to the *Western Watchman*, made no reference to farmer poverty.[13] Letters from perennial *Watchman* correspondents Charles Spears and Sam Patch conveyed a picture of a prosperous farming community, even if the sheep farmers had seen better times.[14]

During the 1880s, an important shift of resources from cereal and livestock farming to dairying had occurred in Humboldt County; by the 1890s Humboldt had become the leading county in a budding California dairy industry. A U.S. Department of Agriculture report, published in 1896, cited estimates from "well informed persons" that over half of the population was employed in the dairy industry.[15] This was almost certainly an overestimate, but the dairy industry was central to the county's economy by the 1890s. Even during the depression, California's dairy farmers continued to prosper. The State Board of Agriculture dwelt on the plight of the California wheat farmers while reporting on the flourishing condition of the state's dairy industry: "No adjunct of farm life offers more inducement for further development and extension than does the dairy business," the 1896 report asserted.[16] Reviewing the county's production and export statistics for 1894, the *Humboldt Times* noted the precipitous decline in lumber production but stated that the dairy industry was "thriving" and that dairy exports had made a "big difference to the county's economy."[17] A short history of the county, written in 1904, spoke of the farmers' dire circumstances in the early 1880s, but stated that, after 1890 and the switch to dairying, there had been "a complete transformation of the financial outlook for the valley farmers" and that "ruination and foreclosures had in great measure been lifted."[18]

To Regenerate a Republic

Most Humboldt County Alliance members saw the Populist movement as a crusade to purify and reform the American body politic and not as a sectarian struggle to restore the supposedly exalted social and economic standing of the American farmer. Humboldt County Populism conforms in many respects with Lawrence Goodwyn's depiction of the national movement as a "movement culture" embodying a "people's movement of mass democratic aspiration."[19] Goodwyn argues that a Populist movement culture derived from years of economic and social cooperation between farmers and that this preceded and was a necessary condition for the emergence of a strong political movement.[20] The case of Humboldt County, however, suggests that the direction of causation was the other way round. Shared political assumptions and discontents generated a movement with broader social ramifications. Moreover, there was nothing unique or distinctive about the social and fraternal manifestations of Humboldt Populism. Impressive as they were, they represented the Populist's ability to utilize and adapt many of the community's existing social customs and rituals to the service of the movement.

For the first half of the 1890s, the Alliance played an important social and political role in the community. The county suballiances organized numerous social events—dances, literary renditions, plays, musical performances, and picnics. On many such occasions, a neighboring suballiance joined the festivities. William Ayres vividly described a visit to a meeting of the Table Bluff Alliance. Following political addresses by several leading members of the county Alliance, there were songs, recitations, and plays that went on until after midnight: "The whole assemblage soon became a regular picnic of friendly greetings, introductions of visiting Alliance brothers and sisters, social intercourse, in fact a veritable lovefeast of good fellowship."[21] Many suballiances organized Fourth of July celebrations. The festivities organized by the Eel River suballiance in 1892 attracted 1,500 people. The customary picnic took place, accompanied by singing, dancing, and foot races, and the day closed with a grand ball in Ferndale Hall.[22] The Island suballiance not only built its own meeting hall but started its own newspaper, the *Alliance Voice*.[23] The paper was edited by a different person each issue and read to the membership every month. The Ferndale suballiance established its own auction market and a warehouse where farmers could store produce.[24] The Table Bluff suballiance founded a cooperative store,[25] and 25 Eel River dairymen bought out the Excelsior Creamery and began operating it as a joint stock concern.[26]

Women played a particularly important role in the suballiances, and male members apparently recognized their contributions. Women staged many social events, and, more important, were elected to official positions. Women contributed as many, if not more, pieces to the *Watchman* than their male counterparts, publicizing the social and political activities of the alliance. After his visit to the Table Bluff Alliance, Ayres reported: "The flourishing condition is acknowledged by all the male members to be due in very large degree to the sisters."[27]

The fraternal spirit and the cooperative ventures of the Humboldt County Alliance did not preclude a serious political orientation. On the contrary, a shared transcendent political vision was the foundation upon which the Alliance was built. All meetings of the Alliance opened with lengthy political addresses and readings. The communications, essays, and articles of Alliance members revealed the explicit nature of their political orientation. The following letter to the *Watchman* from an Alliance member is representative of many such communications:

Be not led by the politicians nor seduced by ambition, but vote to secure the greatest need to the greatest number, without class legislation for any. This is true democracy and pure republicanism. . . . The situation demands reform, and it must come through the ballot box or through a revolution. Then claim your right at the polls and then vote for the heaven born principle of equal rights to all and special privileges to none. No class politics for us.[28]

In February 1892, the Island suballiance offered prizes for the best essays on the Farmers' Alliance. All four prizes went to women, who displayed a thorough knowledge of the history of the Alliance in America. They attacked the national banking system with particular vehemence and expressed the conviction that the country was falling into the hands of the monopolists. Lucie Gallway thought the Alliance would provide for "the protection of the people against the ever increasing monopolies and trusts." She called for the abolition of the National Bank, currency expansion, and the direct election of senators. Della Dunlap began her essay with a forthright statement of the premises on which the Alliance was founded: "Our forefathers held that all men are created equal. This is the fundamental principle upon which the government of our country was founded." Besides listing most of the reforms called for by Lucie Gallway, she called for government ownership of the railroads and telegraph, the Australian ballot, and greater support for public education, "the only salvation of the poor people."[29]

Like an earlier generation of Humboldt County dissenters, the Alliance members' political consciousness reflected an acute awareness of and sensitivity to national social, political, and economic developments. And, while references to the plight of the farmers appeared, they were usually incidental and brought up in the context of the general discussion of the national malaise. The Humboldt County Alliance, the suballiances, and the county and state Alliance lecturers devoted little time to the Humboldt farmer and surprisingly little to the travails of farmers nationwide. In fact, the Humboldt County Alliance displayed as much concern for the working classes as for the American farmer. In the spring of 1892, the county Alliance passed a resolution in sympathy with the Mendocino lumber workers locked in the bitter struggle over the ten-hour day.[30] In 1894, the Alton suballiance passed a resolution blaming the depression on the "unwise and corrupt legislation of the Democrats and Republicans" and "heartily" endorsed "the commonwealth march of J. S. Coxey and his followers."[31] Two months later, the county Alliance denounced President Grover Cleveland's use of troops in the railroad strike and expressed great sympathy with members of the American Railway Union and kindred labor organizations "in their recent efforts to obtain justice at the hands of an organized monopoly."[32]

With the 1892 presidential election approaching, the Humboldt County Alliance hardly needed to be prodded in the direction of political action. Two factors hastened this development. First, at the national level, the Farmers' Alliance founded the People's party in February 1891 and in July held its first convention in Omaha. Second, at the state level, the California legislative session of 1891 proved to be one of the most corrupt in the state's history, and soon became known as the "Legislature of a Thousand Scandals."[33] Humboldt County Alliance members were outraged at the record of their state legislature. In a letter to the *Pacific Rural Press* in October 1891, Charles Devlin reported unanimous sentiment within the Humboldt Alliance in favor of establishing a People's party.[34] The Alliance proceeded to elect delegates to the founding convention of the California People's party to be held later in the month. On July 18, 1892, 400 supporters of the Humboldt County People's party met to nominate and draw up a platform for the fall elections. They endorsed the Omaha platform and that of the California People's party in their entirety. The local platform represented a distillation of the main points in these platforms: a graduated income tax, the direct election of senators, support for the initiative and referendum, expressions of sympathy with the workingman in his battle for a shorter workday, and a resolution condemning the use of Pinkertons and troops in the recent Homestead strike.[35]

The Humboldt County People's party ticket was comprised predominantly of men of relatively humble standing or origin. Fred McCann, the candidate for the California assembly, 2nd District, was born in New Brunswick, Canada, and emigrated to the county in 1873.

He left school at an early age and worked for many years in a logging camp. He managed, however, to continue his education, and in 1884 he became a teacher. The People's party nominee for the 3rd District was B. H. Willsie, a native of the county and the son of a die-hard Greenbacker.[36] At thirty-three years of age, he was a successful farmer thoroughly versed in the principles of the Farmers' Alliance. Nominees for county offices included a ranch worker, a woodsman, a bookkeeper, a mason, and a carpenter. Only the candidates for county surveyor and district attorney were professional men and the latter began life as a farmworker.[37]

The Humboldt County People's party had to contend with two complicating elements in the 1892 campaign. The first was the presence of A. J. Bledsoe on the Republican ticket for the state legislature. Bledsoe had distinguished himself as a maverick Republican in the 1891 legislature determined to expose the corrupt practices of his fellow assemblymen, regardless of party affiliation. On several occasions, the Humboldt County Alliance passed resolutions commending him for his honesty and courage. Thus the Populists found themselves pitting their candidate against a man with a considerable progressive following in the county. The Populists also suffered a setback a few days after their convention in July 1892 when the news arrived that the $1.7 million harbor appropriation bill for Humboldt County had received the presidential signature. The bill had been sponsored by California Democratic Congressman Thomas Geary, whose district included Humboldt County. The community's jubilation following this news was described in the previous chapter, and there can be no doubt that Geary gained some political capital. The *Watchman* praised him, and *Nerve* published a list of people who allegedly would break with their party allegiance and reelect Geary. Several well-known Populists were on the list.[38]

Bledsoe and Geary racked up handsome majorities in the 1892 elections, but the result showed that the People's party had strong roots in the county. The Populist presidential candidate, James Weaver, attracted a respectable 19 percent of the vote, more than double the percentage he received nationally (8.5 percent) or in California (9.4 percent). In only three California counties did Weaver obtain a higher percentage of the vote. On the state ticket, the Humboldt Populist also performed well. Alfred Stimson, Populist candidate for the state senate, garnered 43 percent of the vote; B. H. Willsie got 40 percent of the vote in his fight for a seat in the California legislature; and in the other assembly contest, Fred McCann obtained a creditable 21 percent of the vote against Bledsoe. At the county level, no Populist candidate was disgraced, and even in most three-cornered fights, the Populist got 20 percent of the vote.[39]

Populism, Depression, and the Workingman

The Populist movement in Humboldt County was not simply a rural one. In the 1892 election, Weaver obtained 23.5 percent of the vote in Eureka, a showing that dwarfed his performance in San Francisco, where he received a paltry 4.3 percent of the vote. In almost all state and county contests, Populist candidates performed better or as well as they did in the rural precincts. The strength of Populist support in Eureka indicates the broad-based character of Humboldt Populism and the extent to which earlier dissenting movements had bequeathed a legacy of ideas that the Populists were able to draw on in all areas of the county. The vitality of Populism in Eureka is especially striking in view of the weakness of the county's labor movement in the 1890s, following the collapse of the Knights. It is important to note, though, that in unions that managed to survive the 1890s, such as the Carpenters' Union, the Coast Seamen's Union, and the Typographical Union, a strong current of ideas derived from the radical democratic–republican tradition, and congruent with the Populist program, flourished. Thus, the first paragraph of the Carpenters' Union's formal statement of purpose in 1889 spoke of "wealthy capitalists" who "combine their wealth to monopolize and control the wealth of the world" and "menace . . . our free institutions."[40] A few weeks later, Frank Keyley, the union's recording secretary, stressed the need for political action in rhetoric that anticipated the Humboldt County Alliance almost word for word: "Capital has the army and the navy, the legislature, the judicial and executive departments. Why should the capital control? Why should not the laborer combine for the purpose of controlling the executive, the legislative and judicial departments? They will never find out how powerful they are unless they combine, and use their political power."[41] The carpenters held regular monthly meetings to discuss the principles of trade unionism. But, frequently, political topics were discussed, and an invitation was extended to all crafts and the general public.

In August 1892, "Typo," a self-confessed member of the Printers' Union, expressed his disgust with the Republican party, which he had supported for years. He lambasted the Republican press for its treatment of the Homestead and Coeur D'Alene strikes and alleged that "the money lenders are defiling the temple of pure principles once occupied by the Republican party of Lincoln, Sumner and Steward." The Republican party, he said, had become "too much the party of moneyed aristocracy for the laboring men to follow."[42] In December 1893, the Eureka Typographical Union and the Carpenters' Union forwarded a petition to Congressman Geary calling for the public ownership of all means of transportation and communication.[43]

The onset of the depression of the mid-1890s exacerbated the discontents of many workingmen. By July 1892, the first shock waves of the depression had hit the county. It was reported that times were "very hard" in Eureka, and "the laborers do not attend every picnic . . . [while] all the stores are piled full of goods."[44] The Eel River Lumber Company announced wage cuts of from 5 to 30 percent in April 1892,[45] but the full force of the depression did not hit the industry until midsummer 1893. In early August of that year, the *Watchman* reported large wage cuts and layoffs at many mills.[46] There were isolated instances of resistance. At Scotia, a group of lumber workers walked off the job when informed that their wages had been cut by $5 a month.[47] At the Flanigan and Brosnan mill, too, a walkout occurred after wage reductions were announced.[48] In early May 1894, 60 woodsmen employed by the Pacific Lumber Company struck unsuccessfully to retain the wage rate of the previous summer.[49] More wage cuts and layoffs took place between the summer of 1893 and 1896. In several instances, wages were reduced by more than 30 percent, and unskilled lumber workers were forced to subsist on as little as $15 a month.[50] As early as May 1894, one source estimated that the total number of people employed in the county had shrunk by 2,500 since the outbreak of the depression.[51]

The county's charitable institutions were stretched to the limit. A few weeks after the massive layoffs of August 1893, the *Watchman* reported bands of homeless men gathering every night around the mill slab fires.[52] The *Humboldt Standard*, aware that local charitable institutions were overwhelmed, urged Eureka to follow the example of Stockton and provide work for the needy.[53] In December 1894, the editor of the *Humboldt Standard* overheard a well-respected Eureka "mechanic" saying that if it were not for his little children, he would have committed a crime so that he could obtain a regular meal in the jail. "Will it come to the famine cry 'Bread or Blood,' " asked the editor.[54] "Sockless Simon" complained that "the almost inexhaustible natural resources that are being turned into commercial values by the energy of her people" were "being rapidly concentrated in the hands of a few men." He called for immediate government ownership of railroads, the telegraph, and other "public necessities," and urged people to vote for the People's party.[55]

Both the *Humboldt Times* and the *Humboldt Standard* reported with some consternation that the majority of Humboldt County laborers and citizens were sympathetic to the Pullman railway strikers.[56] Sam Patch noted with sadness a growing "anarchist" sentiment in the community, but, he said, "so long as the rich can dress their pet dogs in silk and satin and have them sleep on eiderdown pillows, while the little rosebuds, the sweet, dimpled babies of the poor are dying in the gutter from hunger and cold, there will be anarchists."[57] When the entire 138-man crew at the Jacoby Creek quarry struck for an increase in wages in July 1894, Sam Patch claimed they had the sympathy of almost every workingman in the county.[58]

After the 1892 election, the Humboldt County Farmers' Alliance continued to thrive, although the total number of suballiances dropped from a peak of 14 to 10 by the time of the 1894 election.[59] Regular quarterly meetings of the county Alliance invariably reaffirmed the main planks of the 1892 platform. The Alliance also passed resolutions calling for stricter enforcement of county liquor ordinances. Several resolutions expressed sympathy for the workingman and welcomed the growing involvement of labor in the California Populist movement. When a county grand jury failed to indict George Hall, a notorious antiunion vigilante on the Humboldt Bay waterfront, for the murder of a union sailor, the Alliance formally expressed its outrage.[60] The Alliance was treated to visits by several prominent western Populist leaders, including Thomas Cator, the leading figure in the California People's party.

The platform of the Humboldt County People's party in 1894 adhered closely to the Omaha platform. It charged the Democratic and Republican parties with "conspiring with foreign bankers to place this nation on a gold basis, thereby reducing our circulating medium, resulting in a depreciated market for the products of all labor." Other demands included the prohibition of immigration "until such time as the home market is relieved," a more economical administration at all levels of government, immediate construction of the Nicaraguan canal under government ownership, and opposition to a bill extending by fifty years the time the railroads had to pay off their mortgages to the federal government.[61] Again, the Populist ticket nominated primarily men of relatively humble standing or origin. Nominees included a mason, a bookkeeper, a shoemaker, a filer in a shingle mill, two other men who had spent most of their lives as lumber workers, a clerk, and two farmers of modest means.[62]

Bledsoe was once more a factor in the campaign. Between 1892 and 1894, he buttressed his reputation as an honest and progressive legislator by supporting legislation to make the Southern Pacific Railroad pay its fair share of taxes and sponsoring a bill to remove three railroad commissioners suspected of dereliction of duty. He also supported bills that would have established initiative and referendum procedures in California and he authored and secured passage of a bill making ten hours the legal working day in California woods and mills,[63] only to see it vetoed by the Republican governor, Henry Markham. Populists knew they had little chance of unseating Bledsoe and put up their weakest performance in the assembly race in the 2nd District.

The 1894 election demonstrated that the Populists had consolidated their position in Humboldt County. J. V. Webster, the Populist candidate for governor, got 36 percent of the vote—one more vote than his Republican opponent and several hundred more than the Democratic nominee. Webster got a higher percentage of the vote in Humboldt than in any other California county. His showing in Eureka was especially impressive; he secured 42 percent of the vote, trouncing his Republican and Democratic party rivals. The Populists elected a district attorney, and although this was their only triumph, Populist candidates at the state and county levels generally obtained 25 percent of the vote when both Republican and Democratic nominees were in contention and over 40 percent when the Democrats did not offer a candidate.

Populism in Retreat

The 1894 elections marked the zenith of both Humboldt County and California Populism. Statewide, Webster got just over 51,000 votes, or 18 percent of the total. This was almost double the number of votes he received in 1892. The 1894 Populist vote translated into fewer seats in the state legislature than in 1892, but in every state and congressional race, Populists constituted the balance of power.[64]

After the 1894 elections, Humboldt and California Populism entered a decline. The Farmers' Alliance in the Golden State was in such poor shape by spring 1895 that it did not have enough money to print the minutes of its state convention.[65] The decline of the Humboldt County Alliance was equally precipitous. The Table Bluff suballiance met in March 1895, and the county Alliance a month later, but these are among the few references of any kind to the continuation of the Alliance after 1894. As early as January 1895, the *Watchman* asked plaintively: "What is the matter with the People's party of Humboldt County? Have they imitated the bears—gone into winter quarters to sleep?"[66]

Undoubtedly, postelectoral apathy contributed to the decline of the Humboldt County Alliance and People's party. This phenomenon also occurred after the 1892 election when the number of suballiances dwindled. The Alliance was sustained by a transcendent political vision of almost millennial proportions. This meant that, in a movement with a pronounced national political orientation, there was a close linkage between the fortunes of the local, state, and national Populist movements. At the state and national levels, the results indicated that the Populist millennium was far from just round the corner. Humboldt Populists had been in the field for almost four years and fought two major election campaigns. The movement could not sustain itself at a euphoric pitch indefinitely, especially in the absence of dramatic, or at least commensurate, gains at the state and national levels. Significantly, in the aftermath of the 1894 elections, even the *Watchman* displayed a distinctly apolitical tendency. A rash of articles and editorials stressing that "cooperation" would be the major vehicle through which the oppressed might find salvation. Finally, after 1894, a full-scale regeneration of the Humboldt People's party was precluded by the increasing drift of the Populist movement at the state and national levels toward fusion and an emphasis on free silver.

As the 1896 election drew nearer, the Humboldt People's party began to show signs of life. In February 1896, the *Watchman* called on Populists to prepare for the upcoming campaign.[67] When William Jennings Bryan was nominated by the Democrats, the *Watchman* expressed reservations about his candidacy; two weeks later, with the Populists' nomination of Bryan, they withdrew their opposition. In August 1896, Humboldt Populists and Democrats cooperated in drawing up a common platform and ticket. All this was somewhat ironic in view of the stridency with which the *Watchman* had denounced the California Populist Congressman Marion Cannon's collaboration with the Democrats in 1893,[68] and it clearly signified that much of the fire that had driven Humboldt Populism between 1891 and 1894 had been extinguished.

From the outset, the tariff and free silver were the main issues of the 1896 campaign. Populists, while opposed to high tariffs in general, had not taken a strong stand on the issue in 1892 and 1894.

By contrast, the Humboldt County Republican and Democratic parties had locked horns on the tariff question ever since the 1884 presidential election. The degree to which the Republican party exploited the tariff as an issue cannot be exaggerated. In the two months before the 1892 presidential election, for example, the Republican *Humboldt Times* published 15 editorials or articles on the benefits of the tariff. A recurring theme was the way in which protectionism was linked with nationalistic and Manifest Destiny tenets of the democratic–republican tradition to equate protectionism with prosperity. The *Humboldt Times* traced the tariff back to the genius of Hamilton and insisted that even Jefferson and Jackson had recognized "the value of the American system."[69] In one editorial, the *Times* asserted: "Republicanism means civilization. It means progress. . . . Republicanism protects—it protects the home, the family, the workshop. It is progressive. And protection is the mystic wand that smoothes the path to progress."[70] It was argued repeatedly that the tariff protected the wages of the American workingman by shielding him from the competition of cheap foreign labor. At the same time a battery of statistics was produced to try to prove that the tariff did not raise price levels. The *Times* argued repeatedly that tariff reductions would devastate the local, regional, and national economies.

In Humboldt County, especially in the midst of a severe depression, the Republican arguments had more than symbolic appeal. Since the Civil War, the American lumber industry had enjoyed considerable protection. During the late nineteenth century, with the increasing development of the Canadian lumber industry, American lumbermen insisted that it was essential to retain the tariff on foreign lumber. In 1888, when lumber appeared to be in some danger of being placed on the free list, Humboldt County lumbermen and the Chamber of Commerce petitioned Congress to resist any such move,[71] and Eureka formed a Protective League with more than 150 members.[72] The *Humboldt Times*, meanwhile, tried to rally the community to the cause by evoking memories of the depressed lumber market of the late 1870s.[73] Similarly, in 1893 and 1894, the *Times* repeatedly warned its readers of the dangers of competition from foreign lumber.[74]

The Wilson-Gorman Tariff Act became law in August 1894 and put lumber and wool, among other items, on the free list. Although its passage occurred after the onset of the depression, this action of a Democratic administration lent plausibility to the Republican charge of a close link between protection and prosperity. In the 1896 campaign, the Republicans argued constantly that the Wilson-Gorman Act had seriously hurt the county's wool and lumber interests.[75] An address by

William Carson blamed the depression in the lumber industry and the country at large on tariff reductions.[76] At a major Republican rally, E. C. Cooper compared wages paid in Humboldt County mills "under the McKinley law with those under the present free trade system."[77] The argument was just credible enough to put Democrats and Populists on the defensive.

Important as the tariff issue was in 1896, it was secondary to the free silver issue. Here again, Populists and Democrats were to have the worst of the argument. The fusionist campaign got off to an inauspicious start when the *Humboldt Standard* repudiated its long-standing support for the Democratic party, largely over the free silver issue.[78] Populists were faced with the awkward task of rationalizing their shotgun marriage with the Democrats and almost totally subordinating their former platforms to the issue of free silver. The *Watchman* insisted that the Democratic party had returned from its "strange wanderings with Cleveland and Carlisle" and that it was once again the party of Jefferson and Jackson.[79] The *Watchman* denied that the emphasis on free silver entailed jettisoning key elements of the Populist program and argued that the issue had sweeping social ramifications. In a strongly worded election-eve editorial entitled "Bimetallism Means the Brotherhood of Man," the *Watchman* stated:

If the morality of bimetallism be not in keeping with the Sermon on the Mount Jesus Christ never taught the brotherhood of man. The men whose interest lie with the Gold standard belong to the same class which Christ drove from the Temple because they had made his house a den of thieves. They have desecrated our Temple of Liberty, gambled on Tables of Law, and are now trying to force a mortgage on our Holy of Holies—the Declaration of Independence.[80]

Notwithstanding such rhetorical flourishes from the *Watchman*, the Democratic party played the main role in the campaign and in the advocacy of free silver. The fusion ticket had to make free silver a credible alternative basis for managing the nation's money supply and allay fears that the system would have the dire consequences predicted by the Republicans. At this task, Humboldt Populists and free silver Democrats failed as badly as their counterparts at the state and national levels.

In Humboldt County, Populists and Democrats had difficulty in stemming the tide of alarmist anti–free silver publicity. The Republicans argued that free silver would put up prices faster than wages, and they cited statistics on the money supply, wages, and inflation during the Civil War and the immediate postbellum period purporting to prove their point.[81] They also argued that any measure to facilitate the monetization of silver would lead to the establishment of a dual currency. Lumber owners would be paid in gold for their lumber and would pay their workers in depreciated silver money. The *Humboldt Standard* reprinted a letter from a laborer alleging that this had happened in neighboring Mendocino County in 1875.[82] The liberal monetization of silver, it alleged, also would destroy the confidence of businessmen in the credit system and thereby lead to economic chaos that would inevitably bring wage cuts.[83] William Carson linked the destitution of the Mexican laborer to the fact that silver was a major component of the Mexican currency.[84]

The Republicans successfully highlighted some of the contradictions and ambiguities in the free silver argument. In an important campaign speech, J. E. Jansen of the Eureka McKinley Club pointed to the absurdity of telling farmers that free silver would raise prices, and at the same time telling laborers that there would be no increase in prices or decrease in real wages.[85] The *Humboldt Times* asked laboring men to consider whether the interests of labor and capital really were totally exclusive. If they were not, and if free silver would hurt the interests of the employers, how would the workingman stand to gain? In the same passage, the *Times* noted that most lumber capitalists attributed the ongoing depression in the lumber industry to "the currency agitation and the lack of proper protective duties."[86]

In another editorial, the *Humboldt Standard* reiterated this argument, but provided it with an interesting twist. It conceded that it was "common talk on our streets, by the advocates of cheap money, that this is a campaign of the poor against the rich, a fight between labor and capital." The *Standard* ridiculed this notion and said that it was the trusts and millionaires who "oppress the people and absorb their earnings." It also pointed tellingly to the contradictions and inadequacies of the free silver argument:

How would free silver prevent continued exploitation? One will tell you that free silver will not depreciate the value of the silver dollar but make it as good as gold; another will tell you that it will be the best thing in the world to have a cheaper money, so that people who owe debts can pay them in fifty or sixty cent dollars, but none of them will point out just how it will curtail the rich and make lighter the burdens of the poor.[87]

At the 1896 elections, the Humboldt County Republicans recorded a comfortable, though not overwhelming, victory. If the Democrats and Populists had been able to muster anything like the support they had received in 1894, they would have swamped the Republicans. Instead, the Republicans beat their opponents by close but secure margins in most contests. Republican presidential electors received a solid 55 percent of the vote. The Republican congressional candidate got a slender, 170-vote margin and a fusionist candidate won a seat on the County Board of Supervisors, but in all other state and county contests, the Republicans won easily.

The Meaning of the Movement

The *Watchman* described the result of the election as a "bitter disappointment" but was philosophical about the outcome. It remained confident that, ultimately, an "earnest, studious population will prove the death knell to the present, usurious monetary system" and called on "each producer" to "continue with might and main at his work with a mightly thinking, and let his thoughts be in the direction of how to make cheap and equitable exchange of his products for his neighbor's products."[88] At a "mass meeting" in February 1897, delegates from the Humboldt People's party passed resolutions declaring the necessity for the continuance of the People's party at the local, state, and national levels.[89] The *Watchman* soldiered on until August 1898, occasionally admonishing the electorate for its stupidity, and reporting sporadically on a Populist party that was little more than a rump after the 1896 elections. In 1898, the Humboldt County Populist party dissolved itself when the dozen or so remaining die-hards voted to cooperate with the Democrats in the upcoming elections. The Republicans triumphed by an even wider margin in the 1898 elections, and no more was heard of the Humboldt County People's party.

The saga of Humboldt County Populism provides insights into important questions about the Populist movement that historians are still debating. It suggests the pitfalls of making sweeping generalizations about the causes of Populism and, in particular, challenges the notion that Populism represented a short-lived political response to the agricultural depression of the late 1880s and early 1890s. Certainly, in many regions, the depression was the midwife of Populism, but in other areas, such as Humboldt, a strong movement developed in the absence of a serious agricultural depression. Conversely, the strength of Populism in Eureka suggests that historians should look further at the appeal Populism had to many workers in urban, and especially small-town, America. The depression of the 1890s hit many workers as hard as it did farmers, and while the union movement was in disarray, the depression may have been a radicalizing experience for them.

Most important, the history of Humboldt County Populism indicates the need to study Populism from a long historical perspective, and to examine not only the social and cultural antecedents of Populism, as such historians as Goodwyn and Hahn have done, but also its political ones. The political history of a county or region, especially the presence or absence of dissenting movements earlier in the Gilded Age, may have been as important a determinant of the strength of Populism as sociocultural antecedents and the severity of the depression.

Unquestionably, the Humboldt County Populist movement was the heir to a rich ideological legacy dating back to the 1870s. The movement represented the denouement of a strong dissenting tradition founded in the radical tenets of the democratic–republican tradition that offered a penetrating critique of Gilded Age capitalism. The Populists offered a program of economic and political reform that was as trenchant as any other reform movement in the mainstream of American history.

Dissenters voiced their political ideas in Jeffersonian and Jacksonian rhetoric partly because this was the language of politics in nineteenth-century America, and partly because they believed the post–Civil War era had produced a serious erosion of economic opportunities and, with it, a grave threat to their cherished political institutions. But they were not starry-eyed idealists who wanted to return America to its early nineteenth-century condition. Although the eras of Jefferson and Jackson provided a reference point, the dissenters did not object to industrialism per se, but rather to the impact of unfettered industrial development on the nation. To them, the restoration of true democracy entailed a degree of government management of the economy that would have been abhorrent to their Jeffersonian and Jacksonian ancestors.

To be sure, the radical democratic–republican tradition contained contradictory and ambiguous elements. To some extent, the persistence of ideas and rhetoric from the late eighteenth and early nineteenth centuries imprisoned Gilded Age dissenters ideologically; that is, although the ideological bequest provided the basis for a class analysis of American society, all but the most radical dissenters in the vanguard of the trade union movement failed to confront the implications of this analysis. They were unwilling to recognize an inherently antagonistic relationship between capital and labor and stressed the primacy of politics as a panacea. By default, they deemphasized the importance of working-class organization, notwithstanding their awareness of the workers' plight. Nevertheless, the radicals and union leaders of the early twentieth century borrowed significantly from the radical democratic–republican ideology, while still departing from it in several important respects.

Chapter 8

The Making of a Union Movement, 1900–1906

A Resurgent Labor Movement

At the dawn of the twentieth century, only sailors, longshoremen, carpenters, and typographical workers belonged to unions in Humboldt County. In a few years, however, a dramatic renaissance of the Humboldt County labor movement occurred, paralleling the resurgence of the labor movement in many parts of the country.[1] By 1906, hardly a trade or occupation in the county had not founded a union; some unions, especially in the building industry, organized almost every member of their trade. The Humboldt County lumber workers established the first international union of lumber workers—the International Brotherhood of Woodsmen and Sawmill Workers (IBWSW)—which organized over 2,000 workers, or approximately half the county's lumber workforce, within two years of its founding in 1905. Within five years, the Humboldt County labor movement acquired a degree of economic and political power that would have been unimaginable to the pioneers of the labor movement in the late nineteenth century.

Almost all unions, including the IBWSW, affiliated with the American Federation of Labor (AFL). The Humboldt County AFL was not a narrow, sectional, or exclusive organization. It attempted, with considerable success, to organize a broad spectrum of the county's labor force and to foster a vibrant union culture. Many union members perceived the labor movement not simply as an agency to extract concessions from employers but also as a social and moral force in the community. Accordingly, they created a set of institutions to give expression to the values represented by this ascending social force.

In 1900, Humboldt County, with 27,104 residents, was the eleventh most populous of California's 58 counties.[2] Eureka contained 7,327 inhabitants and was by far the largest city in the county, and the most important port on the West Coast between San Francisco and Portland. Nevertheless, Humboldt County was almost as isolated from the rest of the state as it had been in 1850. Although the county was well served by an elaborate internal railroad network, it was not connected to the state and national railroad systems until 1914.

The foreign-born made up 22 percent of the Humboldt County population in 1900. The bulk of them came from the following countries: English-speaking Canada (1,698); Denmark, Finland, Norway, and Sweden (1,539); Germany (726); Ireland (604); and Switzerland (409).[3] In Eureka, 28 percent of the city's population was foreign-born.[4] By 1920, when the county had more than 37,000 residents, the proportion of foreign-born remained almost the same. There were, however, some significant shifts in the composition of the immigrant population. The Italian share of the foreign-born increased from 3.7 percent to 15.2 percent, and the Scandinavian countries, led by Finland, surpassed the English-Canadians as the major source of foreign stock.[5]

During the first years of the twentieth century, Eureka experienced unprecedented growth. Between 1900 and 1903, the city's population grew from 7,327 residents to 11,111.[6] The local press made frequent references to a building boom; indeed, between 1902 and 1903, the assessed value of all realty in Eureka increased from $10,720,092 to $13,409,074.[7] Eureka had evolved into a full-fledged city with a diverse array of business, manufacturing, and financial concerns. Some goods were imported from San Francisco and elsewhere, but the range of enterprises in Eureka made it and the county an essentially self-sufficient economic entity. Reflecting the culmination of a trend that had been under way since the 1880s, Eureka was no longer the hub of the county's lumber industry. Logging operations moved farther and farther from Eureka; by 1904, the city contained only 11 of the approximately 50 lumber mills in the county.[8]

A booming economy in Eureka and the county at large occurred in the midst of a sustained national economic recovery after the depression of the 1890s. Humboldt County's economy benefited particularly from a spectacular revival of the lumber industry. At the height of the depression in 1896, lumber production slumped to 100,000,000 board feet, valued at $1,351,577. By 1906, the amount of lumber produced (361,000,000 board feet) and its dollar value ($7,201,000) had more than tripled.[9] The agricultural sector of the county, dominated by the dairy industry, was also thriving; the value of all dairy products increased from $828,991 in 1899 to $1,351,577 in 1909.[10]

Unquestionably, the flourishing economy set the stage for the renaissance of the Humboldt County labor movement. The first two years of the new century saw 20 unions established, embracing not only the trades but many semiskilled and unskilled workers, including bootblacks, stablemen, cooks and waiters, barbers, and laundry workers.[11] In August 1902, the Eureka Federated Trades Council received an AFL charter,[12] and a month later, C. D. Rogers, the general organizer of the California State Federation of Labor, reported that Eureka was a strong union town.[13] The growth of the Humboldt County labor movement owed little to outside organizers. Officials of the California State Federation of Labor made occasional visits to the county, but these were usually for ceremonial purposes. Rarely did such visits spawn new unions or lead to the significant growth of existing ones. The men who played the crucial role as organizers were leading lights in the local labor movement; sometimes, in recognition of their services, they received official appointments from the State Federation of Labor.

Biographical information on leaders of the early-twentieth-century Humboldt County labor movement is sparse. Most of them were relatively new to the community, and their names cannot be found in voting registers or the city and county directories of the 1890s. Some of the newcomers were experienced in the trade union movement before settling in Humboldt County. The most notable of these was Charles Grambarth, who had worked with Samuel Gompers in New York City during the 1870s and was president of the San Francisco Federated Trades Council in the 1880s.[14] There were, however, some continuities between the leadership of the nineteenth- and early-twentieth-century Humboldt County labor movement. For example, Charles Devlin, who had been active in the Knights of Labor and the Populists, was a successful candidate on the Union Labor party ticket in the 1903 Eureka elections. That there were many new union leaders is not entirely surprising, since the county's labor movement had not flourished since the mid-1880s. Moreover, the depression of the 1890s must have forced union pioneers to migrate in search of work. Conversely, the revival of the county's economy drew men such as Grambarth to the community.

Continuities between the two labor movements may have been more pronounced at the rank-and-file level, although in the absence of union membership lists, this is impossible to determine. What can be said is that most unions arose out of the spontaneous efforts of a core of men in a particular trade or occupation. In some instances, however, especially between 1900 and 1902, general organizers, such as Grambarth, and the sailors' and longshoremen's unions played important supportive roles in the embryonic stages of a union's development. A major and largely successful strike by West Coast longshoremen and sailors in 1901 enhanced the power of the Humboldt longshoremen's and sailors' unions. By 1903, the longshoremen's union contained 160 members, almost every longshoreman in the county.[15] The Eureka branch of the Sailors' Union of the Pacific (SUP) was evidently almost as thoroughly organized as the longshoremen's. Both unions lent assistance to the Teamsters, the Painters and Decorators, the Cooks and Waiters, and perhaps other unions in their formative stages. The Teamsters and the Cooks and Waiters passed resolutions expressing their gratitude to the seafaring unions.[16] Indicative of the longshoremen's commitment to supporting unionism was the fact that at one meeting in 1902, they raised $112 in support of the nation's striking anthracite miners; then, not content with their contribution, they continued to raise funds for the miners.[17]

Along with a benign national economic climate, a number of local factors played a part in the flowering of Humboldt County's labor movement in the early twentieth century. The relative isolation of the county labor market strengthened the bargaining power of labor. Humboldt employers had to rely for workers mainly on employment agencies, usually located in San Francisco, but in a booming labor market this did not always compensate for the county's remote location. As a result, wage rates in Humboldt County were higher than in most parts of California, including San Francisco.[18]

Employers seem to have been taken by surprise by the rapid expansion of the labor movement and, at least initially, resigned to it. Employers were poorly organized outside the lumber industry, and often employer organization was a belated and reactive response to the union movement. The Humboldt Lumber Manufacturers' Association (HLMA) did little to oppose the labor movement, and even the most formidable lumber employers seemed bemused by the growth of union power. "Men are demanding more for their labor all along the line, and when it will stop it is hard to guess," lamented William Carson in 1906.[19] Writing in the same year, Irving Harpster, a top official of the Elk River Mill and Lumber Company, was equally despondent: "It seems to be the policy to get as much wages as possible and do as little work as possible. Talk about trusts, these labor unions are the greatest trusts in the world today, and the end is not yet."[20]

Confronted with a resurgent union movement, employers in some trades and businesses responded by drawing up price schedules and passing the cost of wage increases on to consumers. Thus, in 1903, when the Cooks and Waiters' Union demanded a wage increase, the hotel and restaurant owners met informally and agreed to wage concessions. At the same time, they founded the Restaurant and Hotel Keepers' Association of Eureka, which embraced all establishments in the city except one, and they immediately increased the charges for board and meals.[21] Plumbers, drugstore owners, barbers, creamery operators, and many other groups of employers developed various cooperative arrangements.[22] The comparatively few employers engaged in a particular trade or business facilitated agreements, as did Eureka's isolation from the competition of other metropolitan business communities.

The Divine Mission of the Labor Movement

Labor historians have tended to attribute the dramatic growth of the labor movement in the early years of the twentieth century largely to the propitious economic climate. Certainly questions concerning the ideological complexion of the labor movement that enabled and encouraged it to exploit the favorable circumstances have been neglected. In Humboldt County, the labor movement's ability to tap an undercurrent of deeply felt grievances and draw on tenets of nineteenth-century radical democratic–republican tradition, albeit in a modified form, were crucial to its success.[23]

Like their Gilded Age predecessors, and in almost identical rhetoric, leaders of the early-twentieth-century labor movement portrayed the working class as victims of an iniquitous social and political system. In March 1903, the labor movement held a mass meeting attended by at least 500 people to publicize the aims of trade unionism. Grambarth of the Cigarmakers' Union opened the proceedings:

Fifty years ago there were few or no millionaires in the country and a contented and prosperous people. Today there are hundreds, yes thousands of millionaires, and thousands and hundreds of thousands of poverty stricken among the toiling masses. The why: labor has not received its just and equitable compensation.[24]

Grambarth argued that every workingman had a moral duty to his family to join a trade union to secure a "fair wage." He insisted that "whatever concessions capital makes to labor it is forced to do so; labor unions will force capital to treat us with fairness."[25] George Keeling of the Printers' Union spoke in a similar tone: "Labor! Capital! These are in a world called business each seeking advantage. Capital talks of its investments and dividends, and thinks little of sentiment. Labor speaks of its rights, a living wage, and casts an eye in a hazy fashion towards brotherhood."[26]

The labor theory of value remained crucial to the ideology of most workingmen, affirming their belief in the righteousness of the union cause. Labor leaders and workingmen harped on the theme that, for years, capital had been appropriating a larger and larger share of the value of their labor. The following extract from a letter by "Wage Earner" to the *Arcata Union* in 1906 is indicative of this sentiment:

I am a wage earner, and believe that a great majority of the population are in the same position, and consequently we must be the principal consumers, therefore will [sic] say that in the course of a year there are 20,000,000 wage earners engaged in manufacturing $11,000,000 worth in commodities and we receive in wages about $2,000,000 which we must in turn immediately exchange for the necessities of life. Therefore I see we do not share the increase of wealth for the simple reason that our wages do not give us the power to buy back what we have made.[27]

Labor leaders and union members also invoked the memory of the American Revolution to legitimize their cause and to proclaim that full-fledged unionism represented the Manifest Destiny of workingmen born in a country founded on the democratic–republican principles of the Founding Fathers. In 1906, the county's labor movement held its own Independence Day celebration for the first time. In spite of the fact that the occasion took place at Blue Lake, 15 miles from Eureka, 3,000 people attended.[28] Walter Macarthur, of the SUP and editor of the *Coast Seamen's Journal*, opened the ceremonies. Extracts from his speech covered the front page of *Labor News*:

Today we celebrate the greatest event in modern history—the establishment of political liberty. . . . Today upon the one hundred and thirtieth anniversary of American Independence, we reaffirm our faith in the equality of all men and in a "government of the people, by the people." And as an indisputable pledge and proof of that faith we present to the world its greatest, most powerful and prosperous example of national life—our own United States.[29]

In an editorial on the celebration, *Labor News* articulated the connection that many unionists saw between their democratic heritage and the mission of the labor movement:

It was an expression not only of the . . . American ideal of government, but also of a powerful force that is rising in our land today to make its impress on the future of the nation—namely, that of organized labor. . . . It has a mission to perform, the success of which will do more to insure true freedom in our country than any great upheaval that has preceded. Its mission is to emancipate the human race from . . . the remnants of feudal servility and the worse than slave conditions that exist in so many of our industrial centers. . . . The rise of labor to a position of such absorbing importance is a new development, and it is fitting that this rapidly growing army . . . should celebrate Independence Day whose ideals they are pledged to support in their own way.[30]

One cannot overstate the degree to which labor in early-twentieth-century Humboldt County was imbued with a sense of divine mission. In one speech, C. Roberts, president of the Eureka Trades Council, compared the mission of union leaders with that of Christ's apostles.[31] George Keeling likened the labor movement to Rip Van Winkle; after "many centuries" of sleep, it had finally stirred.[32]

Although these labor leaders carried much of the ideological baggage of their Gilded Age predecessors, to a significant degree they broke with this legacy. The ideologues of the early-twentieth-century labor movement in Humboldt County without exception espoused an antagonistic view of class relations and stressed that only through aggressive unionism would workers extract concessions from capital and enjoy a fair share of the fruits of their labor. Furthermore, both obliquely and directly, they attacked elements of the democratic–republican tradition that obfuscated this reality. For example, at labor's 1906 Independence Day celebrations, Keeling repudiated the jingoistic overtones of the occasion: "We as laborers respect the flag as much as any, but if we had entire control we would never let it stand for many things it has almost come to stand for. We would not allow it to have any connection at all with militarism."[33] *Labor News* attacked the notion of reciprocity between employer and worker. Stressing the low standard of living and insecure employment of most workers and the importance of a stable "home influence," it asked: "How is this state of affairs to be brought about? Not by trusting luck, or fortune, or the generosity of employers. No, what workingmen must do is to work out their own salvation."[34] In another editorial, *Labor News* attacked the ideology of social mobility: "The fact is that there is not room for all to rise, and many will have to resign themselves to their station. The best way a young man can elevate his condition is by joining the union."[35]

Some millmen employed by the surviving pioneer lumber entrepreneurs clung to a reciprocal and deferential conception of class relations, but elsewhere such notions were vanishing. Undoubtedly, the influence of newcomers to the community such as Grambarth, Keeling, and Joseph Bredsteen (editor of *Labor News*) was important, but the receptivity of rank-and-file workers to a polar conception of social relations also reflected the depression of the 1890s and the Populist movement. The severity of the depression further undermined the credibility and legitimacy of a political order that had been under fire for two decades. The strong support the Populists attracted in Eureka reflected the increasing dissolution of reciprocal notions of social relations and the growing polarization of class attitudes.

Union Power, Union Culture

The new Humboldt County labor movement demonstrated a commitment to organizing all workers, regardless of sex, skill, or nationality. It strongly endorsed a resolution passed at the 1906 annual meeting of the California State Federation of Labor condemning the high initiation fees charged by some unions. Such a policy, asserted *Labor News*, "is fundamentally selfish and is contrary to the broader minded spirit that lies close to the mainsprings of trade unionism and which welcomes every bona fide worker to the ranks of organized labor." [36] Women were welcome in the union movement, although the fact that they made up a small proportion of the workforce meant that they constituted a fraction of the overall union membership. Nevertheless, they were well represented in the Cooks and Waiters' and the Retail Clerks' unions, and women held important executive offices in both. *Labor News* also provided good coverage of social and political issues affecting women.

The Women's Label League, founded in 1904, played an important role in the social life of the union movement. Membership in the league was open to all wage-earning women and to men in good standing with their union, although men could not hold office or vote. The primary function of the league was to ensure that all merchandise, whether manufactured locally or not, bore the union label. Women delegates visited stores to determine the extent to which a business carried the union label and reported their findings to the Trades Council. The league took its work seriously. In 1906, after an inspection of men's clothing stores, it resolved to fine any league member who could not show at least three items of clothing bearing the union label. [37] The Trades Council attached great importance to the league's work and appointed a Women's Label League Committee. In addition to providing death and illness benefits for its members, league members visited hospitalized union members. At these visitations, women read to patients and brought them flowers. [38] At least once a month, the

Label League held a social at the Union Labor Hall to which all union members were invited. In 1906, the league established a special fund to purchase a $600 piano. The league was such a success that by the end of 1906, it claimed more than 200 members.[39]

The Humboldt labor movement attempted to organize all workers in the county, regardless of their ethnicity or nationality. A concerted effort was made to organize the growing Italian population employed mainly in logging camps and mills outside Eureka. In 1905, the Eureka Trades Council persuaded the California State Federation of Labor to hire someone to translate union literature into Italian.[40] In the same year the Trades Council purchased 1,000 pamphlets printed in Italian from the national AFL to assist in unionizing the Italian workforce;[41] and in June 1906, *Labor News* began printing an Italian-language page. The labor movement may not have been as open to organizing Asians. This was never tested, since there were almost no Asians in the county by the early twentieth century. But resolutions passed by unions, articles in *Labor News*, and the affiliation of some unions with the Asiatic Exclusion League indicate that the Humboldt labor movement shared the racial prejudices toward Asians harbored so fervently by the West Coast labor movement.

Between 1902 and 1906, the Humboldt labor movement consolidated its position. At the 1905 Labor Day parade, 2,500 people represented 25 unions affiliated with the Eureka Trades Council, and 1,250 actual union members marched.[42] In 1906, the Trades Council tripled its membership, boasting at least 4,000 members by year's end.[43] All craft unions won the eight-hour day, and most unions obtained wage increases. Some unions entered into formal collective bargaining agreements, especially in the building trades, where agreements often stipulated that employers could hire only union labor and use raw materials bearing the union label.[44]

Rarely did unions engage in, or even threaten, strikes. The few strikes that did occur were usually prompted by the attempts of employers to use nonunion labor in heavily unionized trades. Carpenters struck successfully over this issue in 1903 and 1906.[45] The boycott was the most commonly employed weapon. Sailors and clerks had tried it in the mid-1880s, but it was used much more extensively and effectively in the early twentieth century. Longshoremen demonstrated the efficacy of this tactic in their critical 1901 strike.[46] Subsequently, barbers, musicians, cooks and waiters, painters, and retail clerks made effective use of the boycott. The Eureka Trades Council sanctioned boycotts and gave them wide publicity in *Labor News*. "Why Dance to Scab Music," read the editorial headline of *Labor News* on April 1, 1905.

Union members were urged to attend only concerts given by orchestras whose members belonged to the Musicians' Union.[47] Employers had an opportunity to appear before the Trades Council to explain why a boycott should not be imposed on them. Most disputes were resolved amicably, either by the parties themselves or after the intervention of the Arbitration Committee of the Trades Council.

Several unions fined or expelled members when they thought they were not acting in accordance with union principles. In 1902, the Clerks' Union passed a resolution warning members that they would be fined $10 if they purchased goods at a nonunion store.[48] In 1906, the Cooks and Waiters levied fines on members who did not attend union meetings, and one member was expelled for working on a nonunion boat during a strike by the longshoremen's and sailors' unions.[49] The Painters' Union expelled a member for smoking nonunion cigarettes and fined two others for using nonunion tobacco.[50] Union discipline and influence expressed itself in other ways that demonstrated union power. The Scandia Hotel, heavily patronized by union members, refused to serve three nonunion longshoremen. A near riot ensued, and union men bundled the longshoremen out of the restaurant.[51]

The Humboldt County union movement represented more than the aggregate of its collective bargaining power. Many members believed that the movement should play a broad social and political role in the community, commensurate with its newfound stature and power. The Eureka Trades Council maintained a Social and Educational Committee to supervise Labor Day, Independence Day celebrations, and union picnics. The committee also organized several well-attended mass meetings to publicize the goals of the trade union movement. Such occasions were part of a deliberate effort to foster and sustain a union culture. These occasions became both educational forums and an opportunity to foster social camaraderie. Representative of this kind of event was a union picnic in 1904 attended by more than 1,000 people. Besides speeches by union leaders preaching the gospel of unionism, there was a diverse program of entertainments, including footraces for the children, a tug-of-war, and a pie-eating contest.[52]

Individual unions also held their own social events. Quite often, after the formal business had been attended to, a union meeting turned into a convivial social occasion with music, plays, and dancing. Frequently, these events lasted into the small hours of a Sunday morning. From time to time, a fraternal invitation was extended to members of another union. Several unions held annual picnics or balls to which the general public was invited. The longshoremen began holding an annual picnic in 1901, and some of their banquets attracted upward of

500 people.[53] The second annual picnic of the Shingle Weavers' Union drew 1,500 people.[54]

In 1906, the Humboldt County labor movement founded the Union Labor Hospital Association. It secured temporary quarters in Eureka and charged union members $10 annually for a hospital ticket. Later in the year, the association decided to finance construction of a $20,000 hospital facility. The project was funded by selling 800 bonds at $25 each to unions and individual union members.[55] *Labor News* boasted that it would be the best-equipped hospital in northern California and hailed the decision to build it: "The aims and purposes of the hospital association touch the mainsprings of brotherhood and fraternity. Such an institution represents one of the leading features of progressive unionism. . . . Long live the hospital and the brotherhood that has given it birth."[56] In 1906, also, the Eureka Trades Council and the Building Trades Council leased a cigar store and established a free employment agency.[57]

The Eureka Trades Council did not attempt to supersede the role of local charitable organizations, but the council responded generously in cases of exceptional hardship. In 1903, the council established a fund for an elderly couple who had lost all their possessions in a fire. Longshoremen opened the fund with a $25 donation.[58] When a single woman with five children appeared before the council to ask for financial assistance, a special committee was appointed "with power to relieve the immediate wants of the above lady and children."[59]

The Trades Council established its own reading room, which it stocked with books on socialism and trade unionism. It also submitted a list of books on these subjects to the Eureka Public Library and provided funds for the acquisition of these works.[60] Individual unions made periodic donations to the union library fund. The founding of *Labor News* was a major achievement of the labor movement. Launched in February 1905, it was one of the first California labor papers established outside the San Francisco Bay Area. Until July 1905, two union officials edited the paper. After this date, and until 1919, Joseph Bredsteen owned and edited the paper, although it remained the official organ of the Trades Council. Unfortunately, there is little biographical information on Bredsteen. He graduated from the University of Wisconsin at the turn of the century and worked for a time as a printer before arriving in Humboldt County shortly before he took over *Labor News*.[61] He was not apparently a member of any Humboldt union, but for fifteen years he played a critical role in the labor movement. An avowed socialist, he was the principal speaker at numerous union and Trades Council functions. The labor movement lent undying support to *Labor News*. Most unions had bloc subscriptions to the paper, which meant that every member of the union subscribed to it.[62] The Trades Council encouraged unions not only to take out subscriptions but also to patronize businesses that advertised in *Labor News*.[63]

By any standard, *Labor News* was an excellent trade union newspaper under the stewardship of Bredsteen. An eight-page weekly, it gave almost equal coverage to local, state, national, and international labor news, but the local labor movement was the main focus of attention. *Labor News* did not simply report on the activities of the Humboldt county labor movement; it candidly analyzed and criticized the movement on occasions, without its loyalty ever being called into question. A considerable amount of space—sometimes the whole front page— covered the labor movement and working conditions in other countries. In its first few months of publication, *Labor News* printed long features on "The Russian Workmen," "New Zealand's Industrial Conditions," and "The Cooperative Store Movement in England."

A Union Debating Club began in 1905.[64] It held meetings on Saturday nights that were open to the general public. It deliberately attempted to cultivate an informal atmosphere. Each meeting selected a new chairman, and people jotted down questions they thought worthy of debate and put them into a specially installed "ideas box." Topics discussed in the early months of the club's existence included the following: Should the National Government Institute a System of Old Age Pensions? Has Organized Labor Any Interest in and a Remedy for Food Adulteration? Should a Working Man Join the Police Force, the Detective Force or the National Guard? Would Municipal Ownership Benefit the Wage Workers?

The Union Labor Party and the Wobblies

The Union Labor Debating Club was founded several years after the Humboldt County labor movement assumed an assertive, independent, and progressive role in politics. As early as 1902, both the labor movement and the Democratic and Republican parties were acutely conscious of the political power of Humboldt labor. The 1902 platform of the Humboldt Democratic party recognized "the strong and growing tendency of the wage earning class of the state, and more particularly of this county, to organize for the better security of their rights and for the improvement of the conditions of labor." Accordingly, the Democrats assiduously courted the labor vote.[65] Republicans appealed to the labor vote just as openly, claiming that the strength of the union movement reflected the prosperity induced by Republican policies.[66]

The Humboldt County labor movement soon made it clear that it would not be seduced by party rhetoric. At a meeting in January 1903, the Eureka Trades Council expressed strong support for referendum and initiative amendments to the California constitution. The council's secretary was instructed to write to county representatives in the state legislature to determine their stance on these issues. The council also resolved to approach the City Council over the use of child labor in street sweeping, and a new committee was appointed to persuade the Eureka City Council to incorporate provisions limiting the hours of labor into a franchise that was shortly to be granted to the operators of Eureka's street railway system.[67] Two county state legislators responded favorably to the request to support the initiative and referendum reforms, but when State Senator Selvage first ignored, then declared his opposition to, such reforms, he infuriated the Eureka Trades Council, which passed a resolution denouncing him as an enemy of organized labor.[68]

Selvage's intransigence on the initiative and referendum was an important factor in the labor movement's decision in April 1903 to form a Union Labor party (ULP) to contest the upcoming Eureka elections.[69] The success of a Union Labor party in San Francisco may also have been a factor. The platform of the party declared that the time had arrived "when the proper solution of all questions affecting the interests of the laboring class of people is to be found in the ballot."[70] The main planks in the platform were support for better schools and compulsory education; a program of civic improvement, including the paving of all streets and the building of more parks and playgrounds; the public ownership of all utilities; an eight-hour day for all public works labor; and the submission of all city franchises to a referendum vote of the people.[71]

Representatives from all 21 unions in the county participated in the ULP convention, and union members made up well over half the ticket. The rest were candidates who had declared their strong support for the party's platform. The ULP was up against the powerful Eureka Civic Federation, formed on May 7, 1903 (and formally incorporated on June 26), which suggests that its establishment may have been prompted by the perceived threat of the ULP.[72] Founded under the auspices of the Eureka Chamber of Commerce with strong support from the *Humboldt Times* and *Humboldt Standard*, the Civic Federation boasted many of Eureka's leading Democrats and Republicans as members. The professed aim of the federation was to encourage further commercial and industrial development in Eureka and to promote a wide range of municipal improvements, including better streets, public parks, and more grandiose public buildings. In a circular issued just before the election, the ULP accused the Civic Federation of being an autocratic clique that had not allowed its membership any say in the selection of candidates, and it appealed directly to the union vote: "Do you favor union labor? Do you favor yourself? If you do, vote the Union Labor ticket, and thereby strengthen unionism. It is the only honestly made ticket." The *Standard* denounced the circular as a "pernicious" effort to "array class against class."[73]

The union leader Joseph Parker's campaign for mayor was hurt by questions about whether he had resided in the city long enough to run for office and by the fact that his rival for the Union Labor party nomination remained in the field. In a four-way race, Parker polled a somewhat disappointing 17 percent of the vote. Other Union Labor candidates performed much more impressively. Three ULP candidates, including Charles Devlin, gained executive offices, and three of five councilmen elected had the endorsement of the party.[74]

The labor movement did not venture directly into politics again until 1906. In the interim, it succeeded in getting most candidates for local and state office to appear before the Eureka Trades Council to explain their stand on important political issues. Resolutions were passed periodically denouncing the California legislature for its neglect of vital issues affecting labor. *Labor News* hailed the results of the 1905 Eureka elections, asserting that the mayor and three of the incoming City Council members had pledged themselves as friendly to labor. Even more important, as far as the Humboldt labor movement was concerned, measures to amend the city charter to provide for the initiative and referendum gained approval.[75]

The labor movement decided to reenter politics in 1906, and in the summer of that year reconstituted the ULP. The party's platform demanded the public ownership of all utilities; an eight-hour day for all workers; the abolition of child labor; the direct election of the U.S. president and senators; restriction on all immigration to the United States; an employer-liability law, and laws providing for better sanitary conditions at the workplace; and the institution of women's suffrage. Virtually all ULP nominees were union members, and they formed part of an almost complete ticket.[76]

The ULP elected only one of its candidates, but its performance was nevertheless impressive. Everett Logan, a carpenter and president of the Eureka Trades Council, won 43 percent of the Humboldt County vote in his battle for a seat in the state senate. Logan obtained 51 percent of the vote in Eureka. Charles Grambarth garnered 38 percent of the vote in his contest for a seat in the California assembly. The ULP elected a sheriff, and in the other county contests the party generally received at least 30 percent of the vote. The Democratic party endorsed some ULP candidates, but in general this was true when it would have been futile for the Democrats to have competed with the ULP. Indeed, in the few contests where the Democrats offered a candidate, they were decisively beaten by the ULP nominees.

The Industrial Workers of the World (IWW) attempted to attract a following in Humboldt County at a time when the AFL was at the peak of its power in the county and successfully organizing the county's lumber workers. In late 1905, Ben Williams, a leading IWW organizer, arrived in Eureka. The Eureka Trades Council cordially offered Williams an opportunity to speak at the Union Labor Hall. Williams's speech was not much more than a recitation of extracts from the IWW's constitution and evidenced little knowledge of the recent history of the county's labor movement. He declared that the IWW stood for the abolition of the capitalist class and argued that the organization of labor based on trades was irrelevant and useless. He described the AFL as an organization of stooges working for the capitalist class and proposed that all labor be divided into 13 industries controlled by a central body of representatives from each industry. Many in the audience challenged the broad assertions of Williams. He was asked specifically to show what the IWW could do that the AFL had not done, or was at least trying to do.[77] *Labor News* commented critically on his speech:

He [Williams] made so many sweeping and rash statements that it is difficult to see how such procedure can gain much sympathy for the cause of the Industrial Workers of the World. To say, as he did, that the AFL and the trade unions of today are useless and never did any good for the workers is absurd. . . . The AFL has its faults and there is room for improvement. The IWW have some good features but these can be adopted by the AFL as soon as the majority of workers are ready to make the change. . . . Many of the claims of the new organization seem visionary and impractical. Instead of taking people and conditions as they are they seem ready to go ahead on the basis of what people ought to be. What any local in Humboldt County would have to gain by joining the new organization it is difficult to see.[78]

The fact that, notwithstanding a concerted effort by Williams and the IWW to establish a rival union of lumber workers, the Wobblies failed to attract a significant following among them or other groups of workers indicates that most Humboldt County workers agreed with *Labor News*'s assessment. The IWW's charges against the AFL elsewhere may have been well founded, but in Humboldt they carried little credibility. Between 1900 and 1906, the county's labor movement, under the auspices of the AFL, established almost from scratch one of the strongest bastions of unionism in California. The Eureka Trades Council and unions affiliated with the AFL made a determined effort to organize workers regardless of their skill, sex, or nationality without any evident support or interference from the national AFL and with only token moral support from the California State Federation of Labor. Imbued with a sense of righteous destiny, the labor movement nurtured a vibrant union culture. And, in most trades and occupations, labor became a formidable bargaining force that was able to secure increases in wages and improvements in working conditions.

Nevertheless, even as the Humboldt County movement was at its zenith, there were portents of the troubled path that lay ahead. Ironically, labor was to some extent the victim of its own success; successful organization efforts soon brought strong counterorganization by employers. Thus, in April 1906, Eureka's builders and contractors established the Employers' Association of Humboldt County,[79] and in October, the Merchants' Association of Eureka was founded.[80] By this time, employers faced the possibility that unions might permanently entrench themselves and further erode employer prerogatives. A worsening economic climate in 1907 stiffened their resolve. Most ominously, lumber employers, confronted by the rapidly growing IBWSW, decided that the new union would have to be crushed when the 1907 season opened. The resulting strike was to have dire consequences for the whole Humboldt County labor movement.

Chapter 9

The Organization of Lumber Workers and the 1907 Strike

In August 1905, when Humboldt County lumber workers received a charter establishing the International Brotherhood of Woodsmen and Sawmill Workers (IBWSW), they had founded the first international union of lumber workers.[1] Between 1905 and 1907, Humboldt lumber workers were as well, if not better, organized than those in any other region. With limited resources, the IBWSW attempted to spread the gospel of unionism to other lumbering regions. Despite its early success and zeal, however, the obstacles to establishing permanent and broad-based lumber workers' unions in Humboldt County and elsewhere were as formidable as they had been in the Gilded Age.[2]

The Big Three and the Company Town

The decentralization of the Humboldt County lumber industry was reaching its culmination in the early twentieth century. During the 1880s, as this process began, a series of epicenters developed in some of the county's remote regions. The transitory nature and relatively small scale of lumber operations militated against the development of company towns. Indeed, sometimes cabins in lumbering and mining regions were put on wheels. The geographic isolation of these logging and mill operations compelled lumber companies to provide rudimentary housing and sometimes a store. With the possible exception of Scotia, these enclaves can best be described as forest camps. By the early twentieth century, however, many of the camps were evolving into full-fledged company towns, and most lumber production was taking place in such settings. Scotia, Samoa, and Korbel developed into archetypical company towns, as did Falk, Newburg, Crannell, and Glendale, albeit on a smaller scale.

Several related factors encouraged the development of company towns. First, many lumber companies secured large acreages of timberlands in the vicinity of their mills in the remote hinterlands. This helped minimize the transitory nature of operations and encouraged lumber entrepreneurs to invest in the infrastructure of a company town. Second, most companies greatly improved their railroad networks. A company with 30,000 acres of timberland had to conduct some logging operations far afield from the mill and, indeed, established some forest camps. Usually, though, loggers could commute between the company town and the scene of logging operations. In Humboldt County, however, distances were great, and the railroad network was neither well integrated nor cheap enough to enable most workers to reside in a major city or town. Finally, not until the late nineteenth and early twentieth centuries did most lumber companies operate on a large enough scale and possess sufficient capital to establish company towns.[3]

The number of workers employed in the lumber industry increased from 2,000 in the 1880s to almost 5,000 by the early years of the twentieth century, and lumber production tripled.[4] In 1906, 50 plants in the county were engaged in some combination of logging, sawmilling, and the manufacture of finished lumber products. Twenty-six mills produced shingles and shakes exclusively, and 10 manufactured doors, moldings, and house finishings. The remainder of the plants specialized in logging and milling, although they often had subsidiary facilities for manufacturing shingles and shakes and finished lumber products.[5] The largest lumber companies owned more than 30,000 acres of timber, employed more than 1,000 workers, and were capable of cutting 600,000 feet of lumber in a day. By most criteria, they were three times the size of their 1880 counterparts. Many mills replaced, upgraded, or expanded their machinery in the early twentieth century. In 1908, the Census Bureau described Humboldt County's mills as among the most modern in the world.[6]

A considerable amount of outside capital, primarily from San Francisco, had been invested in the nineteenth-century Humboldt lumber industry. But until the twentieth century, most lumber concerns had been owned, managed, and not uncommonly financed by the industry's pioneers. The growing interest of outside capital and the industry's increasing capital requirements brought about the demise of many pioneer lumber concerns by the early twentieth century. A few mills and lumbermen survived, but increasingly absentee capitalists, or capitalists, who were new residents of the county, owned and managed the lumber industry. There was also a dramatic increase in the concentration of ownership and production in the industry. By 1904, the Pacific Lumber Company, the Hammond Lumber Company, and the Northern Redwood Lumber Company dominated the industry. The "Big Three" at that date owned 64 percent of the county's timberlands and accounted for almost 60 percent of total milling capacity.[7] The Big Three were so named not simply because of their size but because they acted in concert in almost all matters from marketing arrangements to labor relations.

The metamorphosis of the Humboldt County lumber industry can be illustrated by briefly outlining the histories of the Big Three. It is appropriate to start with the Hammond Lumber Company. Its owner, Andrew Hammond, was probably the most powerful entrepreneur in the county, and certainly nobody played a more important role in shaping the antilabor policies of the county's lumber industry. As early as 1904, William Carson, who was constantly at odds with Hammond, asserted that the Humboldt Lumber Manufacturers' Association "has almost been turned over to Hammond,"[8] and Hammond continued to play a dominant role until his death in 1934.

Hammond was born in the Canadian Province of New Brunswick in 1848. He began work in the woods as a choreboy near Bangor, Maine. After the Civil War, he moved to Montana and engaged in merchandising and lumbering. By the 1880s, he owned the Blackfoot Lumber Company, one of the largest in the state. During the 1890s, his business interests shifted farther westward, and with Collis Huntington and others, he acquired the Oregon Pacific Railroad and three sawmills in Oregon. Hammond's plans in Humboldt County were equally ambitious. In 1900, he took over the management and ownership of the Vance Lumber Company, which had been founded by pioneer John Vance.

Hammond began by incorporating the Vance properties in New Jersey with a capital of $2 million. By the end of 1901, he had virtually rebuilt the Vance mill and tripled its capacity to 300,000 feet a day; by 1904, the physical plant at Samoa had been expanded and modernized to such an extent that the main sawmill and its auxiliaries were capable of sawing 600,000 feet of lumber in twenty-four hours. Approximately 1,000 men were employed by the company, triple the number ever employed by the Vance family. Hammond owned over 36,000 acres of redwood timber by 1902, and he continued to add to his holdings. Every phase of the Vance family's original operation was expanded. In 1901, Hammond acquired a large fleet of steam schooners for the transportation of lumber. The Eureka and Klamath Railroad was extended until it stretched 30 miles north of the mill at Samoa. By 1903, Samoa, which was located on a peninsula across Humboldt Bay a mile west of Eureka, was being transformed from a cluster of dwellings among the sand dunes into a full-fledged company town. Housing was constructed for approximately half of the company's employees; the other half lived in Eureka and commuted across the bay by ferry. Among the facilities established at Samoa were a cookhouse that could feed 300 men at one sitting, a large meeting house, a well-stocked general store, a bakery, and a butcher shop.[9]

The only other company of comparable size in the county was the Pacific Lumber Company, located at Scotia, 30 miles southeast of Eureka. Incorporated in 1869, it was the first major venture by outside capital into the Humboldt County lumber industry, but full-scale operations did not commence until 1887. In the 1890s, it was the largest lumber company in the county, and Scotia was an embryonic company town. During the first decade of the twentieth century, the Pacific Lumber Company dramatically expanded the scope of its operations. By 1904, the company owned 40,000 acres of timberland. The mill, operating on two ten-hour shifts, cut 300,000 feet a day.[10] Following the installation of new equipment in 1909 and the completion of another mill, 450,000 feet could be produced by the two mills in one eight-hour shift. It was one of the largest mills on the Pacific Coast and indeed in the world. By 1904, the company employed over 1,000 workers, and in 1909 one estimate put the total number of employees at 2,000.[11] Scotia's population increased from 454 in 1890 to more than 3,000 in the town and its vicinity by 1910, with most employees living in Scotia.[12] By the early 1910s, Scotia was the county's most-developed company town and one of America's foremost lumber company towns. It contained two churches, two banks, a saloon, a hospital, a schoolhouse, a library, a clubhouse, and a large, company-owned general store. There was an array of social and cultural institutions, including four fraternal orders and a volunteer fire company.[13]

The final member of the triumvirate, the Northern Redwood Lumber Company, was formed in 1903 when the Riverside Lumber Company, owned principally by Harry Jackson of Humboldt County and the San Francisco shipping magnate Charles Nelson, acquired the Humboldt Lumber Mill Company from the Korbel brothers. The Northern Redwood Lumber Company possessed over 15,000 acres of redwood.

The company's two mills produced about 200,000 feet of lumber a day, and by 1906, the company employed 700 men. Like the other large lumber companies in the county, the Northern Redwood Lumber Company was an almost totally vertically integrated establishment, possessing its own railroad, farm, shipping facilities, and wholesale and retail marketing outlets. Company headquarters were at Korbel, 20 miles northeast of Eureka. By the early 1910s, Korbel was a full-fledged company town, ranking only behind Scotia and Samoa.[14]

The Rebirth of Lumber Unionism

In September 1902, Humboldt County lumber workers made their first serious attempts to organize in almost twenty years when they formed a multiplicity of unions. In addition to separate unions of woodsmen and millmen, filers, donkey drivers, and stationary engineers established unions.[15] At almost the same time, the shingle weavers resurrected their union.[16] By 1903, about 1,000 Humboldt lumber workers belonged to a union of some sort, [17] most of which were affiliated with the Eureka Trades Council and the California State Federation of Labor.[18] Several factors prompted the revival of lumber trade unionism. There was a general fear that the growing domination of the county's lumber industry by outside capital might lead to a harsher regime—a fear that was not assuaged by several actions on the part of these companies. Moreover, the expansion of the county's lumber industry drew many new lumber workers to the county, men who did not have the deferential attitudes of their Gilded Age predecessors, especially if they were employed by one of the new titans of the lumber industry. As was true elsewhere in the county, the great demand for labor in the early years of the twentieth century gave lumber workers some sense of their own power. In this context, the union movement spread from Eureka to the woods and mills. It is surely not coincidence that lumber workers began forming unions at the very time the Eureka labor movement was establishing itself and only a few weeks after the founding of the Eureka Trades Council.

The frequency of small strikes and stoppages increased significantly after 1902. An incident in October 1903 involving workers at the Hammond Lumber Company illustrates the growing volatility of labor relations in the Humboldt lumber industry and the assertiveness of lumber workers. A group of about 20 Hammond employees waited for several hours for the ferry to take them from Eureka to Samoa. When the ferry finally arrived, they decided that overcrowding and a dense fog would make it an especially dangerous trip and resolved not to go to work. When the men showed up for work the next day, they were all fired. The discharged workers engaged in a vigorous, and partially successful, effort to persuade their replacements not to go to work. In a long letter to the *Humboldt Standard*, one discharged worker explained the circumstances and added: "We hope that this will set the matter right before the people and workingmen of this section and that they may know the methods of these Eastern lumbermen and beware of them."[19] The San Francisco entrepreneurs who founded the Arcata Barrel Company (to build barrels, wirebound boxes, and wooden containers in 1902) also provoked their workers. In January 1904, they announced that they were increasing the working day from nine to ten hours. In a letter to the *Humboldt Times*, "the crew" appealed to the general public: "We believe our cause is a just one and are of the opinion that we deserve the support of every fair minded and union principled laborer."[20]

Despite these incidents, conflicts continued to be relatively minor. For a few years, the booming demand for lumber and the growing strength of the Humboldt County labor movement encouraged lumber companies to proceed cautiously and avoid major confrontations. Nevertheless, the unions displayed an uneven pattern of development between 1902 and 1905 that contrasted with the steady growth of most unions in this period. The lumber unions tended to flourish during the height of the logging season and decline during the winter months; often they had to be reconstituted at the start of a new season. Thus, the Woodsmen's Union, based at Pepperwood in southern Humboldt County, had to be re-formed in February 1904.[21] In the fall of 1904, in an effort to retain their membership, the union moved its headquarters to Eureka, but over the 1904-1905 winter, it petered out. Indeed, by March 1905, almost all lumber unions in the county were defunct.[22]

The seasonal nature of lumber work and the resultant transient labor force were the greatest obstacles to establishing stable lumber unionism, but there were other hurdles. A significant number of lumber workers found work in the community or sat out the winter in one of Eureka's boardinghouses; in addition, a core of workers was retained by the lumber companies during the rainy season. These men could have sustained lumber unionism, albeit in a skeletal form. Yet this seldom occurred. The spirit of unionism was beginning to take hold in the woods and mills of Humboldt County, but habits of trade union membership are not acquired overnight, especially by seasonally employed workers with little history of unionism. Furthermore, although there were an increasing number of skirmishes between 1902 and 1904, no overriding issue or grievance surfaced that might have galvanized the nascent lumber trade union movement. Finally, the social geography of the Humboldt County lumber industry in the early twentieth century made the task of organizing lumber workers even more daunting than it had been in the 1880s. The dispersion of the lumber industry from Eureka to a group of company towns scattered over a large area presented formidable logistical problems in building and sustaining a union movement. Moreover, the fact that many lumber workers lived in a company town made them vulnerable to victimization, more so than their counterparts living in Eureka in the 1870s, who enjoyed at least some small measure of anonymity.

In January 1905, the Humboldt lumber companies handed the labor movement an issue that ignited lumber unionism. Although the lumber market was still booming, most companies announced wage cuts ranging from 10 to 15 percent.[23] More provocative was the declaration that woodsmen would be charged 50 cents a day, or $15 a month, for board.[24] Some companies agreed to offset the board charge by increasing wages, but the charge was a sharp break with long-established practice. Previously, lumber workers were not charged board regardless of how many days they worked. Under the new system, they would pay 50 cents a day for board whether they worked or not. The system made the wage packet of the lumber worker very uncertain, subject to the vagaries of climate, market forces, and other factors beyond his control.

The discontent provoked by the new system indicates that many lumber workers regarded the old arrangement almost as their birthright. In a front-page article, *Labor News* aired the lumber workers' grievances. It denounced the "Napoleons of finance of this county" for taking advantage of the disorganization of the woodsmen to break with a system established "from time immemorial." *Labor News* added that "it is evident that some of them are making an effort to keep pace with the mark set by the slave drivers of our Eastern cities, and each succeeding year finds another of these privileges taken from them [the lumber workers] and more onerous conditions imposed upon them." It concluded that the new board system would be "the straw that broke the camel's back."[25] The *Arcata Union* and officials of the Dolbeer and Carson and Elk River Mill companies all thought that a general strike at the start of the 1905 logging season was likely.[26] *Labor News* cautioned that if lumber workers were not treated "with justice" there might be a strike, but warned lumber workers not to take any precipitate action.[27]

Some pioneer lumber operators, including William Carson, Dan Newell, and the Elk River Mill and Lumber Company, refused to adopt the new board system for a variety of reasons. An official at Elk River Mill argued that "where there is good profit in a business, it is well to let well enough alone. . . . It takes but a little out of the ordinary sometimes to precipitate trouble."[28] Carson condemned the efforts to change the board system and set wages as not only provocative but unfair: "It is just as vicious a scheme as any that labor unions try to force. These are measures for which the Hammond and Pacific Lumber Companies are largely responsible for no doubt. Those institutions will do more to foster the growth of labor unions here than anything else in this county."[29]

By spring 1905, Carson's forebodings were borne out. In an impassioned and lengthy editorial published on March 4, *Labor News* called on lumber workers to regroup.[30] The response was immediate. By late April, more than 1,000 woodsmen and millmen had organized. Federal labor unions formed at Eureka, Scotia, Blue Lake, Fortuna, and some of the more remote locales in the county.[31] William Owen, former president of the Eureka Longshoremen's Union, spearheaded the organizing drive, acting in his new capacity as a regional organizer for the California State Federation of Labor. Owen was a dedicated and effective organizer whose endeavors bordered on the heroic. Thrown off a lumber company train on one occasion, he trudged miles through pouring rain to keep a speaking engagement. On another occasion, having been evicted first from a cookhouse and then a blacksmith's shop, he proceeded to hold an organizing meeting on some nearby railroad tracks.[32]

Owen received help from some of the leading lights of the Humboldt labor movement, who made frequent trips to more remote sections of the county to implore woodsmen and millmen to join a union. B. Callaghan of the Painters' Union delivered an eloquent plea to the lumber workers of Blue Lake at a general organizing meeting. He heralded the rising spirit of unionism in the woods and mills and called on all workers to set aside the craft prejudices that had divided workers for so long and "create in its stead a spirit of brotherly love." He yearned for the day "when all the working people will be encircled in one common family, and then the watchword will be 'Union.'" Callaghan stressed the need for unity against the growing might of organized capital: "In the great fight for human rights neither religious, racial, nor political lines must divide us. There must be no Catholics, Protestants, Jews, nor Mormons, no Britishers, Scandinavians, Germans, nor Italians, no Republicans, Democrats, Populists or socialists."[33] There were speeches by other Humboldt union leaders, and after the meeting, 233 men signed the roll and established a federal labor union.[34]

The lumber workers' organizing drive received support from some unexpected quarters. The historically antiunion *Humboldt Times* insisted that lumber workers had a right to organize and denied that the establishment of a union would lead inevitably to conflict and strikes.[35] On a number of occasions, *Labor News* denounced the church for its lack of sympathy with working people.[36] Nevertheless, a few pastors gave considerable moral support to the union movement. In a Sunday sermon, the Reverend Teel of the Christian Church explicitly endorsed and legitimized the activities of the lumber workers' unions. He stressed the "indispensable" work the woodsmen were doing in "furthering the advance of civilization" and he invoked the labor theory of value to vindicate their organizing efforts:

We are all agreed that labor creates all wealth, yet the laborer has the smallest amount. "In the sweat of thy face shalt thou eat bread," said Jehovah, but today those who rarely exercise in labor sufficient to cause the brow to perspire are enabled to wine and dine and feed upon dainties and roll in the lap of luxury. Social conditions that produce millionaires and tramps, princes and paupers, are wrong.[37]

By July 1905, the combined membership of the federal lumber unions was approaching the 2,000 mark.[38] Charles Grambarth suggested that the lumber workers apply to the AFL for status as an international union. The pragmatic considerations alone were compelling in that this move would save the federal lumber unions in Humboldt County approximately $2,000 in dues to the national AFL. The money saved could be used to employ a general organizer and provide the basis for an insurance plan.[39] The proposition was unanimously endorsed by the lumber workers, and on August 2, 1905, the AFL issued a charter authorizing the creation of the International Brotherhood of Woodsmen and Sawmill Workers.

The IBWSW embodied many elements of the radical and fraternal union culture that pervaded the Humboldt County labor movement. Like many other Humboldt unions, branches of the lumber workers' union held general social and educational meetings.[40] Leading figures in the county's labor movement usually opened a meeting with an address. Several meetings were open to the general public, with a special invitation to the wives of lumber workers. After the speeches, a program of musical entertainments followed. On one occasion, when a member of the union was killed in an accident, 400 members showed up for the funeral.[41] The IBWSW played the leading role in launching both the Union Labor Hospital and the Union Labor party (ULP).[42] Exactly what percentage of lumber workers voted Union Labor in 1906 is difficult to determine, but *Labor News* reported that, in a straw poll taken before the 1906 election, 95 percent of the Blue Lake woodsmen supported the ULP.[43]

The IBWSW took some tentative steps toward organizing lumber workers outside Humboldt County in 1906. Fully aware that it did not have the resources to launch a major organizing drive outside the county, the union appealed for the assistance of the California State Federation of Labor. Although a formal resolution at the annual convention of the California State Federation of Labor called on the general organizer to assist in the unionization of California lumber workers,[44] the IBWSW received little help from the State Federation of Labor. The union's secretary, Ernest Pape, made organizing trips to Santa Cruz, California, and Washington State, and several locals were subsequently established. Applications for membership also came from places as far away as Maine, Georgia, and Alabama. Even at its peak, however, the IBWSW could boast only 14 locals outside Humboldt County. For all its good intentions, it found it impossible to mount an effective organizing drive outside the county without substantial assistance from the national and California American Federation of Labor.

Strike Prospects and Organizational Problems

As the 1905 logging season drew to a close, the IBWSW honeymoon ended, as it grappled with a host of problems. The first was the perennial problem of how to prevent large losses in membership during the rainy season. The problem was not viewed as entirely logistical or seasonal, but one intertwined with fostering a well-rooted spirit of trade unionism in general. Aside from the problem of out-migration during the winter months, sustaining participation in union activities among the lumber workers during both the logging and rainy seasons presented difficulties. By the fall of 1905, the IBWSW had six locals, all of which, with the exception of the Fortuna local, contained members from camps and mills that were many miles apart. Thus, sustaining an active local, even at the best of times, was hard. Well-attended meetings were not possible on weekdays. Sunday was the only day when all members of a local could meet, and Sunday was the lumber workers' only full day of rest. On Saturdays, many married men left the camp to visit their families, while single men often took the excursion train to Eureka for a night on the town and spent Sunday in the city recuperating from their revelries. The Sunday meeting demanded dedication and commitment, even from men who remained in camp on the weekends. By the time they had trudged several miles to attend a meeting, most of the day was gone.

Labor News suggested the establishment of locals at most camps. This would not only allow weekday evening meetings to take place but would make the union more democratic and more responsive to its membership. Union officials would be more accountable, and more members would be able to hold union office.[45] The first formal meeting of the IBWSW discussed the reform. It was rejected, although the possibility of subdividing some locals in the future was not ruled out; indeed, the following year, some locals did subdivide.[46] By September 1906, there were two locals in Eureka, three in the general vicinity of Scotia, and two at Blue Lake. But this limited structural reorganization did not solve the problem and hardly followed *Labor News*'s recommendation for far-reaching decentralization.

Another problem was the reluctance of millmen to join the union on anything like the same scale as the woodsmen. In part, this reflected the fact that the millmen were not affected by the new board regulations, and, unlike the woodsmen, they had attained the ten-hour day. The IBWSW and *Labor News* alternately exhorted and reproached the millmen, warning them that they would become the next victims of the lumber companies' antilabor policies. Some headway was made in organizing mill workers in the Blue Lake and Fortuna regions during the late summer of 1905, but not until the spring of 1906 was any significant progress made. At that time, a rumor that, in the aftermath of the San Francisco earthquake, many lumber companies would pay men in scrip led to an influx of millmen into the union.[47] Still, the millmen remained much less well organized than the woodsmen, especially in Eureka.

Despite considerable efforts, the IBWSW met with limited success in organizing the Italian lumber workers, who were becoming a significant part of the workforce in southern Humboldt County. *Labor News* began publishing its Italian page on June 16, 1906. Using arguments in favor of unionism that were almost identical to the ones addressed to its English-language readership, *Labor News* stressed that workers of all nationalities were brothers and that because a man could not speak English, he should not be treated "like a dog."[48] Italians, however, did not rush to join the union, although they did engage in small wildcat strikes. In March 1907, 30 Italians were fired for going on strike at a planing mill. *Labor News* lamented that the men would not have lost their jobs if they had been union members.[49] In the spring of 1907, when a major confrontation seemed inevitable, the IBWSW redoubled its efforts to draw Italians into the union fold. A special meeting of Italian lumber workers was held on April 7, 1907, at which Bredsteen and two Italian organizers spoke. There was a "fair-sized attendance," but only 16 men joined the union afterward.[50] Throughout April, the IBWSW held weekly meetings in Italian and announced that some of the top administrative positions on the Union Labor Hospital Board would be reserved for Italians.[51] One Italian organizer beseeched his countrymen to join the union:

We Italians must unite with our American brothers and with those of other nationalities in order to combat the abuses of our oppressors. The Americans of this county know full well that the Italians work in the wood industries in large numbers and that the success or death of the union is up to them. We do not want to draw the anger of our American brothers at this critical moment by not uniting with them and thereby forcing the failure of their cause, which is also our cause. We endeavor to make ourselves esteemed, not hated. If we raise ourselves to their level they will treat us as their equals.[52]

Despite such entreaties, only a trickle of Italian workers joined the union.

By August 1906, signs of stress appeared in the IBWSW. The union had made only modest gains during the year, and the rainy season, combined with mounting apathy and dissension, threatened seriously to erode the membership base. Bitter disputes erupted over the most effective means of utilizing the union's limited financial resources and whether to assess a special levy to hire a general organizer.[53] After an acrimonious debate at the first annual convention of the IBWSW, delegates agreed to raise dues 15 cents a month and to put a 10 percent per capita tax on the locals to support a general organizer. The rank and file ratified both decisions.[54] Shortly after the convention, A. E. Zant of the California State Federation of Labor was hired as a general organizer.[55]

The divisiveness that marked the first annual convention of the IBWSW reflected a growing discontent and restlessness among the lumber workers. The incidence and magnitude of "small" strikes increased in 1906. The most important was a "food" strike at two of Hammond's logging camps. Unlike previous food strikes, this one involved not a handful of men, but 200 woodsmen. Furthermore, the poor quality of the fare was not believed to be the fault of a bad cook but an attempt by Hammond to cut costs.[56] The Eureka Trades Council declared its full support for a general strike of lumber workers, and the IBWSW submitted the issue to a vote of the membership. By a narrow margin (although in conformity with union policy, the results were never published), the membership voted against a strike.[57]

The closeness of the strike vote, and a series of other small strikes, indicate that the patience of lumber workers was wearing thin. In September 1906, *Labor News* admitted that many lumber workers were complaining that the union had done little for them. The IBWSW faced a difficult dilemma. On the one hand, it realized that with only half the county's lumber workers organized, a confrontation with the lumber companies was risky. On the other hand, many lumber workers were anxious to redress their grievances. Strong as the support of lumber workers was for the Union Labor party, the Union Labor Hospital, and the fraternal activities of the union, this could not sustain it indefinitely if bread-and-butter issues were not addressed. The union had derived its initial impetus from the indignation that followed the change in the board system and the wage cuts. The lofty rhetoric and promises of organizers and *Labor News*, combined with the impressive growth of the IBWSW, heightened members' expectations that action would be taken to better their conditions. After almost two full logging seasons of inaction, the credibility of the IBWSW was at stake. As the strike vote indicated, this was not a question that neatly divided the rank and file from the leadership. Furthermore, there is no evidence to show that during 1906 in the context of the Hammond food strike or at any other time the leadership of the IBWSW, the Eureka Trades Council, or *Labor News* tried to discourage a strike.

During the winter of 1906, general organizer Zant made a determined effort to sustain lumber unionism and counteract the apathy and dissension engendered by the often unrealistic expectations of new union members. After visiting most of the major mills and camps in Humboldt County in late November and December 1906, Zant reported that he was struck by the "high degree of intelligence and independence" of the lumber workers, and he insisted that "the material is there for the finest kind of an organization," but, he added, in a somewhat censorious tone:

I am not desirous of having prospective members, who have never belonged to unions, to become over-enthusiastic all of a sudden because such members are not apt to stay enthusiastic very long. Unionism is not learned and comprehended in a day. Those who join without first making a study of the movement are too prone to expect immediate results.[58]

In a report to the *American Federationist* a few months later, Zant reaffirmed his analysis: "There is a splendid spirit of unionism manifest here but we need more complete organization and education on basic principles of federation and discipline."[59] *Labor News* echoed Zant's complaint and reproached lumber workers who grumbled at the IBWSW's lack of accomplishments, insisting that the blame lay with members "who have failed to do anything but pay dues and fail to attend meetings. . . . No set of officers can make headway unless the membership is behind them."[60] But *Labor News* did not confine itself to attempting to instill a greater sense of union discipline and commitment. Simultaneously, it tried to incite the lumber workers by reminding them how, at a time of unequaled prosperity in the lumber industry, wages had been cut and a new board system instituted, while woodsmen still worked a twelve-hour day.

On February 10, 1907, delegates of the IBWSW met to draw up a list of demands before the new season began. The woodsmen's requests included a restoration of the old board arrangement; a return to the 1904 wage scales; a meal schedule in which breakfast would be no earlier than 6:00 A.M., dinner no later than 6:00 P.M.; and a work-day organized in accordance with the meal schedule. The millmen demanded a minimum wage of $40 a month (including board); a 15 percent increase in wages for those earning less than $50 a month, and a 10 percent increase for those earning more, with time and a half to be paid for all overtime.[61] The Eureka Trades Council and the Building Trades Council endorsed the demands.[62] *Labor News* strongly supported the stance of the lumber workers and reiterated that the lumber companies could easily afford to make these modest concessions.

The Humboldt Lumber Manufacturers' Association (HLMA), however, was in no mood to make concessions and immediately rejected the demands of the IBWSW. The association's leading figure, Andrew Hammond, had already evinced a determination to crush the Humboldt labor movement.[63] Fearful of a strike in 1906, he had attempted to flood the county labor market with lumber workers.[64] In November 1906, he was the only employer not to grant workers in the molding mills an eight-hour day and a wage increase.[65] He refused to give the shingle weavers employed by him the increase conceded by the 20 other shingle mill operators in the county.[66] Hammond also spearheaded a protracted, and ultimately successful, drive to crush the Eureka Longshoremen's Union in the closing months of 1906.[67]

The humbling of the once powerful Longshoremen's Union emboldened the lumber owners to take a tough stand against the IBWSW. The indictment of two Eureka Union longshoremen for the murder of a nonunion longshoreman fortified their position. The two men were acquitted in 1909, but sensational and extensive coverage was given to the story in late 1906 and early 1907. Suddenly the labor movement found itself on the defensive in an attempt to preserve the moral standing and reputation it had enjoyed in the community for several years. Revelations about corrupt practices of the San Francisco Union Labor party in early 1907 also received much publicity in the Humboldt press, to the extent that they further tarnished the image of the county's labor movement. In addition, lumber employers drew strength from a mounting open-shop drive against unions at the national level.

Several lumber companies announced small wage increases in an attempt to defuse the resistance.[68] At the same time, the HLMA prepared for a strike. The employers made a major effort to flood the Humboldt County labor market using employment agencies in San Francisco, the Midwest, and the East.[69] *Labor News* reprinted one notice that appeared in an employment agency in Marinette, Wisconsin: WANTED WOODSMEN FOR EUREKA, CALIFORNIA: WORK GUARANTEED THE YEAR ROUND: WAGES $2.25 PER DAY." The advertisement offered to pay half the $50 railroad fare after six months of service.[70] During March and April, hundreds of men flocked to Humboldt County in response to such notices.[71]

Not all Humboldt lumber operators relished the prospect of a confrontation with the lumber workers. Several pioneer lumbermen, such as William Carson and Irving Harpster, dissented from the hard-line position of the HLMA. Carson refused to attend its meetings as a strike began to look inevitable: "I declined, not that I favor strikes, but some of the larger lumber companies [especially the Hammond Company] have not treated their employees fairly and for that Dolbeer and Carson don't care to assume any of their troubles at this time, as we have many friends among the labor unions when Hammond seems to be the bad man."[72] Carson and Harpster believed that the labor policies of the Big Three were not only harsh and unfair but likely to have an adverse effect on productivity and encourage unionism.[73] Harpster wrote that he felt a confrontation was inevitable ever since the new board system was introduced, and he added:

We also believe the mills that have adopted the board propositions have early been the losers all along, for when men are dissatisfied with conditions they are not apt to take the interest they would otherwise do in their work, while on the other hand if the men feel they are treated fairly they in turn will return value received in the way of honest labor. . . . In fact fair treatment lessens the chances of unionization.[74]

The Dolbeer and Carson Company and the Elk River Mill Company did not negotiate with the IBWSW for fear that this would entail tacit recognition. But Carson and Harpster claimed to be granting practically all that the union was asking, and they were confident that the few employees of theirs who had joined the union would not strike.[75]

The Strike

On April 28, 1907, the IBWSW submitted the strike question to the membership. By an overwhelming majority—reportedly 35 to 1 outside Eureka and 5 to 1 in Eureka—members voted to strike.[76] The more benign labor policies of the pioneer lumber companies, and the fact that relatively few of their workers were organized, led the IBWSW to exempt them from the strike.[77] Still more pragmatic was the decision not to call out Hammond's mill workers because of the union's limited following with them. Evidently, Hammond's unabashed policy of repression was beginning to bear fruit and was as effective in containing unionism as the more conciliatory and paternal policies of the pioneer lumbermen. While Hammond was the *bête noir* of the Humboldt labor movement, to have called a strike at a mill where the union had a small following would have been futile. It would also have raised doubts about the union's ability to mobilize a mass following and present the solid front essential for the success of the strike. On May 1, the strike commenced as planned. Newspaper accounts concurred in estimating that about 2,500 lumber workers responded to the strike call. At Scotia, 740 Pacific Lumber Company employees walked out; 625 workers struck the Northern Redwood Lumber Company; and 400 woodsmen employed by Hammond left their jobs.[78]

Even before the strike commenced, lumber companies began evicting workers from company housing and lumber workers left for Eureka in droves. The IBWSW lacked the resources to give much financial support to the strikers. Nevertheless, a committee was appointed to aid the very needy and those who lacked funds to look for work elsewhere.[79] Within a few days, hundreds of striking lumber workers left the county. A large proportion of them were reportedly men who had worked there for many years. *Labor News* confidently predicted that the exodus would persuade the lumber companies to bargain. The out-migration of lumber workers did indeed concern the employers, to the extent that they formally agreed not to bid for each other's men after the strike was over.[80] Notwithstanding these fears, the lumber companies dug their heels in and proclaimed their determination to continue operations "only on an open shop principle." They warned that they were prepared to close down the plants indefinitely rather than submit to the union's demands, and on no condition would they "recognize any union or treat with any committees from the union, now or at any time."[81] Efforts to import fresh labor were redoubled. On May 22, the *Coast Seamen's Journal* estimated that 4,000 workers had "started" for Humboldt County since early 1907.[82] The Eureka Trades Council responded by sending circulars to central labor councils across the country, informing them of the situation in Humboldt. During the strike, pickets were often successful in persuading new arrivals not to go to work, and *Labor News* claimed that some newcomers actively supported the strike.

For several weeks, a barrage of claims and counterclaims was exchanged about the success of the strike by local newspapers, union officials, and lumber company owners. The Humboldt press tended to highlight rumors of a break in the strike, while *Labor News* did its utmost to disprove such reports. The disparate nature of the lumber industry made it hard for the press and the strikers to verify or refute reports. By all accounts, the strike held firm for the first three weeks of May. In the last week of May, it began to collapse. A trickle and then a flow of men drifted back to work, although the Pacific Lumber Company was unable to reopen its mill on May 22, as it had planned.[83]

Friction between the IBWSW and the IWW was responsible for the first and decisive break in the strike. The Wobblies had secured a following of a few hundred lumber workers, concentrated mainly in the Fortuna area of southern Humboldt County.[84] *Labor News* welcomed the IWW's participation in the strike: "It demonstrates that the rank and file of the labor organization is composed of sincere and honest men, no matter how much they may differ with us on the best course to pursue a common aim."[85] The sequence and details of the events that produced the rift between the IWW and the IBWSW are not absolutely clear, and conflicting accounts appeared in *Labor News* and the IWW press. During the third week of the strike, the Eel River Valley Lumber Company, located at Newburg, approximately 2 miles east of Fortuna, indicated its willingness to meet the demands of the strikers, but under no condition would it formally recognize unions. Both the IBWSW and the IWW had a strong following at the Eel River Mill. According to Ben Williams, who had been rushed to the county to lead the strike two days after it began, the IBWSW demanded that any settlement must include union recognition.[86] While there is no hard evidence to support his account, Williams insisted that the IBWSW was also asking for exclusive representation. Williams and the IWW membership decided that in view of the fact that "scale had been offered at Newburg, our men should go to work there, and not cause the IWW to commit suicide by holding out for recognition of the AF of L."[87]

On May 22, the *Humboldt Times* and *Standard* reported that the Eel River Mill and Lumber Company had reached a settlement with the Wobblies and would shortly be reopening with their help.[88] The IBWSW responded by resuming negotiations. Sensing the division, the Eel River Mill and Lumber Company proceeded to retract some of its concessions. Under the agreement reached with the IBWSW, most workers received roughly half what had been demanded originally. The new board arrangements were modified to some extent. Men would not have to pay board if they worked part of the day or were prevented from working by illness, but under all other circumstances, they were to pay full board when not working.[89] Whether, as Williams claimed, the Eel River Mill refused to take back IWW employees is unclear. What is clear is that the Wobblies retaliated by ordering or allowing all their members to return to work.[90] Although *Labor News* reported after the strike that many Wobblies did not return to work, a considerable number did. A significant number helped break the strike at Scotia, and they were also among the first to return to work at the Hammond Lumber company.[91] Simultaneously, the IWW helped drive the last nails into the coffin of the embattled longshoremen. On May 23, 17 Wobblies agreed to work for the Humboldt Stevedore Association, the new shipping agency established by the lumber owners to break the Longshoremen's Union.[92]

Writing in the *Industrial Union Bulletin*, Williams went to great lengths to vindicate the IWW's role in the strike. Without elaborating, he accused the IBWSW of conducting the strike "in the same blind, stupid way." He claimed that the Humboldt County AFL's decision to organize the lumber workers had been inspired by the presence of the American Labor Union (the IWW's predecessor).[93] In a lengthy second article, he accused the IBWSW of refusing to cooperate in prestrike deliberations and holding out for a union shop agreement that would exclude the IWW.[94] He lambasted the IBWSW for not striking in 1906 and for not striking against all the mills in Humboldt County in 1907. Williams divulged the contents of a letter from Secretary Ernest Pape of the IBWSW declining prestrike deliberations. Pape's letter was cordial. He said that he simply assumed the Wobblies would join the strike, that the goals of strike and its timing were clear, and that the general purpose of the two unions the same. Pape had a point, although perhaps the IBWSW can be criticized for not engaging in consultations before and during the strike and thus possibly avoiding the debacle at Newburg. It is also possible, as Williams claimed, that some lumber workers joined the IWW because they were tired of the inaction of the IBWSW. Nevertheless, estimates from all sources, including Williams, do not put IWW membership at more than 300. There can be little doubt that the IBWSW played the predominant role in organizing lumber workers from the summer of 1905 until the strike, while the IWW made no concerted effort. It is hard to escape the conclusion that the Wobblies belated efforts were an attempt to capitalize on the success of the IBWSW and to take a share of the credit if a showdown between lumber workers and employers occurred. To the degree that the IBWSW wanted primary, or even sole, recognition, this was understandable in view of the dominant role they had played in organizing lumber workers. The timing of the strike might have been a mistake, as Williams argued, but on questions of tactics, the IBWSW was far better placed to make difficult decision than Williams, who made only fleeting visits to the county and only showed up there two days after the strike had begun.

While the IWW's return to work occurred at an important juncture in the strike, it did not affect the outcome, given the determination of the major lumber companies not to bargain. During the last days of the strike, and in its immediate aftermath, the Humboldt AFL tempered its recriminations. *Labor News* asserted that a number of Wobblies had refused to return to work, and some had even torn up their membership cards in disgust.[95] In later years, *Labor News* reflected on the actions of the IWW during the 1907 strike with more bitterness. The Wobblies' role in the strike left a legacy of suspicion and anger in Humboldt County that helped circumscribe their ability to attract a significant following among lumber workers.

While Italians joined the IBWSW in relatively small numbers, they strongly supported the strike. In 1907, only the Pacific Lumber Company employed Italians in significant numbers. At Scotia, support for the strike was greater, in terms of total numbers and the proportion of workers striking, than at any other company. *Labor News* reported that the "Scotia contingent of Italians all came to Eureka . . . saying they would never work for a company that treated them the way PL does."[96] Several instances occurred where Italians, used as scabs, were quickly persuaded to honor the strike.[97] In the last days of the strike *Labor News*, while observing that there were some Italian scabs, praised the Italians, saying that "no-one had been more loyal in the present fight."[98] Notwithstanding the failure to draw the Italians into the union in large numbers, the poor treatment that they received from the lumber employers and the continuous efforts of *Labor News* and the IBWSW to explain the broader issues involved in the confrontation, evidently made Italian lumber workers as militant as their counterparts.

Defeat and Decline

The strike dragged on through the end of May. A vote on May 27, at a meeting of about 150 striking lumber workers at Union Hall in Eureka, overwhelmingly favored continuing the strike.[99] But four days later, a referendum vote of the membership reversed the decision. *Labor News* put the best possible face on things, insisting that in many respects the strike had been a success. It praised the solidarity of the lumber workers, asserting that only 100 members returned to work before the strike was officially called off. *Labor News* claimed also that as a result of the strike and the massive exodus of lumber workers from the county, "men were offered individually all the union scale called for, and in some cases more." And it concluded that lumber workers had developed a new sense of their own power and that the future of the union was "bright indeed."[100]

Harry Jackson, the principal owner of the Northern Redwood Lumber Company, lent some credence to the claims of *Labor News* when he admitted that in almost all instances where workers had applied for wage increases on an individual basis, they had been granted.[101] Yet, notwithstanding the courage and solidarity of the lumber workers, the 1907 strike was a disastrous setback for the IBWSW. In all likelihood, only the more skilled lumber workers obtained significant wage increases. Most important, the IBWSW failed to bring the lumber companies to the bargaining table and thereby secure the *de facto* recognition that was essential if it was to retain its credibility. Most union members were disappointed at the fruits of two years of laborious organizational work and a month-long strike. The *Humboldt Times* reported much dissension and talk of a "bungled affair" when the membership met to vote to discontinue the strike.[102]

If the 1907 strike really was a victory, then the IBWSW should have been able to sustain itself in the aftermath in some viable form. But in the wake of the strike, the IBWSW began to disintegrate in Humboldt county, and within a month *Labor News* was warning the whole Humboldt County labor movement that it faced a "grave crisis," and urging the movement to brace itself for a massive open-shop offensive.[103] In July, *Labor News* alluded to a "lull" in the activity of the IBWSW, but tried to draw encouragement from the fact that four locals of the union had decided to affiliate with the Building Trades Council.[104]

In September, Secretary Pape conceded that "our locals in the county are yet somewhat demoralized since our strike of last spring."[105] And at the same time, *Labor News* admitted that both the lumber workers and the longshoremen had been dealt "severe blows."[106]

The total number of locals embraced by the IBWSW increased from 17 to 24 between September 1906 and September 1907. Ironically, at the very time that the IBWSW was being crushed in Humboldt County, it was beginning to attract a wider following from lumber workers in several other important lumbering regions. By September 1908, however, there were only 3 active locals of the union in Humboldt County, and the number of locals outside the county dwindled to 11.[107] The IBWSW held its 1909 convention outside Humboldt County for the first time—in Everett, Washington. Cognizant of the reverses the union had suffered in Humboldt County, the convention decided to relocate union headquarters to Lothrop, Montana. The union struggled on with perhaps 1,000 members, but expired in April 1911 when the AFL suspended its charter.[108]

The outcome of the 1907 strike was a serious setback for the Humboldt County labor movement. In its immediate aftermath, Hammond launched a relentless, countywide open-shop drive. The AFL and the IWW strove to regenerate lumber trade unionism after 1907, but with very little success. A strike in 1906 might have brought more concessions in the short run, but the union had only a limited following among mill workers and understandably believed that it would have to organize more than half the county's lumber workforce to win a strike. They thought that they could consolidate their membership base and tried hard to do so. By 1907, with its credibility at stake, the union was under enormous pressure to ask for concessions from the lumber companies. The demands were modest, and in many respects an attempt to restore the status quo. Tactically, it may have been a mistake to wait nearly three months before striking, for this gave the lumber companies time to prepare for the strike and to flood the Humboldt county labor market and build up inventories. The fact that Humboldt county redwood lumber production was higher in 1907 than in any previous year and that shipments in May and June 1907 were significantly greater than in May and June 1906 indicate a major logistical problem faced by lumber unions. Lumber companies frequently had a large quantity of logs and cut lumber stockpiled. Even when this was not the case, they usually had the capacity to expand production rapidly in the aftermath of a strike. Finally, lumber companies could use a strike to conduct the routine maintenance or upgrading of their machinery that often closed their mills for two to four weeks.

The defeat of the strike cannot be blamed on tactical errors. By 1906, Hammond was determined to crush the Humboldt County labor movement. In 1907, Hammond and other HLMA members recognized that it was vital not to accord the IBWSW even token recognition if it was to be prevented form establishing itself on a permanent footing. In addition to the intransigence of the HLMA, a host of factors militated against a successful strike and the maintenançe of stable trade union-ism in the lumber industry: the transient and seasonal nature of the workforce, the widely dispersed character of lumbering operations, the high degree of organization among the lumber companies, and their dominance of the local economy.

The first decade of the twentieth century witnessed a momentous transformation in the structure of the Humboldt County lumber in-dustry. Within the space of a few years, the pioneer lumber industry that had reigned from the mid-nineteenth century was almost eclipsed by a few giant concerns owned and operated by outside capital. When Hammond commenced operations in Humboldt County, Carson had resided there for fifty years. Hammond hardly ever visited the county. The ascendancy of the Big Three betokened a new era in labor rela-tions. Unencumbered by lingering notions of reciprocal obligations, the Big Three resolved that the most profitable way to run their operations was to cut labor costs to the bone and ruthlessly crush any opposition. In contrast, the surviving pioneers wished to preserve the patriarchial features of nineteenth-century labor relations. Quite aside from any sentiments regarding justice and equity deriving from their own expe-rience in the industry and their longstanding ties to the community, they were convinced that this was the most effective way to counter-act the rising labor movement and preserve harmonious relations that would maximize productivity.

The fact that, during a rising tide of trade unionism in the county, very few workers of the pioneer lumber companies joined a union vin-dicated the analysis of the pioneer lumbermen. Unquestionably, also, the hard-line stance of the large "outside" lumber companies fueled the emergence and growth of lumber unionism generally. But the en-terprises of Hammond and his associates dwarfed those of the pioneers and left them in no position to dictate the tone or content of labor re-lations policy. Ultimately, the strategy of no compromise and outright repression proved successful in stifling the growth of lumber unionism. Effective as this policy continued to be after the 1907 strike, within a few years the titans of the Humboldt County lumber industry ques-tioned whether it was the best way to exact maximum productivity from their workers. Approximately a decade after the strike, they began to see the advantages of fostering a sense of corporate loyalty and, although not abandoning repression as a tool, embraced a scientific paternalism or welfare capitalism as a means to this end. In the meantime, however, they set about the task of extirpating unionism from the lumber industry and the community in general.

Chapter 10

The Open-Shop Offensive

A few days after the 1907 strike ended, lumber magnate Harry Jackson boasted that "the men have unconditionally surrendered and from now on it will be the open shop in Humboldt County."[1] In September 1907, *Labor News* conceded that the longshoremen and lumber workers had been "dealt severe blows . . . by the millowners."[2] Both the lumber employers and the labor movement had no doubt about the broader ramifications of the strike. The lumber companies lost no time in trying to capitalize on their victory. Even as the 1907 logging season drew to a close, they continued to flood the county's labor market.[3] *Labor News* charged that this was part of a deliberate policy to eliminate the last vestiges of lumber trade unionism and reflected bitterly that "some years ago the woodsmen and millmen of this county were treated with some degree of consideration. Now they are treated like so many machines and the whole question of labor is removed from the standpoint of humane consideration, and is reduced to getting the most possible out of the men for the smallest amount of money possible." The article alleged that "slave driver Hammond's methods" would reduce lumber workers to "a state closely bordering on medieval servitude."[4]

This salvo represented the opening shot in a protracted battle by the Humboldt County labor movement to expose the virulently antilabor policies of Hammond and the HLMA and attempt to persuade people of the deleterious effects that the open-shop drive would have on the community. The county labor movement continued to exhort people to join unions, but it believed that the movement's ability to survive a concerted open-shop offensive could succeed only by winning the community's support.

The Lumbermen's Counteroffensive

Hammond and his associates were determined to capitalize on the defeat of the strike. The deepening of the recession and a long-term decline in the fortunes of the lumber industry stiffened the resolve. In 1907, the dollar value of Humboldt County redwood lumber reached a peak of $7,702,205.[5] Between 1908 and 1914, the annual dollar value was consistently less, falling by 21 percent between 1907 and 1908 alone.[6] At the start of the 1908 logging season, most lumber companies cut wages 10 to 15 percent.[7] *Labor News* claimed that lumber employers were able to make the cuts because of the sorry state of the IBWSW and that the lumbermen noted the failure of workers to attend meetings "with unconcealed glee."[8] But even the well-organized shingle weavers received a 21 percent wage cut. The Humboldt shingle weavers struck for almost three months in a desperate but futile effort to preserve wage rates.[9] Adding insult to injury, the Big Three decided in 1908 that they would pay their men every 90 days rather than every month, although credit was to be granted liberally at company stores between paydays.[10] William Carson, however, continued to pay his workers in cash every month, and no pressure was put on workers to patronize the company store.[11]

After 1907, lumber companies refused to give workers a holiday on Labor Day,[12] and on at least one occasion, went so far as to sponsor a rival Labor Day celebration.[13] But the attempt by lumber employers to undermine the Union Labor Hospital constituted the most flagrant and bitterly resented attack on the labor movement. In 1908, several large companies, including the Hammond and Pacific Lumber companies, announced they would establish their own hospital facilities and insurance plans.[14] Carson refused to have any part in this scheme.[15] The decision came shortly after the labor movement had decided to expand and upgrade the Union Labor Hospital. The outraged Humboldt County labor movement obtained an injunction forbidding the lumber companies from proceeding with their hospital plans, but in 1910 this was overturned by the California Supreme Court.[16]

Of more long-term consequence to the labor movement was the decision of lumber companies to accelerate the development of their company towns. The initial establishment and growth of company towns, it should be reiterated, resulted primarily from the need to bring workers closer to the point of production, which, because of the receding forest, was moving farther and farther from towns such as Eureka and Arcata. In the context of increasingly bitter labor conflict, especially in the wake of the 1907 strike, lumber companies saw that a company town setting would enhance their ability to control their workforce. Many Pacific Lumber Company employees lived in company-owned housing from the outset. In the very early twentieth century, Hammond had allowed his workers at Samoa to own their homes, but soon he reversed this decision. Hammond expanded company housing at Samoa so that the proportion of his workforce living in Eureka declined steadily. By 1909, well over half his employees resided in Samoa.[17] The population of Blue Lake declined from 507 to 441 between 1910 and 1920. The *Arcata Union* attributed the decline to the fact that many men working for the Northern Redwood Lumber Company were obliged to move into company housing at Korbel.[18] Fortuna's population declined in the same period, partly because of the growth of Scotia and the company towns of Newburg and Metropolitan.

The Big Three also expanded their mercantile facilities at Scotia, Samoa, and Korbel and began putting pressure on their employees to patronize these facilities exclusively.[19] Married men, and any others who preferred to do their own cooking, had to eat at the company cookhouse.[20] Many foreign workers, especially the Italians, resisted this. In 1913, 100 Italian workers at Scotia went on strike, demanding the right to eat in their own homes.[21] The quality of the fare at many lumber camps also deteriorated. John Pancner, a leading IWW organizer who was sent to Humboldt County in 1910, supplied graphic reports to the *Industrial Worker* of the poor food and harsh and unsanitary living conditions at many lumber camps in the county.[22]

Labor News also provided periodic reports on deteriorating working conditions in the woods and mills. In 1910, the Pacific Lumber Company extended its working day by half an hour. The company magnanimously agreed to allow employees to stop work an hour earlier on Saturdays, but in order to ensure a full working day it began work an hour earlier, which meant waking the workers at 4:45 A.M.[23] *Labor News* asserted that while the millman worked a ten-hour day, "the introduction of pacemaking and the speeding of machinery" reduced him to a "physical wreck" twice as fast as had been the case ten or twenty years earlier under a more benign regime. Moreover, it alleged, the risk of injury was much greater because of the new technology and the extensive use of inexperienced men.[24]

Most lumber companies became systematically more repressive after the 1907 strike. Employees were asked not only whether they had ever belonged to a union but also to sign a yellow-dog contract.[25] Blacklisting was employed more thoroughly than ever to weed out union sympathizers. A few months after the 1907 strike, Ernest Pape reported to the *American Federationist* that the most prominent members of

the IBWSW had been blacklisted.[26] Organizers Pancner, "Rugger," and
W. B. Lane of the IWW made numerous references to the blacklist
in their reports to the *Industrial Worker* and related several incidents
where union men or sympathizers were instantly dismissed.[27] The
IWW organizers also charged that the Hammond Lumber Company
made extensive use of company spies.[28] A Pacific Lumber Company
employee who was rash enough to distribute circulars publicizing a
meeting of the Socialist party was fired immediately.[29] A letter from
a woodsman employed by the Pacific Lumber Company eloquently
expressed the sense of powerlessness felt by many people:

There is no way to avoid the tentacles of the corporation as every foot of ground
. . . is owned by the company. All over this vast baronial estate the "pluck-
me" stores flourish like the proverbial green bay tree, and instances of families
whose head has worked for twenty years or more that are in perpetual debt
to these stores are numerous. The man or family working for this or similar
corporations is always in danger of becoming peoned through inability to get
out of debt.[30]

Fighting the Open Shop

Labor News devoted an enormous amount of space to exposing the
policy of many of the county's lumber companies in an attempt to
win the sympathy and support of the community. Front-page articles
repeated a host of charges with almost monotonous regularity. *Labor
News* appealed both to the community's sense of justice and to its
economic self-interest. The attack on the Union Labor Hospital was
highlighted as a prime example of lumber company ruthlessness. *Labor
News* insisted that real wages in the lumber industry had declined since
1907, thus diminishing the community's overall purchasing power and
hurting local business.[31] The paper portrayed the lumber companies
as greedy, impersonal corporations with few roots and little sense of
obligation to the community. The old days were recalled nostalgically:

Most of the men . . . worked in the mills and woods [and] made Humboldt
their home. The man who owned the lumbering plant also superintended it
and was generally intimately acquainted with his employees. He realized he
depended upon them for his success and treated them well. In most instances
the manufacturer of lumber was not so far removed from the time when he
himself was a working man. . . . He [the lumber worker] was recognized by his
employer as a human being with opportunities before him and entitled to the
free exercise of rights that since have been greatly abridged.[32]

Labor News warned that the county was in danger of falling under the total social and economic hegemony of the lumber companies, claiming that by 1910 the Big Three accounted for three-quarters of the county's lumber operations. In 1908, *Labor News* asked melodramatically, "Shall Eureka Be a Company Town?" The article asserted that if present trends continued, Eureka would become another Scotia or Samoa. The labor organ confessed ignorance of the precise extent of company ownership or involvement in nonlumbering businesses in Eureka, but cautioned that there was abundant evidence that the lumber companies' direct interest was significant and growing. The article also dwelt on the fact that many lumber companies were transforming their company towns into self-contained communities, thus drawing business away from Eureka and some of the county's other towns.[33]

Labor News insisted that there was no rationale for maintaining the 50 woods camps, or "hell holes," that existed in Humboldt County. The camps could be abolished overnight if the lumber companies ran regular train services to the nearest towns. Under the wood-camp system, married woodsmen could see their families only on Sundays, while single men had little opportunity to develop stable family relationships and thus had no alternative but to resort to the Saturday night debauches at the saloons and brothels of the nearest town.[34]

One of the favorite arguments used by *Labor News* was that "the independent and family citizens" of Humboldt were being replaced by a "floating" population of single men. Good family men had been driven out of the county by low wages and the open-shop policy of Hammond and his allies.[35] The new floating labor force not only had less money to spend but was also less likely to spend its limited savings in the community. The men spent their money in the company towns and took their savings with them when they left the county at the end of the logging season. *Labor News* produced some statistics to support its contention, noting that Eureka's rate of population growth had slowed dramatically between 1904 and 1908.[36] Using school census figures, *Labor News* estimated that the population of Eureka had declined by 800 people between May 1907 and May 1908.[37] In 1909, *Labor News* drew attention to the fact that in the two years following the strike, the school population of Eureka had declined for the first time since the beginning of the century. All told, the number of schoolchildren in Eureka diminished by 275 between 1907 and 1909.[38] The 1910 census showed that the population of Eureka declined from 12,147 persons in 1908, when the city took its own census, to 11,845.

Andrew Hammond visited Humboldt County in late May 1909, his first visit in four years.[39] A vigorous exchange of views took place in the pages of the *Humboldt Times* between him and Joseph Bredsteen. Hammond initiated the exchange. Stung by criticisms of his land-acquisition practices in the *Humboldt Times*, Hammond attempted to divert attention from the issue by lashing out at the Humboldt County labor movement, claiming that the issue of trade unionism dwarfed all others in importance. He argued that Eureka was on the verge of being run by corrupt and ruthless union bosses of the type that had dominated San Francisco before their activities were exposed.

Hammond denied he was opposed to organized labor on principle, but at the same time he argued that only in an open-shop environment could the community's economy flourish. He pointed to the rapid growth of Los Angeles as an example of a place that thrived in an open-shop climate. He insisted that Humboldt labor demanded wages and conditions that made it hard for the county's industries to compete in national markets.[40] Bredsteen rehashed many of the arguments he had used since the 1907 strike, and critically reviewed Hammond's labor policies since he commenced operations in Humboldt County. Bredsteen insisted that "a strong organized labor movement means better wages, shorter hours in all the saw mills of the county, steadier employment, more homes, more families, more business," and he asked, "Would an eight hour day in Samoa injure anybody in Eureka?"[41]

The debate served only to intensify Hammond's determination to crush the Humboldt County labor movement. Not satisfied with having played the leading role in crushing the once powerful Longshoremen's Union and the IBWSW, he broadened the scope of his attack on labor. Only a month after the debate, Hammond began using his influence in the banking community to persuade Eureka businessmen to cooperate with the open-shop drive.[42] Securing the cooperation of the banking community was probably not difficult. Hammond controlled the First National Bank of Eureka, and at least one prominent lumber employer served as an officer or director at each of the four other banks in Eureka.[43] It is unclear precisely what pressure was put on merchants in Eureka to join the open-shop crusade, but the story was treated seriously by the *Humboldt Times*, and the labor movement appealed to the merchants not to collaborate with Hammond.[44]

In August 1909, Hammond pressured local businesses not to hire union carpenters.[45] Emboldened by Hammond's intransigence, the Eureka foundry employers forced the Machinists' Union to accept a nine-hour day. The *Eureka Herald* described this concession as a "triumph for Eureka" and a blow "to an arrogant policy by the local union labor leaders."[46] Two months later, the Hammond Lumber Company forced caulkers and carpenters to accept a ten-hour day,[47] and in the spring of 1910 all shipyard workers employed by Hammond agreed to work a nine-hour day.[48] At the conference of the California Building Trades Council (BTC) in 1910, the delegate from the Humboldt BTC succinctly described the problem facing the county's labor movement:

Our most persistent, unrelenting and malicious enemy is one Hammond, the Monster of Samoa—head, shoulders, fore and hind feet of the movement to crush unionism. This man has enlisted bankers and tradesmen, and he has established a satellite of open shop committees all over the county. Merchants of Eureka have been pressured by the banks to succumb.[49]

At the convention of the Pacific Coast Maritime Builders' Federation held in Eureka later in 1910, President Cheffers commented that "the people of this port must like Hammond for they let him hold them and nearly everything there is here in his arms. . . . I hardly understand how he got such a hold."[50]

Cheffers's assessment was somewhat harsh and did scant justice to the efforts of the Humboldt County labor movement to fight Hammond. Indeed, a year earlier, in July 1909, the Eureka Trades Council had established a special open-shop committee, composed of one representative from each member union of the council.[51] Within weeks, thousands of handbills were printed stressing the adverse effects of the open shop on the community's economy and threatening to boycott any merchant who cooperated with Hammond.[52] The theme of the 1909 Labor Day celebration was the open shop, and every speaker addressed the question.[53] Hammond declined an invitation to debate Bredsteen on the occasion. In December 1909, a campaign was launched to publicize the importance of the union label as a means of combating the open-shop drive.[54]

It is difficult to gauge precisely the extent to which the labor movement won community support. It is significant, however, that the historically antilabor, pro-Republican *Humboldt Times* not only gave coverage to the open-shop debate but, for a time, echoed many of the arguments used by *Labor News*. In January 1911, the *Humboldt Times*, disappointed at the county's sluggish growth, attacked Hammond's open-shop policies with particular vehemence in a series of articles. The *Times* harkened back to an age when employees of the lumber companies provided a steady demand for Eureka's products: "These men, in those days, were well paid. A large proportion of them were family men, whose families resided in Eureka, patronized the local grocers and retail goods merchants in all other lines." The *Times* conjured up images of frugal lumber workers queuing at banks to deposit their savings on Saturdays, in the days when wages gave the lumber worker "a fair and just return for their labor." Then, sighed the *Times*, "came the change of policy on the part of the big three companies," and wage levels plummeted and local trade suffered terribly.[55] The *Times* dismissed a rebuttal letter from George Fenwick, manager of the Hammond Lumber Company, claiming that real wages had not declined and that many Hammond employees still shopped in Eureka. The *Times* insisted that Eureka had suffered a heavy loss of business, and added: "The laboring men of Eureka . . . can tell you of scores, doubtless hundreds, of their former friends and acquaintances—good family men, or single men of the best type—who have left Humboldt because of the unsatisfactory wages and the conditions imposed upon them." Rows of empty houses bore "mute but impressive testimony to the truth of these statements."[56] In a subsequent article, the *Times* starkly contrasted the policies of the Big Three with those of William Carson:

William Carson has never found it necessary to build, equip, and operate a company town. Eureka has been his town. . . . Many of the woodsmen and millmen employed by William Carson today have been with him from one to three decades—some perhaps longer. A large number of these have their permanent homes in Eureka. Many have raised their families here, acquired property and are among the prosperous men of the town. Mr. Carson hasn't been bothered by strikes and labor difficulties. . . . He hasn't sought to reduce the laboring men upon whom the merchants depend to serfdom and impecunious misery.[57]

Notwithstanding the polemics of the *Humboldt Times*, the labor movement received little overt support from the Eureka business community. In his report to the annual convention of the California State Federation of Labor in 1912, Joshua Dale, who had visited Humboldt County the previous year, stated that Hammond had succeeded in coercing many businessmen into cooperating with the open-shop drive.[58] Precise data on the fate of all unions and general membership levels are not available. Undoubtedly, even outside the lumber industry, the labor movement encountered setbacks in the decade after the 1907 strike. Overall union membership almost certainly declined, and union shop and eight-hour agreements were sometimes breached. The hod carriers, clerks, longshoremen, and a host of smaller unions representing unskilled workers struggled to survive.

Nevertheless, the Humboldt County labor movement remained a defiant force of considerable influence in the community in spite of the open-shop drive. Even Joshua Dale, in his pessimistic appraisal of the state of the county's labor movement, complimented the building trades for putting up a "heroic fight." The building trades managed to retain the gains achieved in the early years of the twentieth century. The minutes of the Eureka Trades Council reveal that the labor movement continued to make effective use of the boycott. Many unions also continued to hold social gatherings, and Labor Day celebrations were usually well attended. Unquestionably, though, the position of the Humboldt labor movement after the 1907 strike was essentially defensive.

The Socialist Party and the Unions

In the political arena, the Humboldt County labor movement ceased to participate as directly and cohesively as it had in 1906 under the auspices of the Union Labor party. No attempt was made to reconstitute the ULP. In part this reflected the beleagured position of the labor movement, and in part it resulted from revelations of corruption in the San Francisco Union Labor party, which had statewide repercussions. Certainly by the 1910s, the growing responsiveness at both state and national levels of most of the major political parties to issues affecting unions and working people negated the prospects for a union labor party. At the national level, Republicans, Democrats, and Progressives, confronted with a more class-conscious and better-organized labor movement than before, and the increasingly impressive performance of the Socialist party, vied for the working-class vote. In California, where the labor movement was strong in many areas, the Progressive party one of the most powerful in the nation, and the Socialists had substantial support, the competition for the working-class vote was especially keen. Ultimately, the gains attained by labor at both the state and national levels were limited, but the major political parties had to address labor's grievances more seriously than they had during the Gilded Age.[59]

In Humboldt County, labor did not withdraw from politics. The Eureka Trades Council took a strong stand on local and state issues, especially measures to provide for the initiative and recall. The council asked state legislators to explain their records on labor issues, and *Labor News* gave extensive coverage to the growing role of labor in English and Australian politics. At the 1908 Labor Day picnic, a four-cornered political debate took place between spokesmen for the Republicans, Democrats, Socialists, and Union Labor party, with Bredsteen speaking for the latter and George Keeling on behalf of the Socialists.[60] But the ULP did not offer a slate at the 1908 elections; instead, *Labor News* tacitly endorsed the Socialist ticket.[61]

The embattled state of the local labor movement and the appeals of the major parties siphoned off some of the labor vote and undermined the cohesive voting bloc that was taking shape in 1906, but the long-standing tradition of dissent in Humboldt County politics did not expire. There was significant and growing support for the Socialist party. Aided by the endorsement of *Labor News*, the Socialists greatly improved their electoral performance in 1908. Between 1904 and 1908, Eugene Debs increased his share of the presidential vote from 9.2 percent to 13.3 percent. After the election, the relationship between Humboldt labor and the Socialists became increasingly close. *Labor News* unequivocally endorsed the Socialist party for the next decade. It is impossible to calculate exactly what percentage of union men voted Socialist. But certain facts are not in question. First, the Socialist party's program was almost identical to the one offered by the ULP in 1906. Keeling and Bredsteen could have swapped speeches on Labor Day, 1908, and nobody would have noticed the difference. Second, many of the leading unionists in Humboldt County were registered Socialists, and at least half of the Socialist party ticket was usually composed of union leaders. Third, several unions, including the Carpenters and the Cooks and Waiters, specifically endorsed the Socialists.[62] Finally, *Labor News* was the official paper of the Eureka Trades Council, and the council was prohibited by its constitution from making partisan political endorsements. Yet it did not question or repudiate *Labor News* for its unabashed support of the Socialists.

The index to the Humboldt County Register of Voters for 1914 indicates that the Socialist party constituency was predominantly working-class. The voting register listed people's party affiliations after the passage of the California primary law in 1909. Table 2 shows the number of registered Socialists for each occupational group that had five or more registered Socialists.[63] A high proportion of the registered Socialist voters were laborers, woodsmen, millmen, and carpenters. Seventy-four farmers also registered Socialist. Unfortunately, it is impossible to know whether they owned farms or were farm laborers, although the Humboldt Socialist party made a deliberate effort to appeal to small farmers and farm laborers.[64] All told, 387 housewives or housekeepers registered Socialist; most of them wives of working-class Socialist men. It is important to point out that the register represents only about half the people who actually voted Socialist. This is apparent if one takes the total Socialist vote for Debs in 1912 or the total vote for the victorious Socialist mayoral candidate for Eureka in 1915. This indicates that, even though voters had the option of declining to state party affiliation, a number of Socialist voters were fearful of registering

Table 2

Registered Socialist Party Voters, Humboldt County, 1914, for
Each Occupation with Five or More Registered Socialists

Occupation	No.	Occupation	No.
Laborers	130	Cooks and chefs	10
Woodsmen	87	Dairymen	8
Farmers	74	Clerks	7
Carpenters	43	Shoemakers	6
Mill workers	37	Barbers	6
Ranchers	19	Painters	6
Engineers	15	Longshoremen	6
Blacksmiths	13	Teachers	5
Miners	11	Gardeners	5

SOURCE: Index to the *Affidavits of Registration of Humboldt County, 1914, To and Including October 3, 1914.*

their affiliation. Indeed, in 1910, when voters were asked to declare party affiliation for the first time, the Humboldt County Clerk, George Cousins, found many voters unwilling to do so.[65]

The IWW resented the strong foothold that the Socialist party had established among the Humboldt working class. John Pancner, the IWW organizer in Humboldt County in 1910, complained bitterly: "In almost every camp I find a group of political socialists. All they seem to know is vote, vote, and read the "Appeal." They disgrace the fair name of socialism. . . . The working man whose brain is not clogged up with political dope can easily understand industrial unionism."[66] Another IWW organizer, M. B. Butler, complained that one of the Wobblies' biggest handicaps in Eureka were the "Berger worshippers."[67] In 1910, Pancner, who on several occasions was granted a forum by the local Socialist party, greeted the first electoral successes of Humboldt County Socialists with sarcastic derision: "Here I am living in a new Socialist republic," he wrote to the *Industrial Worker*. He added that he believed "the killing of a Ferrer does more for the Social Revolution than the election of a thousand socialists." Pancner concluded by arguing that "the doctrine of direct action is simple; it is easy for the slave to understand, while Political Socialism winds through the swamps of confusion."[68]

Pancner's disparaging judgments reeked of the sectarianism the IWW had displayed during the 1907 strike and can hardly have endeared many working-class Socialists in Humboldt County to the Wobblies' cause. Ironically, the refusal of the majority of the Humboldt County Socialist party to support the expulsion of IWW leader Bill Haywood from the party's National Executive Committee in 1913 and the radical political stance of local party leaders caused a split in the Humboldt Socialist party. The fact that the allegedly "pro-syndicalist" wing of the party emerged as its dominant and official branch did not allay the hostility of the Wobblies. At a Socialist-organized May Day celebration in 1914, an IWW organizer proceeded to incense most of the assembled company with an intemperate attack on the local AFL, the Socialists, and the American flag—"a rag unworthy of respect."[69]

In 1909, the Socialists recorded their first triumph when George McDaniel was elected to the Eureka City Council. The following year saw John Moore, president of the Eureka Trades Council, elected police judge on the Socialist ticket. In 1911, the Socialist party and the labor movement almost singlehandedly opposed a new charter for Eureka providing for a city commission and manager form of government.[70] Under the proposed charter, the only elected city officials would be five commission members, who would appoint a city manager and all other executive officials. The power to recall local officials would have been severely circumscribed, and the ability of the city to acquire ownership of utilities greatly hindered. The city press praised the new charter as an excellent means of taking the politics out of local elections, but the charter was rejected overwhelmingly by 1,048 to 124 votes. The *Humboldt Times* acknowledged the decisive role of the Socialists in defeating the charter and noted that in the Socialists' stronghold in the Fifth Ward, only 1 of 19 people voted in favor of the new charter.[71]

The fortunes of the Socialist party were clearly rising. When Bredsteen ran for mayor of Eureka on the Socialist ticket in 1909, he garnered a meager 9 percent of the vote in a three-way fight.[72] In 1911, in a two-way contest, he got 40 percent of the vote.[73] The following year, the Socialists succeeded in getting all their amendments to the Eureka charter passed at a referendum election, while all the amendments offered by the majority on the City Council went down to defeat. The Socialists defeated proposals that would have provided for the election of officials every four years, instead of every two; the abolition of the ward system in favor of city elections at large; and a measure that would have allowed the mayor to fill vacancies for elective office by appointment rather than special election. The Socialists passed amendments that greatly facilitated Eureka's ability to municipalize utilities, that established a superintendent of public works with clearly specified duties, and that provided for open-market bidding on public contracts.[74]

In the early 1910s, the Humboldt County labor movement may have been on the defensive in the industrial arena, but in the political sphere a radical culture flourished. The Socialist party, *Labor News*, and many leading union members played the major roles in sustaining this culture, which amounted to more than a good turnout for the Socialists on election day. The Socialists created what can best be described as a counter sociopolitical culture. Beginning in 1912, the Socialists held their own Fourth of July celebrations. In 1912, 2,000 people attended an International Labor Day picnic.[75] Leading trade unionists, including Keeling, spoke on the compatibility of trade unionism and Socialist political action.

The Socialists sponsored numerous special events, such as a "Women's Day" celebration at Union Labor Hall in 1911. There were musical selections, a play, poetry recitations, and a rousing speech in favor of women's suffrage.[76] A special meeting at Union Labor Hall protested the arrest of the editor of the *Appeal to Reason*.[77] On weekends, a "red auto," carrying leading Socialist and labor officials, drove through the county distributing literature and copies of speeches.[78] Debs and Haywood both spoke in Humboldt County, as did many leading California Socialists and trade unionists, including Stitt Wilson, the Socialist mayor of Berkeley, and Archie Mooney, secretary of the Los Angeles Building Trades Council. Mooney's address, before one of the largest labor audiences in Humboldt County history, urged labor to support the Socialist party.[79]

A Union Political Club formed in April 1912 with delegates representing 700 union members. Organizing the club circumvented a rule that prohibited the discussion of politics at union meetings, for the club was not to be a branch of any political party. Nevertheless, the club's first chairman, W. H. Hemsted, a leading figure in the Carpenters' Union, was a well-known Socialist.[80]

The Socialist councilman George McDaniel fought valiantly for the interests of labor. At a Eureka City Council meeting, he complained bitterly when the city contracted a painting job to nonunion labor. With much applause from the floor, he warned the council that the labor party had elected him and that if such practices continued, there would be "something doing."[81] He also objected to the omission of an eight-hour clause from a contract the City Council had given to a quarry mining firm.[82] When 30 quarry workers went on strike for the eight-hour day, the Socialist party vowed to use "all honorable means to assist the strikers."[83]

The close affinity between the Humboldt Socialist party and the labor movement could be seen in the 1912 platform of the Socialist party. Although it was a presidential election year, the platform contained many planks that were of direct interest to Humboldt labor. The Socialist party pledged to make a special effort to fight for a shorter working day in the California legislature, with particular emphasis on obtaining an eight-hour day for lumber workers. The platform also pledged to fight for legislation providing for better conditions in the lumber camps and a law prohibiting the use of the blacklist. Significantly, the platform called for California to establish a network of banks and loan offices. It denounced "the present wage scale paid to the working classes of Humboldt County as inadequate and demoralizing," and pledged "both politically and economically to aid the workers of Humboldt County to better their condition by every honorable means at our command."[84]

At the 1912 elections, the Humboldt Socialist party had to contend with strong competition from the Progressive party. *Labor News* denounced the record of both Theodore Roosevelt and Hiram Johnson, the Progressive governor of California,[85] but it seems likely that the Progressives cut into the Socialist vote. Nevertheless, the Socialist performance in Humboldt County was creditable. Debs obtained 21 percent of the vote, more than three times the percentage he achieved nationally. Bredsteen garnered 18 percent of the vote in his battle for a seat in Congress, and George Keeling won an impressive 34 percent in the state assembly contest.[86]

The Eureka Socialists scored their greatest triumph when a millman, Elijah Falk, was elected mayor of Eureka in 1915. Falk had worked in the Humboldt County lumber industry since 1878. His technical skill as a millwright soon won him great respect, and he assisted with the design of several county mills. In 1906, he abandoned the Republican party and became a devout supporter of the Socialists.[87] Falk obtained 41 percent of the vote in a four-way race, edging out his main rival by seven votes. In addition, two Socialists won City Council seats, including Bredsteen. Socialist candidates for street superintendent and school supervisor also were successful. The latter, Newell Palmer, a machinist, was elected president of the Eureka Trades Council a few weeks later.[88]

The election results demonstrated that the Socialist party had a very strong constituency in Eureka in the early 1910s. It should be noted, however, that in 1915 the Socialists achieved their victory by diluting their program to the point where it was almost indistinguishable from those of the Progressive and the Democratic parties. All references to the broader emancipatory role of the Socialist party were dropped from the 1915 platform. In previous elections, Eureka Socialists had pledged municipalization of all public utilities, a public works program for the unemployed, and a municipal free employment agency. The Socialists' 1915 platform modestly called for the public owner-ship of the local rock quarry, improved street-lighting and firefighting equipment, and more thorough inspection of slaughterhouses. Falk reiterated these demands in his inauguration address and stressed the need for greater efficiency in the administration of local government.[89]

The Eureka Socialists accomplished relatively little. They got bogged down in acrimonious and tedious debates with other City Coun-cil members about whether the city should acquire its own rock quarry, what kind of materials should be used to pave the streets, and minu-tiae relating to the organization and administration of local govern-ment. Doubtless, many Socialist party supporters were not indifferent to such matters, but the Socialists failed to press for measures that might have strengthened their ties with the trade union movement and their working-class following. In April 1915, two months before the Socialists' electoral success, union leader George Keeling implored the City Council to adopt a public works program to alleviate the dis-tress caused by high levels of local unemployment.[90] A few days later, 300 workers descended on City Hall demanding such a program.[91] Be-tween 1915 and 1917, the Socialists failed to make a single proposal for public works, in spite of continuing high levels of unemployment. In large part, this reticence reflected the fact that the Socialists were in a minority on the City Council and that, in spite of their moderation, they were constantly on the defensive. Indeed, a recall drive was launched against them in February 1916 alleging that they were re-sponsible for the poor maintenance of Eureka's streets and general incompetence in local government administration. The recall drive, however, petered out after a few weeks.

Notwithstanding these constraints, the Socialists' failure to pro-pose measures that might have appealed more directly to their working-class and union constituency revealed a lack of political courage and imagination. The Socialists neglected to exploit the considerable po-litical influence they wielded in Eureka. In a special referendum elec-tion in November 1916, all eight measures proposed by the Socialists passed, including one providing for Eureka's acquisition of the local rock quarry, while all three measures initiated by their opponents were defeated, including a proposal to have City Councilmen elected at large.[92]

In the last analysis, however, the saga of the Eureka Socialists illustrated the limits of municipal Socialism. Even if the Socialists had been able to provide public works to the unemployed at union wage levels and to municipalize all public utilities, it would have made relatively little difference to the balance of power between labor and capital in the community. Quite simply, the scope and functions of local government were such that there was little that the Socialists and the labor movement could do to translate their political power into the economic power necessary to thwart Hammond's open-shop drive. The ascendancy of Hammond and his allies showed the degree to which employers, notwithstanding the presence of a defiant labor movement, could dominate an essentially single-industry community. The Eureka Socialists' decisive defeat in the 1917 elections was primarily the result of their opposition to American involvement in World War I, but it also reflected their inability to translate political power into economic power at the local level.

Chapter 11

The Makings of Stability

Lumber Unionism in Disarray

After the 1907 strike, both the AFL and the IWW did their utmost to regenerate trade unionism in the Humboldt County lumber industry. As Hammond's open-shop offensive gathered momentum, the Eureka Trades Council realized more clearly than ever before the link between the health of the county's labor movement as a whole and the strength of trade unionism in the woods and mills. The IWW's organizational activities in Humboldt County lapsed for almost three years, but in 1910 they renewed their efforts to organize lumber workers in Humboldt County and other lumber centers in the West.

In spite of some limited gains during the First World War, the AFL and IWW attempts to revive trade unionism in Humboldt County during the 1910s and 1920s ended in failure. At no time could either organization claim more than a few hundred members, and for most of the period they had only a token following. The IWW and AFL had little more success in organizing lumber workers elsewhere in California, or in Oregon and Washington. Before 1917, notwithstanding repeated efforts, the Wobblies attracted no more than 1,000 members at any one time in a Pacific Northwest lumber industry that employed at least 300,000 workers.

Of course, the part played by repression and an unpropitious economic climate in the failure of the unions cannot be overemphasized. But these factors alone do not account for the inability of the IWW and AFL to attract a larger and more enduring following in the lumber industry. It suggests that lumber employers did not rely exclusively on repression to stifle trade unionism in Humboldt County during the 1910s and 1920s. Perhaps as important in inhibiting the growth of unionism was a series of newly conceived policies by the lumber companies designed to divide workers and foster a spirit of corporate loyalty. After almost a decade of reliance on repression, and an outright repudiation of the paternalistic policies of the pioneer lumbermen, several factors prompted the "outside" capitalists to reconsider this stratagem. The lumber companies began to cultivate an image of beneficence, even though it entailed making concessions and improvements. Although the motivations of the pioneer lumbermen and the "outside" capitalists were similar, the "new" paternalism was in many respects different from the old. To begin with, companies had to manage a much larger labor force, and the old bonds at the workplace and in the community could not be re-created, especially among workers, foremen, and employers new to the county. In addition, novel theories of scientific management and welfare capitalism greatly influenced the lumber employers.

With almost monotonous regularity, *Labor News* exhorted the lumber workers to reorganize. Unable to spark an indigenous revival, the Humboldt County labor movement appealed to the California State Federation of Labor for assistance at its annual convention in 1912.[1] In 1913, the federation sent Joshua Dale to help rebuild the Humboldt lumber union movement. Dale found the situation grim: "There is not a class of workmen in the entire country, outside the agricultural and migratory workers, that is more in need of organization than men in the lumber camps." He was struck by the unsanitary living conditions and the dangerous working conditions: "Empty pant legs and coat sleeves, fingerless hands and sightless eyes, are a common sight in the woods."[2] Dale succeeded in founding a Eureka branch of the newly chartered International Union of Shingle Weavers, Sawmill Workers and Woodsmen.[3] But he did not manage to establish branches anywhere else in the county, and the Eureka branch, which had started with only 100 members, made little headway over the next few years.[4] At the start of the 1915 logging season, the lumber companies increased the price of a worker's board from 50 to 60 cents a day, and cut wages.[5] *Labor News* reproached the lumber workers for their submissiveness, and later expressed total exasperation with them: "It would be difficult to find any place in the whole country where the company hirelings submit as meekly as they do in Humboldt."[6]

In 1909, the IWW launched a drive to organize the lumber workers of the Pacific Northwest. For several years, the *Industrial Worker* had carried stories about the plight of lumber workers and appeals to organize. The Wobblies attracted small pockets of support among lumber workers, mainly in the vicinity of Seattle, Portland, and Vancouver, Canada. During the summer of 1910, the IWW resumed organizational activities in Humboldt County.[7] For almost three years, the veteran IWW organizer John Pancner lived in Eureka and attempted to rally the lumber workers of Humboldt and neighboring counties. On his arrival, he had reported "a strong undercurrent of discontent and class hatred" among the Humboldt loggers.[8] He furnished the *Industrial Worker* with graphic accounts of the deplorable living conditions and wages in the county's lumber industry. With the assistance of other IWW die-hards, Pancner held street meetings every Saturday and Sunday night.[9] On December 18, 1910, he established LU 431 in Eureka.[10] He appealed continually for fellow Wobblies to come to Humboldt to aid him, insisting that "this place is the 'key' to the lumber industry around here."[11] But, after eight months, the IWW local had only 175 members.[12] By the winter of 1912, Pancner's patience was wearing thin. In a testy letter to the *Industrial Worker*, he said he was tired of "the old cry . . . 'we had one strike in Humboldt and we lost.' Is this any reason why we should remain contented slaves?"[13]

In May 1913, the IWW decided it was time for a show of strength in the Pacific Northwest lumber industry. The Wobblies demanded an eight-hour day, a minimum daily wage of $3; time-and-a-half pay for overtime, and greatly improved sanitary and safety conditions.[14] In a highly melodramatic fashion, the IWW called on the lumber workers of the Pacific Northwest to strike in favor of these demands. The IWW strike call provoked a negligible response from the lumber workers of the Pacific Northwest, even according to reports in the *Industrial Worker*.[15] In Humboldt County, few, if any, lumber workers took notice of the strike call. The county press, *Labor News*, and the *Industrial Worker* reported no stoppages or walkouts. A few months later, *Labor News* asserted that the strike call "failed to get even a ripple started in Humboldt County."[16]

New Methods in an Old Fight

The AFL and IWW faced not only the time-honored methods used by lumber employers against unions since the 1880s but also a range of new and sophisticated ones designed especially to counter the serious threat posed by the union movement in the early twentieth century. To begin with, employers took a more systematic interest than before in the composition of the workforce and the backgrounds of individual workers.

Lumber employers in Humboldt County and northern California exploited the growing heterogeneity of their labor force. For most of the

Gilded Age, the lumber workforce in Humboldt County was made up of Americans and Canadians for the most part and, to a lesser extent, immigrants from the British Isles. In all likelihood, lumber employers had some national prejudices, but experience in the lumber industries of the Maritime Provinces, Maine, and the Great Lakes states, plus family ties to the company and community, were almost certainly more important criteria for employment. There is no evidence that lumber employers systematically considered nationality in choosing workers. By the late 1880s, Scandinavian immigrants were playing an increasingly important role in the county's lumber industry, but the real fragmentation of the lumber workforce began in the early twentieth century and coincided with the wave of "new" immigrants, from southern and eastern Europe.

As early as 1903-4, the county press commented on the influx of new immigrants, especially Italians.[17] Many of the immigrants went to work in the woods and mills, especially in southern Humboldt County. In the Hydesville census precinct, most lumber workers were employed by the Pacific Lumber Company. Information from this precinct, obtained from the 1910 Manuscript Census, indicates how diverse the Pacific Lumber Company workforce was then. Only one-third of the lumber workers were native-born. Italians made up 16 percent of all lumber workers living in the precinct and 25 percent of the foreign-born. Lumber workers from Finland, Sweden, and Norway combined made up the second-largest segment, with Austrians ranking third. A majority (58 percent) of lumber workers from the three best-represented foreign national groups—the Italians, Finns, and Austrians—had emigrated to the United States in the five years preceding the 1910 census, and 92 percent had arrived in the United States after 1900. A surprisingly high proportion of Swedes and Norwegians were also recent arrivals: 38 percent of them emigrating to America after 1905 and 81 percent after 1900. Less surprising was that the vast majority of these immigrants were aliens. Only 14 percent of Italians, Finns, and Austrians were naturalized or had filed citizenship papers.[18]

The lack of comprehensive lumber company employee records makes it hard to determine precisely how representative the Pacific Lumber Company's workforce was of other lumber companies in Humboldt County. *Labor News* made scattered references to the employment of Italians in the Eureka area by 1906. A partial list of workers employed by the Hammond Lumber Company in 1914 reveals that a considerable number had southern and eastern European names.[19] In 1911, when the *Humboldt Times* was berating Hammond for his antilabor policies, the *Times* accused him of driving "sturdy American and first class Europeans out of the woods and out of the county."[20]

The Pacific Lumber Company workforce may have been more heterogeneous than most companies in the county, but there is considerable evidence to suggest that it was broadly representative of the northern California lumber industry as a whole. For example, Italians constituted 24 percent of the labor force of the Union Lumber Company (the giant of the Mendocino County lumber industry) in 1909.[21] In 1911, IWW organizers claimed that 60 percent of the Mendocino woodsmen were Italians.[22] From accounts of the 1909 strike at the McCloud River Lumber Company in Siskiyou County (about 150 miles northeast of Humboldt County), it is evident that roughly half of the labor force was Italian.[23] In 1914, the California Bureau of Labor Statistics issued a 100-page report on the California lumber industry and found that most of the large lumber companies in the northern redwood district had "very cosmopolitan pay rolls, embracing men from all quarters of the globe." Americans predominated in the California lumber industry as a whole, with Italians ranking a close second. In the northern redwood lumber district, Russians, Finns, Portuguese, and Austrians also made up large segments of the labor force.[24]

In part, the diversification of the redwood lumber region's workforce resulted from a calculated policy of the lumber employers. In 1911, an important article by E. A. Blockinger, the general manager of the Pacific Lumber Company, published in the *Pioneer Western Lumberman* (a trade journal of the Pacific Coast lumber industry), advised: "Don't have too great a percentage of any one nationality. For your own good and theirs mix them up and obliterate clannishness and selfish social prejudices."[25] In his statement to the annual convention of the California State Federation of Labor in 1911, the Eureka Trades Council vice-president, John Ericksen, asserted that "since the woodsmen's strike here in 1907, men speaking many languages have been imported to make harmony among the workers hard to obtain."[26] He appealed to the federation to print labor literature in Italian and to hire an Italian-speaking organizer. Three years later, Joshua Dale reported that the Humboldt County lumber companies "studiously selected" men of different nationalities.[27] The California Bureau of Labor Statistics report on the California lumber industry stated that at least one employer had freely admitted to investigators that the labor force was judiciously mixed to inhibit labor organization.[28]

The heterogeneity undoubtedly compounded the difficulties of organizing lumber workers. "The problem of mixed nationalities is not nearly as difficult as it seems," declared *Labor News* in 1910,[29] but this and similar proclamations in *Labor News* and the IWW press acknowledged the extent of the problem while trying to minimize it. Their repeated calls for union literature written in Italian and for Italian-speaking organizers indicate the importance they attached to organizing Italians. Given the failure of lumber unionism to gain an established foothold in the northern California lumber industry among workers of almost all national and ethnic groups, it would be wrong to place too much weight for this failure on the values and attitudes of any one immigrant group. Nevertheless, because Italians were the largest immigrant group employed in the Humboldt and northern California lumber industry by the 1910s, and attempts to bring them into the union fold met with little success, the question deserves attention.

Although the Eureka Trades Council and the IBWSW can be criticized for making little use of Italian-speaking organizers, pamphlets printed in Italian and the Italian-language page of *Labor News* showed a serious effort to persuade Italians to join the union movement. As stated earlier, Italians strongly supported the 1907 strike, but they joined labor unions in limited numbers. There were several instances of Italians engaging in wildcat strikes in the years after the 1907 strike, and 700 Italians played a leading role in the well-publicized McCloud River Lumber Company strike of 1909 in Siskiyou County.[30] But in northern California, as in many other places in the United States, episodic expressions of militance by Italians did not translate into a willingness on their part to become trade union members.[31] The indifference of most Italians to unions was the result of a number of factors. First, Italians encountered prejudice both within and outside the labor movement. The recollections of Julio Rovai, who worked in the Humboldt lumber industry for many years, confirm this. A combination of prejudice, strong familial bonds, and a general feeling of powerlessness helped nurture a very self-contained Italian community. Under the company town regime, recalls Rovai, "one was condemned, confined, and compelled to live their way of life." He observed: "The Italians only strength was the family and relatives . . . [and] making it stronger by allying it to other families, and to protect it."[32] It is not without significance that one of the most serious incidents at Scotia occurred in 1913 when 100 Italians struck, demanding the right to eat in their homes and not at the company cookhouse. The Pacific Lumber Company acceded to their demand, although another 100 workers, who were protesting the quality of the fare, were fired.[33]

In 1922, an IWW organizer at the Hammond Lumber Company

reported that "there are many Italians, but they are leery of men who do not speak their language."[34] As much, or more, than any other immigrant group, Italians saw themselves as "birds of passage" who would return to their native country after they had accumulated sufficient savings to buy land there. Over 60 percent of Italian emigrants to the United States did return to Italy, and Rovai cites examples of Humboldt Italians who did so. Finally, many Italians had little experience of unionism before coming to America. According to Rovai, a large number of Humboldt Italians came from the province of Lucca in northwest Italy where trade unionism was almost unknown.[35]

Lumber employers were by the 1910s intent on accumulating as much information as possible about the personal histories of their workers. Employees and prospective employees filled out forms with a host of questions concerning their family status, total number of dependents, health, accident history, English-language ability, previous occupation, and amount of savings.[36] A primary purpose of the questionnaire was to identify the thrifty and responsible worker, one who either had a family to support or had aspirations. Blockinger believed that "the steadiest man is the one with a small savings account which he is trying to make bigger so he can get married, build a home, or lay up against a rainy day or old age." He urged his fellow lumber employers to "encourage savings accounts either by small banks or through your pay offices."[37]

During the nineteenth and early twentieth centuries, almost all lumber workers were paid a flat hourly or daily rate of pay. In the 1910s, lumber companies began experimenting with a range of other systems of payment. Lumber trade journals and lumber employers' conference reports are full of accounts of systems that had the dual purpose of providing productivity incentives and dividing the workforce. In 1913, the Hammond Lumber Company became one of the first lumber companies in the West to introduce the bonus system. W. Peed, the company's superintendent, gave a detailed and glowing account of it to the Pacific Logging Congress in 1914. The system guaranteed workers a base wage rate. Production quotas were set for crews in different departments and a bonus paid to the crew according to how far they exceeded the quota. To enhance a spirit of competitiveness, Hammond Lumber took the additional step of posting the performance of each crew on a bulletin board. Peed exulted that, under this new system, productivity in some departments had increased by as much as 40 percent in the first year of the experiment. A further advantage, stressed by Peed, was that under the bonus system, the "poor man" could be detected and weeded out much more effectively by the men on the job than by the foreman.[38]

The printed summary of the proceedings of the 1914 Pacific Logging Congress noted the "widespread interest" aroused by the discussion of the bonus system and observed that "there is undoubtedly a rapidly growing sentiment in the various forms of industry where it is possible to devise some direct plan of participation by the workers in the returns of industry it should be undertaken."[39] In 1916, H. L. Henderson, a leading management official in the Hammond Lumber Company, gave a further progress report on the bonus system to the Pacific Logging Congress. He was as enthusiastic about its application and results as Peed had been, asserting that in logging operations, "efficiency perhaps finds its greatest device to be the bonus system."[40]

Used judiciously, the bonus system was an ingenious means of increasing productivity and fostering a spirit antithetical to the development of trade unionism. It divided workers into groups of competing entities and encouraged them to blame foremen, malingering, or incompetent fellow workers, rather than the company, for a small wage packet. Conversely, if the group worked efficiently and received a large bonus payment, the system was liable to persuade workers that their fat paycheck was the result not only of their endeavor but also of the benevolence of the company. Indeed, many lumber employers, such as D. S. Painter of the McCloud River Lumber Company, saw the bonus system as an important means of fostering a corporatist ethos among the workers.[41]

Similar to the bonus system was the contract system, by which a senior worker in a particular logging or milling function would be paid a lump sum to produce a certain quantity. The effects of this system were much like the bonus system in that it induced the contracting worker to be especially concerned with the work performance of his crew. Finally, where the bonus system was not used, or where the individualization of some tasks made it impractical, workers were paid under a basic piece-rate system.[42] Carrying the principle of incentives and accountability to their logical extremes, some companies went so far as to fine workers for wastefulness and carelessness.[43] The introduction of these incentive schemes antedated the establishment of the eight-hour day for all lumber workers in March 1918, but *Labor News* and the San Francisco *Labor Clarion* alleged that lumber employers made more extensive use of such methods after the passage of the law in order to maintain production levels with the reduced working day.[44] These new payment systems were popular with many employers in the West Coast lumber industry and persisted well into the 1920s.[45]

Toward a New Paternalism

Important as employers regarded the policies of judiciously selecting workers, mixing ethnic and national groups, and "incentive" wage payments, these were not their only new tactics. There was a fear that such tactics might not be sufficient or, in the case of wage-incentive schemes, could even backfire if not applied carefully and along with other stratagems. A growing number of employers believed in fostering a sense of corporate identity among their workers. Beginning in the 1910s, lumber employers experimented with a range of welfare plans to achieve this goal. Like the pioneer lumbermen of the nineteenth century, they saw, albeit after a decade or so of confrontation, that inducing a degree of company loyalty could help preempt trade unionism. As the secretary of the Pacific Logging Congress put it in his 1912 report: "The best cure for the IWW plague—a people without a country and without a God—is the cultivation of the homing instinct in men." [46] In addition, the doctrine of social environmentalism, which attained popular currency during the Progressive era, also influenced lumber employers. In short, many were persuaded that safe, sanitary, and reasonable working and living conditions would result in a more contented and productive labor force. [47]

One of the most important factors that inspired lumber employers to experiment with welfare capitalism derived from their own experience. Before becoming owners, managers, or foremen in one of the giant lumbering concerns of the twentieth century, many had worked in the pioneer lumber industry of the nineteenth century. As labor relations grew increasingly antagonistic, they attributed the deterioration to the impersonalization of relationships between themselves and the workers caused by the massive growth of many lumber enterprises. Peed eloquently expressed this view in a speech before the Pacific Logging Congress:

The logging business has grown from a camp handled or owned by one man, and working only a few men with a small equipment of teams, up to the large operations of the present time, wherein the organization involves a great number of men and a heavy investment in machinery, equipment and rolling stock. With the earlier small operations the manager was able to keep in a close personal touch with all the details of the work and with the men employed by him. The present conditions are such that, with the large and complex organizations, scattered over a more or less extended territory, it is not possible for the manager to maintain the close relations that heretofore existed. [48]

Another lumber employer echoed Peed's sentiments: "Ten years ago, when we had but 75–80 employees, I knew each one by name, and frequently the members of their families, but today we have a crew of 700. I am overloaded in the office and about the only ones I know are the few that are left from the original crowd."[49] Edwin Van Sycle, who worked in the Pacific Northwest lumber industry for many years, concurred. He observed that with the eclipse of the small logging concerns, "the close personal relationship was gone and, with working or living conditions no better, the logger began to grouse, then bedamn . . . under the spur of the union organizer, to rebel."[50]

While the scale of many lumber operations and the employers' lack of ties to the community precluded any replication of the bonds that nineteenth-century pioneer lumbermen had with their workers, the development of full-fledged company towns by the 1910s created a promising environment for using welfare capitalism to instill a sense of company loyalty among employees. T. H. Simpson, industrial chaplain of the logging industry of Grays Harbor, Washington, summarized the twin elements of the welfare capitalist thrust: "First, the physical, which has to do with camp sanitation, bunk house accommodation, bathhouses, light, heat, bedding and food. Second, the mental or morale of the workers . . . which builds up or destroys loyalty to the company."[51] Lumber employers realized that improved working and living conditions were necessary if they were to instill a spirit of corporate loyalty. This would help nurture contentment and increase labor productivity by reducing accident rates, illness, and labor turnover. Employers came to this conclusion partly because of the prodding of state legislatures through laws and administrative agencies. At the 1914 Pacific Logging Congress, the Washington State commissioner of health spoke on "camp sanitation." Referring to the rapid industrialization of America, he stated that "little or no attention was paid to the human element—the worker. But during the past two decades experience had shown that aside from the personal interest of the worker, the prosperity of the industry itself necessitates an ever-increasing attention to the worker's physical welfare."[52]

Some of the attempts by the lumber companies to foster loyalty bordered on the crass. With derisive comments, *Labor News* and the *Industrial Worker* reprinted a circular that the Pacific Lumber Company distributed to its workers in 1913: "Men are valuable just as in proportion they are willing to work in cooperation with other men. Harmonious cooperation is organized efficiency. . . . Bear in mind that the Company's success means your success."[53] In general, however, the methods were more subtle. Some companies made deliberate efforts to personalize relationships with the men. Blockinger gave the following advice to fellow managers:

Learn to know your men by name or as many by name as possible. Speak to each from the highest to the lowest. A group can be addressed as boys and somehow it makes them feel better. Let the men feel you are taking an interest in their work. Compliment them when they are doing anything especially well. Keep your foreman always in the position of authority but that don't [*sic*] mean that you must see everything through his eyes. Correct faults through the foreman yet let the men feel that any suggestion for the good of business can be made to you directly.[54]

The heart of the strategy for promoting company loyalty lay in the attempt to build a new moral order in lumber camps and towns. The proverbial Paul Bunyan blanket stiff, who recklessly whored, drank, and brawled his way through life, would be replaced by a man of stable and sober habits, and somewhat more lofty aspirations. In this endeavor the Pacific Lumber Company was in the vanguard. Blockinger's recommendations are again highly instructive:

A reading room with facilities for letter writing and any games, except gambling, is easily and cheaply put into any camp. Arrange subscription clubs for papers and periodicals or let the company do it for the men. If you can have a circulating library among your camps and at the mill plant, it will be much appreciated. Let the daily or weekly papers be of all nationalities as represented in your camp. Lumber trade journals are especially interesting to the men and they can and will readily follow the markets for lumber and appreciate that you have some troubles of your own.

Organize fire departments among your men. The insurance companies will give you reductions in rates for such additional protection while it offers another opportunity for your men to relax and enjoy themselves.

Shower baths at the camps or mill are easily and cheaply installed. They will be used and appreciated after a hot, dusty day's work.

Make your mill town beautiful. Spend some money for paint and fences. Encourage the planting of trees, shrubs, and flowers. Offer prizes for the best kept front yards. . . .

Get your men loyal and keep them so. Let this replace loyalty to a union. The spirit is what you want in your men. Ten good men will accomplish as much as fifteen ordinary laborers if the spirit and good will is there. Treat them right and they will treat you right.[55]

In 1909, as the Pacific Lumber Company commenced a great expansion of its plant operations, it also began encouraging a whole range of social and cultural institutions to improve the moral order of Scotia. A second schoolhouse was built in 1909, but more symbolic was the decision in 1910 to close the company saloon and establish the First National Bank of Scotia.[56] In a letter to *Collier's National Weekly* in 1913, P. A. Rosetti described the great change that had taken place in the moral tone of the community. He recalled that when the company was running the saloon "wide open," many men spent most of their leisure time there, "cursing, quarelling and fighting." After access to the saloon was drastically restricted in 1908, a social club was organized. Clubrooms were furnished with chairs, tables, a piano, a phonograph, billiard and pool tables, and a gymnasium. Singing and debating were encouraged, and there was a special evening for ladies. All these facilities were furnished for a 50-cent monthly membership fee. In addition, between 1903 and 1913, four fraternal societies were founded, two churches built, and another bank established. Rosetti reflected:

I walked into Scotia on a Sunday morning 14 years ago and I could see men under the influence of liquor in all directions. . . . I again walked into Scotia on a Sunday morning six months ago, and I could see well-dressed men with respectful countenances, pleasant and cheerful, and afterward I learnt that practically everyone had a bank account. I could see bright, neatly dressed children coming from Sunday school, men and women going to church or on their way to visit neighbors.[57]

The Pacific Lumber Company had a well-stocked library with a good selection of books in Italian.[58] In addition, the company awarded cash prizes to families with the best-kept lawns and gardens.[59] Many companies sponsored baseball teams to promote social integration and corporate identity. During the 1910s, teams representing the Pacific Lumber Company, the Hammond Lumber Company, the Northern Redwood Lumber Company, the Little River Redwood Company, and the Arcata Barrel Company, among others, competed in the Industrial Championship league. The games attracted large crowds, and baseball in Humboldt County soon was of a semi-professional standard. As early as 1909, the manager of the Pacific Lumber Company team was complaining that rival teams imported players.[60] In 1910, the company put all the "sawdust babies," as the players were called, on the company payroll. The company's athletic budget for the last six months of 1923 allocated $2,600 to baseball, $1,750 of which was spent on salaries.[61]

The new interest of the lumber companies in organizing the recreation of their employees was also evident in the increasing practice of showing movies in company towns and wood camps. In December 1911, the Pacific Lumber Company became the first to show movies in Humboldt.[62] Providing movies for workers was just one more means, according to one commentator, "of keeping the workman contented and preventing the debauches which so often wreck camp operations."[63] In 1920, the Pacific Lumber Company completed construction of the Winema Theater in Scotia.

Even before 1910, the Hammond Lumber Company provided its workers at Samoa with an assembly hall, reading rooms, and other social and recreational facilities.[64] The recollections of Elsie Miller, who worked for Hammond during the early twentieth century, suggest that his social and recreational programs were not unlike those of the Pacific Lumber Company, and that the money spent on such ventures was not wasted:

There's always been a kind of family atmosphere in the company and the town. I always declare there's never another place in the world like it, because in time of disaster, everybody rushes to everybody's aid. If there's illness, or any trouble of any kind, the company always comes forth, and so do all the rest of us. The company built us a lovely clubhouse here for the youth, the PTA and the Woman's Club.[65]

The general pattern for the lumber companies was to improve living conditions and provide social and recreational facilities in the company towns first and then to implement such reforms at the logging camps. By the early 1920s, Hammond had extensive social facilities at some of his larger logging camps. At one camp there was a school, social center, and a free library. There were facilities for showing movies, and dances were held regularly; women had their own social club. Cabins became more individual when companies stopped building them in symmetrical rows. The *Humboldt Standard* asserted that this was part of an attempt to encourage men to bring their families with them to the woods, and it added that companies provided "cosy little cottages and garden spots."[66]

In 1913, the Pacific Lumber Company sponsored a benefit ball for an employee with a severe case of diabetes.[67] A year later, Humboldt lumber companies instituted the first annual Lumbermen's picnic, which was attended by approximately 2,000 people.[68] The Pacific Lumber Company demonstrated its benevolence at Thanksgiving in 1917 by treating its employees to a lavish turkey dinner.[69] It is difficult to know how workers responded to these gestures of benevolence. Some employees evidently did not view them any more cynically than Elsie Miller did. To take one example, on March 6, 1918, a large number of mill employees from the Hammond Lumber Company appeared at the house of George Fenwick, who had been general manager of the company for eighteen years, to serenade him on his birthday and present him with a gift.[70]

Lumber employers became increasingly concerned with labor turnover rates in the late 1910s. High turnover rates in themselves were a direct cost;[71] equally important, they minimized the potential for nurturing a loyal and socially disciplined cadre of employees. The subject arose with increasing frequency in lumber trade journals and at logging conferences. There is little empirical data on turnover for most American industries before 1920,[72] but turnover rates in the lumber industry apparently were among the highest. The California Bureau of Labor Statistics reported in 1913 that at one of the lumber camps providing the best conditions in California, 391 of 1,694 workers quit during the peak month (August) in the lumbering season.[73] In 1915, the Federal Industrial Relations Commission estimated annual turnover in logging camps at about 500 percent; records of a Washington lumber camp for 1919 to 1921 revealed an annual turnover rate of 564 percent.[74] In 1917, Colonel Bryce Disque, the man sent by the War Department to try and resolve the labor problems in the Pacific Northwest lumber industry, estimated the turnover rate at almost 1,000 percent annually.[75]

In Humboldt County, the Pacific Lumber Company made the earliest and most concerted effort to reduce the turnover rate. In 1918, the company introduced a "continuous service plan." Under the plan, a man who stayed with the company for one year got an annual bonus amounting to 2 percent of his salary; after five years of service, the bonus amounted to 7 percent.[76] While the Pacific Lumber Company introduced the plan during the acute labor shortage of World War I, it was retained after the war, and during the 1920s turnover rates fell to half their previous levels.[77] By the early 1920s, if not before, the Hammond Lumber Company had introduced a similar plan, except that workers received a 3 percent bonus after only six months and 4 percent after a year. The *Industrial Worker* commented that "a system like this sure breeds stool pigeons."[78]

In many regions, lumber employers harnessed the services of the industrial department of the YMCA. Almost every session of the Pacific Logging Congress during the 1910s and 1920s contained a detailed report of the work of the YMCA in lumber camps, and frequently the Congress featured a YMCA welfare dinner. The aims of the YMCA dovetailed neatly with lumber employers' interest in engineering a new moral order in their workforce. John Goodell, Northwest Industrial Secretary of the YMCA, summarized these goals in a speech before the Pacific Logging Congress in 1911:

The YMCA recognizes the threefold nature of man—body, mind, and spirit. . . . The YMCA seeks . . . to develop the threefold nature of man in the construction and logging camps of the Northwest. The physical side is developed by recreative games, such as baseball, boxing, wrestling. . . . The mental side is developed by providing reading matter in the form of daily papers, magazines, circulating libraries etc. . . . . A talk on "Savings" by some banker has always been profitable. The spiritual work . . . usually consists of a gospel song service some evenings in the week, and a gospel talk and song service on Sunday evenings.[79]

The following year, Goodell stressed "the particular need of the lumber industry" to remedy problems caused by "the vanishing personal relationship between employer and employee." He reiterated that the YMCA could play an important role in producing healthy, efficient, and loyal lumber workers.[80]

The YMCA supplied library materials to Humboldt logging camps in the late 1910s, but a Eureka branch of the YMCA, founded in 1894, had lapsed by the twentieth century, and despite the appeals of the *Eureka Herald*,[81] the YMCA did not reestablish itself in Eureka until 1920. Anticipating the branch opening, the *Humboldt Times* praised the YMCA and linked its activities to the general interest being shown in employee welfare:

Many of us can remember when no employer ever was expected to give a thought to the health or welfare of his employees. . . . Men were only so much timber for use of employers—driven dumb creatures without souls. But times have changed—laborers are no longer to be thought of as "Chinks," "Dagoes," or "Wops." They are human beings with souls. The Trotskys, Lenins, Mooneys and McNamaras are the product of neglected moral social and religious surroundings. Their minds have been poisoned from youth by false teachings.[82]

The Eureka YMCA began with a charter membership of 775 people. Mrs. George Fenwick, wife of the general manager of the Hammond Lumber Company, became one of the vice-presidents, and Mrs. Milton Carson, the wife of the owner of the Dolbeer and Carson Lumber Company, served on the board.[83] A month before the founding of the YMCA, the future secretary talked with officers of the Pacific Lumber Company about holding Sunday school meetings in the logging camps and found them amenable to the idea.[84] By January 1921, there were branches of the YMCA at Eureka, Arcata, Fortuna, and Scotia. At Scotia, the Pacific Lumber Company converted an old movie theater into a gymnasium, which the YMCA used for physical education classes.[85]

Labor Legislation to the Aid

Although the lumber employers' interest in the moral and material welfare of their workers was partially inspired by the growing volatility of labor relations in the early twentieth century and the general influence of Progressive values in social welfare and scientific management, these were not the only forces making for a new departure in labor relations policy. Improvements in material conditions and efforts to reshape the moral order of the company town and the logging camps occurred at different times and varied significantly according to county, state, and employer. While lumber employers were aware of the potential and danger of strikes and unionism, they also knew that lumber trade unionism was weak. Furthermore, social environmentalism and other Progressive ideas associated with management only began to gain currency in the early 1910s. To a significant degree, as Daniel Nelson has argued, the new concern for employee welfare was prompted by state labor legislation.[86]

In California, the Workmen's Compensation Act and the Camp Sanitation Act of 1913, in conjunction with other legislation, put pressure on lumber employers to be more concerned about the welfare of their workers. The Camp Sanitation Law, which was amended and reinforced in 1915, established strict guidelines for improving camp living conditions and gave agents of the labor commissioner considerable powers.[87] Agents were given access to camps and workplaces and "all the powers and authority of sheriffs and other peace officers to make arrests for violations of the provisions of this act."[88] In 1915, the California Commission of Immigration and Housing assumed all responsibility for enforcement of the act.

In 1913, shortly after passage of the Camp Sanitation Act, the California Bureau of Labor Statistics began an extensive investigation into the California lumber industry. In the northern redwood district, 40 camps were visited and statistics compiled on 7,198 workers. The report indicated that in the California lumber industry as a whole, few improvements had taken place since the passage of the Camp Sanitation Act. Sanitary and living conditions were usually little better than they had been in the nineteenth century. In the northern redwood lumber district, conditions were especially bad. Only one camp had installed steel bunks (as required by the 1913 law), and the commissioner reported that "generally speaking the premises were greatly in need of attention," while "the sanitary condition in many of the camps deserved severe criticism."[89] Only one camp in the region supplied a shower bath.[90]

The records of the California Commission of Immigration and Housing indicate that the Commission did an extremely effective and conscientious job in enforcing camp sanitation laws.[91] Lumber camps in Humboldt County were visited annually by inspectors from 1913 until the mid-1920s. The inspectors compiled lengthy reports on all lumber camps; summaries of the reports were sent to the lumber companies, and the commission firmly asked the companies to remedy deficiencies. During 1917 alone, 1,003 camps were examined by commission inspectors, and by January 1, 1918, the commission had investigated 4,239 labor camps and made 2,720 reinspections. By that date, 74 percent of the camps were in compliance with the law, compared to only 34 percent when the commission made its first inspections.[92]

By the early 1920s, the commission reported dramatic improvements in conditions at Humboldt lumber camps. In 1920, the *Humboldt Times* gleefully quoted Edward Brown, director of the Bureau of Labor Camps, extolling the lumber employers for all the improvements they had made.[93] A letter by the director of camp sanitation, written in 1921 to Henry Cole of the Little River Redwood Company, praised the lumber operators for making "wonderful strides in improving the lumber camps."[94] In 1923, in its published report, the commission recalled that in 1914, when inspectors first visited Humboldt County, they were told of a "nut" who provided a bath for his men and that inspectors in the county were looked upon as "crazy men and their suggestions were openly called extravagant dreams."[95] By 1922, the commission reported, "there was not a lumber camp of any importance in the entire state which did not have adequate bathing facilities."[96]

The relationship between the commission and the lumber companies seems to have been a remarkably harmonious one. Edward Brown asserted that "the camp managers of Humboldt have nearly all shown a willingness to cooperate."[97] The 1919 annual report of the commission quoted Donald McDonald, vice-president of the Pacific Lumber Company:

We are heartily in accord with the campaign which has been carried on by the State Commission of Immigration and Housing for the improvement of camp sanitation. The results are not measurable in dollars and cents alone. Proper conditions about the wood camps not only make for better men, but better service, and in our judgement the work which has been carried on by your commission has been a distinct help, not only to the employee, but the employer.[98]

The lumber companies' cooperation with the California Commission of Immigration and Housing reflected their shared motives and assumptions. "If men are housed comfortably and not, as is the case in some lumber camps, in a less healthful and decent manner than a good farmer houses his animals, the morale of the men is sustained and they stick by the job instead of drifting the moment they make enough money to leave the camp," stated Edward Brown.[99] The Commission was preoccupied from the outset with defusing working-class discontent over conditions and, with an increasing number of lumber employers, shared the much-cherished notion of many Progressives that the solution to the labor problem lay in improving working and living conditions.[100] If some lumber companies did not initially welcome the intrusion of the commission, most employers realized by World War I that the commission's approach to the labor problem dovetailed in many respects with their own.

The First World War also helped convert a significant number of lumber employers to welfare capitalism and new management policies. The lumber industry benefited as much as any other from the wartime boom in the economy. West Coast lumber employers were suddenly faced with severe labor shortages. This encouraged them to introduce, or use more extensively, policies designed to reduce labor turnover and attract new workers. The greatly enhanced bargaining power of labor also led to increasing militancy by lumber workers, especially in the Pacific Northwest. For a time, the IWW and the International Union of Timber Workers (IUTW) were able to disrupt production and expand their membership base. In Humboldt County, although the labor movement experienced a revival during the war, the lumber industry was not affected by the rash of strikes and slowdowns that hit the Pacific Northwest. In part this may have been because California lumber employers experimented with new policies earlier than their counterparts in Oregon and Washington, and, in particular, had gone further toward improving living conditions. Writing in 1918, Paul Scharrenberg, a leading figure in the California labor movement and a member of the California Commission of Immigration and Housing, commented that "it is a significant fact that while the lumber regions and construction camps of the Pacific Northwest have had a long series of labor difficulties, California has been singularly free from any such disturbances since the camp sanitation policy has been in force."[101] But the militancy of lumber workers elsewhere in the West reawakened lumber employers to the potential threat of a revival of lumber trade unionism and the need for preemptive measures.

During World War I, the federal government was anxious to stem the rising tide of lumber trade unionism and militancy. Confronted with serious lumber production bottlenecks that threatened the war effort, the War Department put pressure on lumber employers to improve working conditions and shorten the working day. Most employers yielded to the pressure. In March 1918, they agreed to grant workers the eight-hour day. Simultaneously, the federal government and the Pacific Northwestern lumber employers sponsored the Loyal Legion of Loggers and Lumbermen to compete with the IWW and IUTW.[102] The union proved a great success, boasting 70,000 members by spring 1918. This was far more than the IWW and IUTW combined ever attracted at any one time, although from 1917 onward, savage repression by private organizations and local, state, and federal government authorities greatly circumscribed the IWW's and IUTW's ability to function as unions.[103]

Lumber employers, like most others, did not welcome the unprecedented degree of federal government intervention in labor management and production during World War I. But the intervention spurred lumbermen who had been dragging their feet to improve conditions in the industry and experiment with welfare capitalism. After the war, when the market slumped, many lumber companies cut wages and increased the working day. They did not abandon welfare capitalism, however; indeed, like the Pacific and Hammond Lumber companies, they expanded their programs. And as the California Commission of Immigration and Housing reports indicate, working and living conditions improved, rather than deteriorated, despite the virtual absence of trade unionism and a generally weak lumber market during the 1920s.

It would be facile to suggest that by the 1920s all lumber workers were corporate automatons who viewed the company's interests as synonymous with their own. Julio Rovai's colorful recollections of life during the 1920s in Rio Dell, which was inhabited primarily by Italians working for the Pacific Lumber Company, hardly depicts residents as puritanical corporate zombies. Even allowing for a measure of exaggeration, bootlegging, gambling, and prostitution flourished in the community. So universal was bootlegging that when a major fire broke out in 1928, many denizens broke open barrels of wine to douse the flames after the water supply had been exhausted.[104] But Rio Dell, located 2 miles from Scotia, was not a company town, and Rovai, while glorifying the illicit recreational activities of his fellow Italians, writes of the "powerlessness" they felt vis-à-vis the Pacific Lumber Company. In Rio Dell it was one thing to be a bootlegger and debaucher and another to challenge the prerogatives of the company on fundamentals of labor policy. Despite the much more intrusive role of employers in the social life of company towns, such as Scotia and Samoa, workers may have been able to carve out some measure of autonomy and social space, but the obstacles to doing so were infinitely greater. In a situation of virtual powerlessness, it was tempting for workers to submit to the dictates of the company, and to be reduced to a state of apathy, particularly when employers were not totally indifferent to their "welfare."

By the late 1910s, as David Gordon, Richard Edwards, and Michael Reich have suggested, employers in many industries realized that it was not always advisable to depend on repression and the "drive system" to maximize profits and harmonize labor relations.[105] Welfare capitalism, scientific management, bonus and incentive schemes, and more time-honored methods of segmenting the workforce along national, ethnic, and racial lines could be used effectively to both divide labor and placate it. The lumber employers ability to implement many of these policies, especially welfare capitalism, was enhanced by the company town or single-industry setting in which most lumber production occurred. Indeed, as Elizabeth Fones-Wolf has argued persuasively, welfare capitalism may have been an important factor in American labor relations in general until at least the mid-twentieth century.[106] Finally, during the 1920s, a weak lumber market and a conservative political climate made the prospects of reviving trade unions even more formidable than in the 1910s.

Postscript

During World War I, the Humboldt County labor movement made a fleeting recovery. The membership of all unions affiliated with the Eureka Trades Council doubled in the first five months of 1917.[1] Unions that had been virtually moribund for a decade experienced a sudden influx of members, while the building trades unions were powerful enough to establish the closed shop in Eureka by May 1917.[2] In contrast to the tame rituals that marked Labor Day rallies earlier in the decade, the 1917 rally attracted well over 3,000 people.[3] Many workers obtained the eight-hour day and wage increases that at least kept pace with inflation.

Several factors accounted for the rejuvenation of the Humboldt County labor movement. The county was hit by a severe labor shortage that affected much of the nation during the war years. The lumber industry operated at full capacity to meet wartime production needs, while a massive shipbuilding program, employing upward of 1,000 additional men, put stress on a labor market deprived of 2,000 Humboldt County men who enlisted.[4] As America entered the war, the *Humboldt Times* predicted that there would be a shortage of 3,500 men by the fall of 1917.[5] The decision of San Francisco Mayor James Rolph to operate his new shipbuilding operations on Humboldt Bay under the closed shop also gave the union movement a boost. *Labor News* heralded Rolph as the savior of the Humboldt County labor movement.[6] Finally, the federal government's unprecedented intervention in labor relations during World War I, especially in the shipbuilding and lumber industries, gave the county's labor movement a sense of legitimacy and self-confidence that it had lacked over the previous decade. *Labor News* highlighted the pressure that the federal government exerted on lumber and shipbuilding employers to improve conditions.[7]

Despite these signs of revival, lumber trade unionism in Humboldt lagged behind the recovery of many other sectors of the county's labor movement. Humboldt's lumber workers did not participate in the wave of strikes that buffeted the Pacific Northwest lumber industry in

July 1917. The Wobblies did not establish an office in Eureka until late July, and it closed within two months.[8] Wobbly organizers were active in the county in the early months of 1918, but they failed to attract more than a token following during the war and in the early 1920s. The AFL International Union of Timber Workers (IUTW) had more success in organizing Humboldt lumber workers. Estimates of the IUTW's membership in the county varied greatly. The *Humboldt Standard* put the figure at between 2,000 and 3,000 by March 1918.[9] J. T. Woods, a general organizer for the California State Federation of Labor, estimated that the IUTW had 800 members, which was probably nearer the mark.[10] In January and February 1918, Humboldt County lumber workers pressed for the eight-hour day at a series of rallies. Under extreme pressure from their workers and the War Department, the county lumber employers and their Pacific Northwest counterparts grudgingly conceded the eight-hour day in March 1918.

The war's end halted the resurgence of the Humboldt labor movement. In 1919, severe dislocations to the local economy resulted from the end of the government orders that had prompted the growth of a large shipbuilding industry. The redwood lumber market also began to slacken at a time when the county was trying to absorb returning servicemen. By 1920, the Humboldt labor movement had suffered a sharp loss of membership and was in much the same state as before the war.

The recovery of the lumber trade union movement was especially ephemeral. In the spring of 1919, most Humboldt County lumber companies reinstituted the nine-hour day with little resistance.[11] The IUTW fought vigorously during 1919 to maintain its base in the county. In June it sent one of its leading organizers, Harry Call of Seattle, to Humboldt County to boost the sagging fortunes of the local IUTW branch.[12] The crucial test of strength for the lumber trade union movement in Humboldt County came in September 1919 when more than 500 Hammond Lumber Company employees walked out in support of two workers who had been discharged for demanding time-and-a-half rates for all hours worked in excess of eight.[13] The strike originated as a spontaneous affair, but within a few days strikers, including many women, flocked into the IUTW. The IUTW demanded time and a half for all work over eight hours, reinstatement of all strikers, and equal wage rates for men and women. The county labor movement gave its wholehearted support and the Mayor of Eureka offered to mediate, but Hammond was intransigent. He accused Call and other IUTW leaders of past links with the IWW. Revelations that the charge proved to have some degree of substance hurt the strikers' cause. In October, Hammond secured an injunction that effectively broke the strike. Disillusioned by the defeat of the strike and proof of past affiliation of some of the IUTW's leadership with the Wobblies, many Humboldt County lumber workers tore up their IUTW union cards.[14] Hammond gloated over his victory and was emboldened to demand the closing down of *Labor News*.[15]

Throughout 1920, Call strove desperately but vainly to rekindle the spirit of unionism in the lumber industry. In 1921, most Humboldt lumber companies cut wages by from 10 to 15 percent, and some of the county's lumber workers were forced to accept a ten-hour day. The union movement all but vanished from the woods and mills of Humboldt County during the early 1920s. The IUTW, after meeting with similar failures in other lumbering regions, formally dissolved in 1923. Undeterred by a local criminal syndicalism ordinance and frequent arrests of their members, the Wobblies made a stubborn effort to establish a foothold in Humboldt County up until 1926.[16] But for all their valor and persistence, the Wobblies were no more successful in attracting a following than they had been since early in the twentieth century. Often the Wobblies expressed exasperation at the difficulty and magnitude of their task. Writing to the *Industrial Worker* in 1922 from Humboldt County, one Wobbly complained that "it would take a Sherlock Holmes to find any militancy in these tame apes."[17] Another correspondent to the *Industrial Worker* reported that in his Humboldt camp 10 percent of the men were IWW members or sympathizers, 10 percent company stool pigeons, and the other 80 percent "scissorbills"[18]—the derogatory Wobbly term for workers lacking class consciousness or militancy. During the early 1920s, the Wobbly journal *Industrial Pioneer* devoted several pieces to the plight of the redwood lumber workers. In a feature article entitled "The Tragedy of the Redwoods," the author reproached the lumber workers for their quiescence. He called the Pacific Lumber Company and the Hammond Lumber Company the "Octopus" of northwestern California and described the massive deforestation of the redwood lumber region and the victimization of labor leaders. But, he said, the saddest feature of the situation was the "apathy" of the workers.[19] In a subsequent article, "Californian" entitled his piece on the redwood lumber region "The Land of Sunshine and Serfdom."[20]

Although the IWW was the harshest critic of the Humboldt County lumber companies during the early 1920s, several correspondents to the Wobbly press admitted that, notwithstanding the wage cuts and the abrogation of the wartime eight-hour day, conditions in the lumber camps were substantially better than they had been before the war. In 1922, George Duville reported that the Hammond and Pacific Lumber companies provided greatly improved living conditions, which were superior to those of other county lumber companies.[21] Two years later, a lumber worker returning after an absence of five years informed the *Industrial Worker* that a striking transformation in living conditions had taken place at almost all Humboldt County camps.[22]

Whatever weight one gives to the roles of state camp sanitation laws, welfare capitalism, repression, scientific management, and divisions within the workforce, the quietude of the Humboldt County lumber workers was not exceptional. For most of the interwar period, not only was lumber trade unionism weak nationally, but there were also comparatively few strikes in the industry. In 1917, for example, there were 299 strikes in the nation's lumber industry, more than the total number (232) between 1918 and 1926. The incidence of strikes declined over the same period in other industries, but, with few exceptions, the tapering off was most dramatic in the lumber industry, in which, nationwide, only six strikes were recorded in 1924, nine in 1925, and three in 1926.[23] The incidence of strikes and their severity, as measured by the number of workers involved and "man days idle," continued to be low from the late 1920s until the mid-1930s in most states. In California, there were only 27 strikes, of relatively short duration, and involving a limited number of workers, between 1927 and 1936.[24]

In Humboldt County, the serenity of labor relations was disturbed only in 1935 by a violent but brief strike of a small number of the county's lumber workers.[25] It was reported that 95 percent of Hammond's day crew at Samoa opposed it, while, at Scotia, 733 Pacific Lumber Company employees signed a loyalty pledge, with only 38 abstaining. Workers at the Dolbeer and Carson Company offered their employer a loyalty pledge. They stated that they had been employed by the company for from one to fifty years and that they had "always received the greatest consideration from our president and friend, J. M. Carson, and do not need a union . . . to make demands for us." A month later, the vast majority of employees at Mendocino's two most important lumbering concerns—the Union Lumber Company and the Casper Lumber Company—signed similarly worded petitions. There is no evidence that these pledges were either solicited or coerced. In 1938, workers at the Union Lumber Company voted 599 to 290 against any kind of union representation in elections supervised by the National Labor Relations Board. At another NLRB election in 1941, Hammond employees voted 546 to 417 against union representation.[26] During the 1930s in Humboldt County, the AFL Sawmill and Timber Workers Union (STWU), which operated under the jurisdiction of the

United Brotherhood of Carpenters and Joiners (UBC), secured only a small following.

In the late 1930s, labor relations in the Pacific Northwest lumber industry were more turbulent than in Humboldt County and most other lumbering regions. In 1937, dissident lumber workers, mainly from Oregon, Washington, and British Columbia, chafing under the conservative leadership of the UBC, founded the International Woodworkers of America and affiliated with the CIO. In Oregon and Washington, the IWA and the STWU engaged in a bitter struggle to secure jurisdiction over the discontented lumber workers. The IWA, however, had even less success than the STWU in establishing a foothold in Humboldt County. Although much of the IWA's energy was consumed by fighting between its pro- and anti-Communist wings, it nevertheless succeeded in attracting the majority of workers to its fold by the early 1940s.[27] The booming demand for lumber, and acute labor shortages during World War II,[28] saved the lumber workers from the consequences of prolonged and acrimonious intra- and interunion disputes. The extensive intervention of the National War Labor Board in the lumber industry forced employers both to recognize and bargain with unions in accordance with the National Labor Relations Act of 1935. The consequent institutionalization of labor relations, and a sustained demand for lumber after World War II, established trade unionism in the lumber industry as a relatively stable entity for the first time. During the war years, the STWU made enormous gains in Humboldt County and other parts of the Redwood Empire. Shortly after the war ended, the STWU felt strong enough to call out all its members in the redwood region in pursuit of the union shop and a substantial wage increase.

The militance of lumber workers in some regions during the late 1930s and the 1940s, and the establishment of more enduring unions, by no means reversed the subordinate position of labor in the redwood industry. Most employers could not countenance a union shop and some of the other demands made on them. In April 1948, after a strike that lasted twenty-seven months, the STWU was forced to concede defeat.[29] Nationally, although lumber trade unionism remained a factor after World War II, it did not wield the same power as unions in most other industries. In 1947, only 16.5 percent of lumber workers were organized and in 1953 only 21.1 percent. In both these years, the percentage of workers organized in the other sectors of the economy except government and service was significantly higher.[30]

The reasons for the comparative weakness of lumber unionism in the mid-twentieth century, and indeed today, are complex but in many respects similar to those that prevailed in the late-nineteenth and early-twentieth century. Union drives of the IWA and the STWU were undoubtedly assisted by the sanctification of collective bargaining initiated by the National Labor Relations Act. Furthermore, the automobile freed lumber workers from the confines of company towns and single-industry communities. But the gains made by the IWA and the STWU after the Second World War were due in large part to a buoyant lumber market that lasted until the early 1970s. The fact that lumber companies dominated the economies of the communities they operated in after the war to same extent that they had before limited the gains of the union movement even in a benign economic climate. When the lumber market collapsed in the late 1970s and early 1980s, lumber unionism in the Redwood Empire and elsewhere proved vulnerable to an antiunion offensive, and the accompanying plant closings devastated the economies of many lumber-dependent communities.

Notes

Introduction

1. *Humboldt Times*, January 3, 1884.
2. There is a brief autobiography of Keller's early life in the Kaweah Collection, Folder C. F. Keller, CA 302, Bancroft Library, University of California, Berkeley.
3. *Democratic Standard*, May 29, 1880.
4. See Robert V. Hine, *California's Utopian Colonies* (San Marino: Henry E. Huntington Library, 1953).
5. For one of the best review articles on how community studies have contributed to our knowledge of American history, see Kathleen Neils Conzen, "Community Studies, Urban History, and American Local History," in Michael Kammen, ed., *The Past Before Us: Contemporary Historical Writing in the United States* (Ithaca, N.Y.: Cornell University Press, 1980), pp. 270–291.
6. Steven Hahn and Jonathan Prude, eds., *The Countryside in the Age of Capitalist Transformation: Essays in the Social History of Rural America* (Chapel Hill: University of North Carolina Press, 1985), p. 3.
7. Melvyn Dubofsky, "The Origins of Western Working Class Radicalism, 1890–1905," *Labor History* 7 (Spring 1966): 131–154. See also Carlos A. Schwantes, "The Concept of the Wageworkers' Frontier: A Framework for Future Research," *Western Historical Quarterly* 18 (January 1987): 39–55. Schwantes has written a useful review on the labor history of an important subregion of the American West: "The History of Pacific Northwest Labor History," *Idaho Yesterdays* 28 (Winter 1985): 23–35. Among other things, Schwantes notes the preoccupation of social historians with the region's most violent episodes, the overall neglect of the labor history of the Pacific Northwest, and a "time lag" by the historians of the region in using the conceptual insights and frameworks of the new social history.
8. U.S. Bureau of the Census, *Census of Manufacturing, 1905* (Washington, D.C.: GPO, 1907), pt. 1, p. clix.
9. Vernon Jensen, *Lumber and Labor* (New York: Holt, Rinehart & Winston, 1945), p. 7.
10. U.S. Department of Labor, Bureau of Labor Statistics, Bulletin 211 (Washington, D.C.: GPO, 1917), p. 8.

11. Charlotte Todes, *Labor and Lumber* (New York: International Publishers, 1931), p. 80.

12. The best of the very few studies of lumbering communities is Norman H. Clark, *Mill Town: A Social History of Everett, Washington, from Its Earliest Beginnings on the Shores of Puget Sound to the Tragic and Infamous Event Known as the Everett Massacre* (Seattle: University of Washington Press, 1970). William G. Robbins has also published several articles that prefigure his forthcoming book on Coos Bay, Oregon. Among them are "Timber Town: Market Economics in Coos Bay, Oregon, 1850 to the Present," *Pacific Northwest Quarterly* 75 (October 1984): 146–155; and "The Social Context of Forestry: The Pacific Northwest in the Twentieth Century," *Western Historical Quarterly* 16 (October 1985): 413–427.

13. Howard Brett Melendy, "One Hundred Years of the Redwood Lumber Industry, 1850–1950," doctoral dissertation, Stanford University, 1952, p. 15.

14. Gareth Stedman Jones, *Languages of Class: Studies in English Working Class History, 1832–1982* (Cambridge, England: Cambridge University Press, 1983), especially "Rethinking Chartism," chap. 3, pp. 90–178. The important works of Sean Wilentz, Bruce Palmer, Alan Dawley, and Leon Fink, notwithstanding, in recent years British social historians have attached more importance to political ideology and the "language of class" than their American counterparts. As Michael Frisch and Daniel Walkowitz observed in their introduction to a recent collection of essays in American working class history: "Interest in political ideas and activity has not generally characterized labor history; this interest was patronized as utopian and immature in the most traditional works and dismissed as superficial and tangential by recent historians more concerned with social structure." Michael H. Frisch and Daniel J. Walkowitz, eds., *Working-Class America: Essays on Labor, Community, and American Society* (Urbana: University of Illinois Press, 1983), pp. xiii–xiv.

15. Melvyn Dubofsky says that "loggers were perfect IWW recruits" in his *We Shall Be All: A History of the IWW* (New York: Quadrangle, 1967), p. 129. Philip Foner writes of the lumber industry as "an ideal field for the IWW" in his *The Industrial Workers of the World, 1905–1917* (New York: International Publishers, 1965), p. 218, although he confronts the failure of the IWW to obtain a large following among the lumber workers more directly than most authors. For a recent book celebrating the supposed militancy of lumber workers, see Jerry Lembcke and William M. Tattam, *One Union in Wood: A Political History of the International Woodworkers of America* (New York: International Publishers, 1984).

16. George Bain and Robert Price, *Profiles of Union Growth: A Comparative Statistical Portrait of Eight Countries* (Oxford, England: Basil Blackwell, 1980), p. 95.

17. Many articles and essays could be cited. Among the most recent and important are Thomas Bender, "Wholes and Parts: The Need for a Synthesis in American History," *Journal of American History* 73 (June 1986): 120–136; William E. Leuchtenburg, "The Pertinence of Political History: Reflections

on the Significance of the State in America," *Journal of American History* 73 (December 1986): 585–600; and Spencer C. Olin, Jr., "Toward a Synthesis of the Political and Social History of the American West," *Pacific Historical Review* 55 (November 1986): 599–611. David Brody has addressed the problems of arriving at a synthesis in the field of labor history in a number of essays, among them "The Old Labor History and the New: In Search of an American Working Class," *Labor History* 20 (Winter 1979): 111–126; and "Working-Class History in the Great Depression," *Reviews in American History* 4 (June 1976): 262–267. For a provocative and interesting attack on the clarion call for synthesis, see Eric H. Monkkonen, "The Dangers of Synthesis," *American Historical Review* 91 (December 1986): 1146–1157.

Chapter 1

1. The best account of Humboldt County's early history is Owen C. Coy, *The Humboldt Bay Region, 1850–1875* (Los Angeles: California State Historical Association, 1929). See also, W. W. Elliott & Co., *History of Humboldt County, California* (San Francisco: W. W. Elliott, 1881); Leigh H. Irvine, *History of Humboldt County, California, with Biographical Sketches* (Los Angeles: Historic Record, 1915); Lynwood Carranco, ed., *The Redwood Country: History, Language, Folklore* (Dubuque, Iowa: Kendall & Hunt, 1971).

2. For the history of the lumber industry in Humboldt County, see Coy, *Humboldt Bay Region*; Lynwood Carranco and John T. Labbe, *Logging the Redwoods* (Caldwell, Idaho: Caxton Printers, 1979); Lynwood Carranco, *Redwood Lumber Industry* (San Marino, Calif.: Golden West Books, 1982); Howard Brett Melendy, "One Hundred Years of the Redwood Lumber Industry, 1850–1950," doctoral dissertation, Stanford University, 1952.

3. Coy, *Humboldt Bay Region*, pp. 107–110.

4. The following contain many biographical sketches of early Humboldt County pioneers: John Carr, *Pioneer Days in California* (Eureka, Calif.: Times Publishing, 1891); Elliott, *History of Humboldt County*. The *Humboldt Historian*, published by the Humboldt County Historical Society since 1953, is a good source for biographical sketches, as is the *Redwood Researcher*, published by the Redwood Genealogical Society.

5. Coy, *Humboldt Bay Region*, pp. 107–110.

6. Statistics compiled from the Manuscript Census of Population for Humboldt County, 1860.

7. *Humboldt Times*, August 8, 1857. The *Humboldt Times* was the county's first newspaper and commenced publication in September 1854 at Eureka as a weekly. In December 1854 it moved to Arcata, but in 1858 returned to Eureka. It became a daily publication on January 1, 1874.

8. *Humboldt Times*, January 26, 1861, and June 7, 1862.

9. Ibid., September 5, 1863.

10. Ibid., September 13, 1856.

11. Ibid., November 19, 1859.

12. U.S. Bureau of the Census, *Twelfth Census of the U.S., 1900, Statistics of Population* (Washington, D.C.: GPO, 1901), vol. 1, pt. 1, table 5, p. 75.

13. *Reports of the California Surveyor General*, 1879–1881.

14. U.S. Bureau of the Census, *Twelfth Census of the U.S., Statistics of Agriculture* (Washington, D.C.: GPO, 1902), vol. 5, pt. 1, table 44, p. 592.

15. U.S. Bureau of the Census, *Census of Manufacturing, 1905* (Washington, D.C.: GPO, 1908), pt. 111, pp. 644–645.

16. U.S. Bureau of the Census, *Ninth Census of the U.S., 1870, Statistics of Wealth and Industry* (Washington, D.C.: GPO, 1872), vol. 3, table 11, p. 639; *Statistics of Agriculture* (Washington, D.C.: GPO, 1872), vol. 3, table 4, p. 104.

17. *Humboldt Times*, January 1, 1891.

18. *Report of the California Surveyor General*, 1870, p. 84. The size of the lumber workforce was calculated from the Manuscript Census Schedules of Population for Humboldt County, 1870.

19. *Humboldt Times*, June 8, 1878.

20. *Report of the California Surveyor General*, 1880–1881, p. 69. The appendix to Carranco, *Redwood Lumber Industry*, contains a chronological list of the major mills established in Humboldt County.

21. J. M. Eddy, *In the Redwood Realm* (Eureka: Times Publishing, 1893), p. 37, cites one estimate of 190 million feet of logs sawn in the 1887 season. Even after the California State Board of Harbor Commissioners began keeping statistics on the export of lumber from Humboldt Bay in 1889, estimates of lumber exports from the county varied according to source. Estimates of the lumber workforce appeared in *Humboldt Standard*, December 24 and August 2, 1887; *Times-Telephone*, April 20, 1888.

22. Thomas R. Cox, Robert S. Maxwell, Phillip Drennon, and Joseph Malone, *This Well-Wooded Land: Americans and Their Forest from Colonial Times to the Present* (Lincoln: University of Nebraska Press, 1985), p. 115. This book is the most comprehensive and up-to-date general survey of American forest history and contains a useful bibliographical essay.

23. Eddy, *In the Redwood Realm*, pp. 34–41; Melendy, "One Hundred Years of Redwood Lumber," pp. 275–315. The county press invariably provided statistics on annual lumber production and the amount shipped to a specific port. See also, Thomas R. Cox, *Mills and Markets: A History of the Pacific Coast Lumber Industry to 1900* (Seattle: University of Washington Press, 1974).

24. According to the 1880 Manuscript Census Schedules for Humboldt County, 211 lumber workers resided in Eureka and 231 in Arcata and the Arcata Precinct.

25. Carranco, *Redwood Lumber Industry*, p. 138; Eddy, *In the Redwood Realm*, p. 31.

26. This was true of most large lumber companies in the Pacific Coast states by the late nineteenth century. Cox, *Mills and Markets*, pp. 128–129.

27. Melendy, "One Hundred Years of Redwood Lumber," p. 305. On the history of the U.S. lumber industry and its failure to achieve order and stability,

see William G. Robbins, *Lumberjacks and Legislators: Political Economy of the U.S. Lumber Industry, 1890–1941* (College Station, Tex.: Texas A & M University Press, 1982); and Vernon Jensen, *Lumber and Labor* (New York: Holt, Rinehart & Winston, 1945).

28. The available studies indicate that a majority of America's leading lumbermen in the nineteenth century came from relatively humble origins. An interesting source is American Lumberman, *American Lumberman: The Personal History and Public and Business Achievements of One Hundred Eminent Lumbermen of the U.S.*, 3 vols. (Chicago: American Lumberman, 1905). See also Frederick W. Kohlmeyer, "Northern Pine Lumbermen: A Study in Origins and Migrations," *Journal of Economic History* 16 (December 1956): 529–538; and Kohlmeyer, "Social Origins of Lumbermen," in *Encyclopedia of American Forest and Conservation History*, ed. Richard C. Davis (New York: Macmillan, 1983), pp. 610–612.

29. Irvine, *History of Humboldt County*, pp. 607–610; *Humboldt Standard*, February 20 and 27, 1912; *Humboldt Times*, February 28, 1912.

30. Irvine, *History of Humboldt County*, pp. 1167–1169.

31. Elliott, *History of Humboldt County*, p. 143.

32. Irvine, *History of Humboldt County*, pp. 314–316.

33. *Humboldt Times*, October 23, 1889. Howard Libby, who worked in the Humboldt County lumber industry for many years, states that "many of the resident managers of the various companies are men who came up through the ranks." Interview with Howard Libby, 1953, transcript, Bancroft Library, P-W, vol. 3, p. 5.

34. Calculated from Manuscript Census of Population for Humboldt County, 1860, 1870, 1880. For a detailed breakdown of the nativity of the Humboldt County lumber workforce, see Daniel Cornford, "Lumber, Labor, and Community in Humboldt County, California, 1850–1920," doctoral dissertation, University of California, Santa Barbara, 1983, pp. 67–69.

35. Some women worked as cooks at logging camps and in mill towns, but most cooks were male. By the early twentieth century, and perhaps before, several mills employed women as clerical workers.

36. *Frontier Journal* (Calais), July 17, 1851.

37. Alan A. Brookes, "The Exodus: Migration from the Maritime Provinces to Boston during the Second Half of the Nineteenth Century," doctoral dissertation, University of New Brunswick, Fredericton, 1979; Brookes, "Out-Migration from the Maritime Provinces, 1860–1900: Some Preliminary Considerations," *Acadiensis* 5 (Spring 1976): 26–55.

38. Brookes, "The Golden Age and the Exodus: The Case of Canning, Kings County," *Acadiensis* 11 (Autumn 1981): 57–82; Jon Humboldt Gates, *Falk's Claim: The Life and Death of a Redwood Lumber Town* (Eureka: Pioneer Graphics, 1983), pp. 39–42.

39. Interview with Frank Fraser, 1953, transcript, Bancroft Library, P-W 57, vol. 3, p. 4.

40. Eugene F. Fountain, "The Story of Blue Lake" (unpublished manu-

script, n.d.), vol. 2, p. 204, available at the Humboldt Room, Humboldt State University Library.

41. Stewart Holbrook, *Holy Old Mackinaw: A Natural History of the American Lumberjack* (New York: Macmillan, 1938), pp. 71–72 and 152.

42. Graeme Wynn, *Timber Colony: A Historical Geography of Early Nineteenth Century New Brunswick* (Toronto: University of Toronto Press, 1981); David C. Smith, *A History of Lumbering in Maine, 1861–1960* (Orono: University of Maine Press, 1972).

43. Statistics compiled from the Manuscript Census of Population for Humboldt County, 1860, 1870, and 1880.

44. *Arcata Union*, April 12, 1917.

45. Ibid.

46. *Labor Enquirer* (Denver), September 18, 1886.

47. For a fuller description of logging, see Carranco and Labbe, *Logging the Redwoods*; and Carranco, *Redwood Lumber Industry*. For a good general description of technological changes in the West Coast lumber industry during the late nineteenth century, see Cox, *Mills and Markets*, pp. 227–254. Logging terminology differed according to region, with significant differences between the redwood lumber industry and that of the Pacific Northwest. For example, the men who worked in the woods were called "loggers" in Oregon and Washington but "woodsmen" in Humboldt County.

48. Descriptions of sawmilling in the Humboldt County lumber industry are not nearly so detailed and frequent as those of logging, but see Melendy, "One Hundred Years of Redwood Lumber," pp. 56–64; *Humboldt Times*, November 3, 1889; Gates, *Falk's Claim*, pp. 85–87. As Cox et al. note in their bibliographical essay in *This Well-Wooded Land*, p. 309, there are very few studies of sawmill technology for the post-1850 years.

49. Wynn, *Timber Colony*, p. 78; Smith, *A History of Lumbering in Maine*, pp. 21, 225–226; Jensen, *Lumber and Labor*, pp. 39–40; *Ninth Biennial Report, California Bureau of Labor Statistics, 1899–1900* (Sacramento: State Printer, 1900), pp. 57–63.

50. Dolbeer and Carson Records, Bancroft Library, C-G 164, vols. 1 and 12.

51. This was particularly evident from an examination of the census, Special Schedules of Manufactures for Humboldt County, 1880.

52. U.S. Bureau of the Census, *Report on Manufacturing Industries, Eleventh Census of the U.S., 1890* (Washington, D.C.: GPO, 1895), vol. 6, pt. 1, table 3, pp. 624–625. Most Humboldt County lumber company records indicate that few mills operated for more than 250 days a year.

53. *Humboldt Times*, November 20, 1889.

54. Dolbeer and Carson Records, vols. 1 and 12.

55. Melendy, "One Hundred Years of Redwood Lumber," pp. 326–329.

56. See Joseph Conlin, " 'Old Boy, Did You Get Enough of Pie': A Social History of Food in Logging Camps," *Journal of Forest History* 23 (October 1979): 165–185.

57. W. H. Wilde, "Chronology of the Pacific Lumber Company, 1869 to 1945" (unpublished manuscript, n.d.), p. 24, available at Bancroft Library; Ben Shannon Allen, "From the Penobscot to the Eel" (unpublished manuscript, 1949), available at Humboldt State University Library.

58. *Humboldt Times*, January 12, 1897.

59. The Eureka City Census of 1904 was reprinted in *Humboldt County Souvenir* (Eureka: Times Publishing, 1904), pp. 199–201.

60. *Western Watchman* (Eureka), September 24, 1887, July 7, 1888, April 25, 1891. Typescript, "History of the Pacific Lumber Company as Told by the Late George Douglas," Pacific Lumber Company files at Scotia, unmarked folder. See also Allen, *Penobscot to the Eel*, chap. 14, pp. 7–8.

61. According to the 1880 Manuscript Census Returns, 41.2 percent of millmen were married and 32.6 percent of woodsmen.

62. Holbrook, *Holy Old Mackinaw*, p. 87.

63. *Humboldt Standard*, July 6, 1896.

64. On the occupational hazards of lumber work, see Andrew M. Prouty, *More Deadly than War: Pacific Coast Logging 1827–1981* (New York: Garland, 1985).

65. Strikes by lumber workers were relatively rare in the nineteenth century. There was little effective organization among lumber workers until the coming of the Knights of Labor in the mid-1880s, and the Knights only succeeded in organizing lumber workers briefly. The first major recorded strike of American lumber workers occurred in 1872 in Pennsylvania. Nancy Lee Miller, "Sawdust War: Labor Strife in Lumber-Mills," *Pennsylvania Forests* 72 (March–April 1982): 6–8, 13. Federal government statistics indicate that there were only 275 strikes involving 73,626 workers in the "lumber and timber products" industry between 1881 and 1905; Florence Peterson, *Strikes in the United States, 1880–1936* (Washington, D.C.: Department of Labor Bulletin 651, 1938), p. 30. The number of strikes and workers involved in them was far greater in such industries as coal, iron and steel, boots and shoes, the building trades, tobacco, and textiles.

66. *Humboldt Times*, October 29, 1881.

67. For recent studies on the inequalities of wealth in post–gold rush California, see Ralph Mann, *After the Gold Rush: Society in Grass Valley and Nevada City, California, 1849–1870* (Palo Alto: Stanford University Press, 1982); and Robert A. Burchell, "Opportunity and the Frontier: Wealth-Holding in Twenty-Six Northern California Counties, 1848–1880," *Western Historical Quarterly* 18 (April 1987): 177–196.

Chapter 2

1. Leon Fink, *Workingmen's Democracy: The Knights of Labor in American Politics* (Urbana: University of Illinois Press, 1983), p. 26. In an important review essay, David Montgomery stressed the prominence of independent po-

litical activity in the Gilded Age and the need for further work in this field. David Montgomery, "To Study the People: The American Working Class," *Labor History* 21 (Fall 1980): 485–512.

2. Among the more important of these studies are Eric Foner, *Tom Paine and Revolutionary America* (New York: Oxford University Press, 1976); Paul G. Faler, *Mechanics and Manufacturers in the Early Industrial Revolution: Lynn, Massachusetts, 1780–1860* (Albany: State University of New York Press, 1981); Sean Wilentz, *Chants Democratic: New York City and the Rise of the American Working Class, 1788–1850* (New York: Oxford University Press, 1984); Bruce Laurie, *Working People of Philadelphia, 1800–1850* (Philadelphia: Temple University Press, 1980); Edward Pessen, *Most Uncommon Jacksonians: The Radical Leaders of the Early Labor Movement* (Albany: State University of New York Press, 1967); Howard B. Rock, *Artisans of the New Republic: The Tradesmen of New York City in the Age of Jefferson* (New York: New York University Press, 1979). Alan Dawley's *Class and Community: The Industrial Revolution in Lynn* (Cambridge: Harvard University Press, 1976) spans the antebellum and postbellum period till the early twentieth century.

3. Herbert G. Gutman, *Work, Culture, and Society in Industrializing America* (New York: Knopf, 1976). On Gutman's secondary concern with explicit political ideology and activity, see David Montgomery, "Gutman's Nineteenth Century America," *Labor History* 19 (Summer 1978): 416–429, especially pp. 426–427.

4. Valuable contributions to our understanding of Gilded Age labor and radical politics before the advent of the Populists have been made in the following books, although they differ in the degree to which they focus on politics: David Montgomery, *Labor and the Radical Republicans, 1862–1872* (New York: Knopf, 1967); Steven J. Ross, *Workers on the Edge: Work, Leisure, and Politics in Industrializing Cincinnati, 1788–1890* (New York: Columbia University Press, 1985); Richard J. Oestreicher, *Solidarity and Fragmentation: Working People and Class Consciousness in Detroit, 1875–1900* (Urbana: University of Illinois Press, 1986); Nick Salvatore, *Eugene V. Debs: Citizen and Socialist* (Urbana: University of Illinois Press, 1982); Fink, *Workingmen's Democracy*.

5. Faler, *Mechanics and Manufacturers in the Early Industrial Revolution*, p. 186.

6. Wilentz, *Chants Democratic*, pp. 14–15, 61–103, 157–167, 182–216, 237–254, 271–286; Foner, *Tom Paine and Revolutionary America*, pp. 39–41, 88–102, 123–124, 134–138.

7. Historians of nineteenth-century America, especially the Gilded Age, are divided as to the relative degree to which local, state, or national politics were people's major frame of reference. Eric Foner's *Free Soil, Free Men, Free Labor: The Ideology of the Republican Party Before the Civil War* (New York: Oxford University Press, 1970) was deservedly highly acclaimed. Besides having much to say about the roots and nature of the democratic–republican tradition, Foner demonstrates the extent to which politics had been "nationalized" by the 1850s. Yet the consensus of most social and political historians is that peo-

ple were animated mainly by local political issues during the Gilded Age. In the oft-quoted phrase of Robert Wiebe, they inhabited "island communities" in terms of their political frame of reference. Robert Wiebe, *The Search for Order, 1877–1920* (New York: Hill & Wang, 1967). In reviewing the historical literature, Thomas Bender reflects this consensus while trying to reconcile it with contradictory evidence. Thomas Bender, *Community and Social Change in America* (New Brunswick: Rutgers University Press, 1978), pp. 86–120.

8. *Humboldt Times*, December 13, 1863.

9. Letter Book of James Beith, February 19, 1857, p. 13, Bancroft Library.

10. Ibid., February 4, 1861, p. 52.

11. *Humboldt Times*, February 27, 1858.

12. Ibid., August 7, 1858.

13. Ibid., January 14, 1860.

14. Ibid., March 26, 1864.

15. Letter Book of James Beith, January 24, 1862, p. 162.

16. Rowland Berthoff, "Writing a History of Things Left Out," *Reviews in American History* 14 (March 1986): 1–16.

17. Letter Book of James Beith, January 24, 1862, p. 162.

18. *Humboldt Times*, July 13, 1861.

19. Diary of James Beith, vol. 5, July 9, 1881, p. 166.

20. *Humboldt Times*, December 21, 1867, and January 4, 1868.

21. Ibid., January 11 and 18, 1868.

22. Ibid., November 14, 1868.

23. Ibid., January 8, 1868.

24. Ibid., July 15, 1871.

25. *Northern Independent* (Eureka), July 13, 1871.

26. Ibid., August 26 and September 1, 1869.

27. Ibid., August 19, 1869.

28. *Humboldt Times*, March 11, 1871.

29. Ibid., April 15 and August 26, 1871.

30. *West Coast Signal* (Eureka), July 9, 1873.

31. This party is sometimes referred to as the Independent party or the Dolly Vardens. The secondary literature on it is sparse, but see Curtis E. Grassman, "Prologue to Progressivism: Senator Stephen M. White and the California Reform Impulse, 1875–1905," doctoral dissertation, University of California, Los Angeles, 1970, pp. 17–22; and Walton E. Bean, *California: An Interpretive History* (New York: McGraw-Hill, 1978), p. 261.

32. *West Coast Signal*, August 6, 1873.

33. *Humboldt Times*, August 30, 1873.

34. Ibid., July 5, 1873.

35. Ezra Carr, *The Patrons of Husbandry on the West Coast* (San Francisco: A. L. Bancroft, 1875).

36. *Humboldt Times*, September 20, 1873.

37. *West Coast Signal*, September 24, 1873. The local press printed official election returns about two weeks after an election. Local and state election

returns are also available at the California State Library, Sacramento. Returns for 1849 to 1916 are on microfilm at the University of California, Berkeley Library.

38. Biographical information on Sweasey was obtained from T. J. Vivian and D. G. Waldron, *Biographical Sketches of the Delegates to the Convention* (San Francisco: Francis & Valentine, 1878), pp. 29–30; *West Coast Signal*, September 24, 1873; *Democratic Standard*, January 1, 1879; *Humboldt Times*, October 1, 1893; *Western Watchman*, October 7, 1893; and *Nerve*, October 7, 1893.

39. *Humboldt Times*, January 24, 1874.

40. Ibid., January 6, 1877.

41. Ibid., January 20, 1877.

42. *Pacific Coast Wood and Iron*, a trade journal of the Pacific lumber industry, published a review of redwood lumber prices for the previous thirty years in 1899, which was reprinted in the *Humboldt Standard*, December 13, 1899.

43. *Humboldt Times*, February 10, 1877.

44. *Daily Evening Signal*, July 3, 1877; *Humboldt Times*, July 7, 1877.

45. *Mendocino Democrat*, March 2, 1878.

46. *Humboldt Times*, July 21, 1877.

47. Ibid., July 21 and October 13, 1877, March 2, 1878.

48. Ibid., March 2, 1878.

49. *Democratic Standard*, November 3, 1877.

50. *Humboldt Times*, August 25, 1877.

51. *Daily Evening Signal*, August 18, 1877.

52. Eugene F. Fountain, *The Story of Blue Lake* (n.p., n.d.), vol. 3, pp. 589–592.

53. The study named all landholders possessing 500 acres or more in every California county. The *San Francisco Chronicle* began serializing the findings of the *Sacramento Daily Record* on October 28, 1873, and the findings for Humboldt County were published in the *Humboldt Times*, November 8, 1873.

54. *Humboldt Times*, November 8, 1873. See also obituary of Joseph Russ, *Times-Telephone*, October 10, 1886.

55. *San Francisco Chronicle*, October 28, 1873.

56. Ibid., November 1, 1873.

57. On the concentration of land ownership in California, see Carey McWilliams, *Factories in the Field* (Boston: Little, Brown, 1939); and Cletus E. Daniel, *Bitter Harvest: A History of California Farmworkers, 1870–1941* (Ithaca: Cornell University Press, 1981).

58. See E. B. Willis and P. K. Stockton, *Debates and Proceedings of the Constitutional Convention*, 3 vols. (Sacramento: J. D. Young, Superintendent of State Printing, 1880).

59. *Humboldt Times*, April 27, 1878.

60. Ibid.

61. Ibid.

62. Ibid., May 11, 1878.

63. *Democratic Standard*, November 23, 1878.

64. *Humboldt Times*, May 9, 1874; *Pacific Rural Press*, July 14, 1877.

65. *Humboldt Times*, October 21, 1876.

66. Ibid., November 18 and December 2, 1876.

67. *Daily Evening Signal*, March 15, 1878.

68. The fullest account of the California Workingmen's party is provided by Ralph Kauer, "The Workingmen's Party of California," *Pacific Historical Review* 13 (September 1944): 278–291. An important book on the California labor movement and reform politics in the late nineteenth century is Alexander Saxton, *The Indispensable Enemy: Labor and the Anti-Chinese Movement in California* (Berkeley: University of California Press, 1971). Also useful on the history of the California Workingmen's party are Royce D. Delmatier, Clarence F. McIntosh, and Earl G. Walters, *The Rumble of California Politics, 1848–1970* (New York: Wiley, 1970), pp. 70–98; and Ira B. Cross, *A History of the Labor Movement in California* (Berkeley: University of California Press, 1935), pp. 88–129. These studies, however, focus mainly on the San Francisco Workingmen's party and the anti-Chinese agitation.

69. *Humboldt Times*, September 22, 1877.

70. Delmatier et al., *Rumble of California Politics*, p. 83.

71. U.S. Bureau of the Census, *Tenth Census of the U.S., Statistics of Population* (Washington, D.C.: GPO, 1883), vol. 1, table 14, p. 498; idem, *Ninth Census of the U.S., Statistics of Population* (Washington, D.C.: GPO, 1872), vol. 1, table 3, p. 90.

72. *Evening Star* (Eureka), January 17, 1877.

73. Lynwood Carranco, "The Chinese Expulsion from Humboldt County," *Pacific Historical Review* 30 (November 1961): 329–340; idem, "The Chinese in Humboldt County, California: A Study in Prejudice," *Journal of the West* 12 (January 1973): 139–162.

74. Statistics compiled from the Manuscript Census of Population for Humboldt County, 1880.

75. *Humboldt Times*, June 4, 1878; *Democratic Standard*, June 1, 1878; *Ferndale Enterprise*, June 1, 1878.

76. *Humboldt Times*, May 11, 1878.

77. *Democratic Standard*, May 25, 1878.

78. *Humboldt Times*, July 6, 1878. In 1878, the bulk of lumber workers, as well as laborers, artisans, and businessmen, resided in Eureka and, to a lesser extent, Arcata. Farmers constituted the majority of the electorate outside these precincts. Unfortunately, even later in the nineteenth century and the early twentieth century, there were no clearly identifiable "lumber worker precincts," which limits the utility of precinct analysis per se to gauge the voting behavior of lumber workers. Unquestionably, farmers constituted a larger proportion of the registered voters in relation to their numbers than lumber workers and most other occupational groups. Nevertheless, lumber workers made up a significant

proportion of registered voters. The geographic stability of a sizable core of lumber workers, and the relative leniency of residency requirements imposed by California law, both before and after the 1879 constitution, facilitated this. While farmers tended to "persist" longer on the voting registers than most other occupational groups, they too were fairly transient. On the above issues, see Robert A. Burchell, "Opportunity and the Frontier: Wealth-Holding in Twenty-Six Northern California Counties 1848–1880," *Western Historical Quarterly* 18 (April 1987): 189–190.

79. Willis and Stockton, *Debates and Proceedings of the Constitutional Convention*, vol. 2, p. 1144.

80. *Democratic Standard*, May 3, 1879.

81. Ibid., May 24, 1879.

82. Ibid., April 5, 1879.

83. Ibid., May 10, 1879.

84. Ibid., June 7, 1879.

85. Ibid., April 12 and June 28, 1879.

86. Ibid., July 5, 1879.

87. Biographical sketches of the men on the Workingmen's party ticket appeared in the *Democratic Standard*, July 19, 1879.

88. *Democratic Standard*, August 16, 1879.

89. Ibid., July 5, 1879.

90. Ibid., September 6, 1879.

91. Saxton, *Indispensable Enemy*, p. 152.

92. *Democratic Standard*, March 13, 1880.

93. Ibid., April 24, 1880.

94. Ibid., May 15, 1880.

95. Ibid., April 17, 1880.

96. Ibid., January 8, 1881.

97. For critical responses to Sweasey's land-reform proposals, see the *Humboldt Times*, May 4, 11, and 18, 1878. Sweasey strongly defended his proposal in the *Daily Evening Signal*, June 12, 1878.

98. *Arcata Union*, August 14, 1886.

Chapter 3

1. Michael B. Katz, Michael J. Doucet, and Mark Stern, *The Social Organization of Early Industrial Capitalism* (Cambridge: Harvard University Press, 1982), p. 130.

2. Robert Sharkey, *Money, Class, and Party: An Economic Study of Civil War and Reconstruction* (Baltimore: Johns Hopkins University Press, 1959), p. 197.

3. In addition to Sharkey, *Money, Class, and Party*, for accounts of national monetary and economic policy in the immediate post–Civil War years, see Irwin Unger, *The Greenback Era: A Social and Political History of Ameri-*

can Finance, 1865–1879 (Princeton: Princeton University Press, 1964); Walter K. Nugent, *Money and American Society, 1865–1880* (New York: Free Press, 1968); Allen Weinstein, *Prelude to Populism: Origins of the Silver Issue, 1867–1878* (New Haven: Yale University Press, 1970). For a good discussion of the interest of labor leaders in currency reform, see David Montgomery, *Beyond Equality: Labor and the Radical Republicans, 1862–1872* (New York: Knopf, 1967).

4. Quoted in Sharkey, *Money, Class, and Party*, p. 195.

5. See, however, John D. French, " 'Reaping the Whirlwind': The Origins of the Allegheny County Greenback Labor Party in 1877," *Western Pennsylvania Historical Magazine* 64 (April 1981): 97–119. For a brief but important overview article on the relationship between the labor movement and the state, see David Montgomery, "Labor and the Republic in Industrial America: 1860–1920," *Le Mouvement Social* 3 (April–June 1980): 201–215.

6. *Democratic Standard*, June 1, 1878.

7. Ibid., May 29, July 3 and 31, 1880.

8. Ibid., July 24, 1880.

9. *Reports of the California Surveyor General*, 1879–1882.

10. *Democratic Standard*, February 28, 1880.

11. *Reports of the California Surveyor General*, 1879 and 1880.

12. *Arcata Leader*, August 7, 1880.

13. *Reports of the California Surveyor General*, 1880–1882.

14. *Democratic Standard*, September 27, 1879.

15. Ibid., July 10, 1880.

16. *Humboldt Times*, September 24, 1881.

17. Ibid., December 25, 1880.

18. Kaweah Collection, CA 302, Bancroft Library, C. F. Keller Folder.

19. *Democratic Standard*, May 29, 1880.

20. This view is well developed in one of the most sophisticated critiques of the Populists' ideology: Bruce Palmer, *"Man Over Money": The Southern Populist Critique of American Capitalism* (Chapel Hill: University of North Carolina Press, 1980).

21. *Democratic Standard*, September 13, 1879.

22. Ibid., March 19, 1881.

23. Ibid., July 22, 1882.

24. The occupation of most delegates can be established by the 1880 Manuscript Census of Population for Humboldt County or L. M. McKenney & Co., *Eight County Directory of Humboldt, Napa, Marin, Yolo, Lake, Solano, Mendocino and Sonoma Counties* (San Francisco: L. M. McKenney, 1885). Data for this directory were collected in 1883.

25. *Democratic Standard*, May 15, 1880.

26. Ibid., September 25, 1880.

27. Humboldt Times, September 11, 1880.

28. Ibid., March 26, 1881.

29. Ibid., November 20, 1880.

30. Ibid., November 25, 1882.

31. Humboldt Times, October 22, 1881.

32. Democratic Standard, August 19, 1882.

33. Ibid., August 26, 1882.

34. Ibid.

35. *Humboldt Times*, August 26, 1882.

36. Ibid., September 2 and 9, 1882.

37. *Democratic Standard*, March 27, 1880.

38. Ibid., May 29, 1880.

39. Ibid., October 2, 1884.

40. *Truth*, March 25, 1882.

41. *Truth*, March 25, 1882; *Industrial Worker*, June 21, 1924.

42. *Humboldt Times*, March 11, 1882.

43. *Democratic Standard*, May 8, 1880; *Arcata Leader*, May 22, 1880.

44. *Democratic Standard*, August 26, 1882.

45. *Humboldt Times*, June 17, 1882.

46. Ibid., October 28, 1882.

47. For an account of the issues surrounding the Debris Bill, see Robert L. Kelley, *Gold Versus Grain: The Hydraulic Mining Controversy in California's Sacramento Valley* (Glendale: Arthur H. Clark, 1959)

48. *Democratic Standard*, March 12 and 26, 1881.

Chapter 4

1. On the history of the California labor movement from the gold rush to the early twentieth century, see Ira B. Cross, *A History of the Labor Movement in California* (Berkeley: University of California Press, 1935). On the origins of the labor movement in the Pacific Northwest, see Carlos A. Schwantes, *Labor, Socialism, and Reform in Washington and British Columbia, 1885–1917* (Seattle: University of Washington Press, 1979); and Harry W. Stone, "Beginning of the Labor Movement in the Pacific Northwest," *Oregon Historical Quarterly* 47 (June 1946): 155–164.

2. On the industrialization of the American West and the rise of a militant labor movement, see Melvyn Dubofsky, "The Origins of Western Working Class Radicalism, 1890–1905," *Labor History* 7 (Spring 1966): 131–166.

3. *The Annual Report of the Secretary of the Interior, 1879–1880* (Washington, D.C.: GPO, 1880) asserted that "much trespassing is reported upon the redwood pine found on the public lands of Humboldt and Mendocino Counties" (p. 577). Many lumber companies acquired land and timber by getting people to file "dummy" entries under existing homestead laws or by simply cutting on the public domain. The *Annual Reports of the United States Commissioner of the General Land Office* are replete with accounts of such practices in California and elsewhere. The abuses of federal land law by lumber interests are examined in Harold H. Dunham, *Government Handout: A Study in the Administration of Public Lands, 1875–1891* (Ann Arbor, Mich.: Edward Brothers,

1941); and John Ise, *United States Forest Policy* (New Haven: Yale University Press, 1920).

4. S. A. D. Puter, *Looters of the Public Domain* (Portland: Portland Printing House, 1908).

5. *Ferndale Enterprise*, April 7, 1882.

6. The fullest account of this episode is in *House Executive Documents*, 50th Cong., 1st sess., Exec. Doc. 282, pp. 1–21. See also *Annual Reports of the United States Commissioner of the General Land Office* for the following years: 1885, pp. 59–60; 1886, pp. 94–95; 1887, pp. 79–81.

7. *Annual Report of the United States Commissioner of the General Land Office, 1886*, p. 95.

8. House Exec. Doc. 282, p. 2.

9. *Annual Report of the United States Commissioner of the General Land Office, 1886*, p. 95.

10. *New York Times*, April 20, 1886.

11. *Democratic Standard*, January 13, 1883.

12. Ibid., March 24, 1883.

13. Kaweah Collection, CA-302, Keller folder, Bancroft Library. Hereinafter cited as Keller Autobiography.

14. On the general problem faced by lumber entrepreneurs in acquiring timberlands, see Thomas R. Cox, Robert S. Maxwell, Phillip Drennon Thomas, and Joseph J. Malone, *This Well-Wooded Land: Americans and Their Forests from Colonial Times to the Present* (Lincoln: University of Nebraska Press, 1985), pp. 138–142. The authors state that there was "a considerable measure of both public support and official understanding—even sympathy—for lumbermen who had to break the law" (p. 141).

15. *Democratic Standard*, March 3, 1883.

16. Ibid., March 31, 1883.

17. Ibid., March 24, 1883.

18. Intermittent references to Ayres's involvement appeared in the county press from the mid-1880s to the mid-1890s. Ayres's involvement was most fully exposed by C. F. Bergin, who served as a special agent for the General Land Office investigating the California Redwood Company, in an article in the *Berkeley Daily Advocate*, May 23, 1892.

19. *Times-Telephone*, May 5, 1883.

20. *Ferndale Enterprise*, August 3, 1883.

21. Herbert G. Gutman, "The Workers' Search for Power," in *The Gilded Age*, ed. H. Wayne Morgan (Syracuse: Syracuse University Press, 1970), pp. 31–53.

22. Keller Autobiography, p. 3.

23. *General Land Office Report*, 1886, p. 95.

24. Ise, *United States Forest Policy*, p. 76.

25. *Democratic Standard*, August 11, 1883.

26. For more details on the history of the IWA, see Cross, *History of the Labor Movement in California*.

27. *Democratic Standard*, August 11, 1883.

28. IWA Records, CA 306, Bancroft Library, unmarked folder, Keller to Moore.

29. *Democratic Standard*, September 1, 1883.

30. IWA Records, unmarked folder, Keller to Haskell, October 9, 1883.

31. *Truth*, August 25, 1883.

32. IWA Records, Amelia Jones to Haskell, October 5, 1883.

33. IWA Records, Keller to Burgman, October 9, 1883; Keller to Haskell, October 9, 1883.

34. IWA Records, unmarked folder.

35. Ibid.

36. Cross, *History of the Labor Movement in California*, p. 161.

37. In an analysis of 147 IWA members in San Francisco, Bruce Dancis concluded that the organization was unsuccessful in attracting unskilled and semiskilled workers. Bruce Dancis, "Social Mobility and Class Consciousness: San Francisco's International Workingmen's Association in the 1880s," *Journal of Social History* 1 (Fall 1977): 75–98.

38. IWA Records, unmarked folder, Keller to Haskell, October 9, 1883.

39. *Democratic Standard*, May 29, 1883.

40. *Truth*, September 1884, pp. 228–231.

41. Ibid.

42. Keller Autobiography, p. 3.

43. For an account of the Kaweah Cooperative Colony and the respective roles of Keller and Haskell, see Robert V. Hine, *California's Utopian Colonies* (San Marino: Henry E. Huntington Library, 1953).

44. *Truth*, January 12, 1884.

45. IWA Records, unmarked folder, August Glatt to Haskell, April 16, 1885.

46. Diary of Burnette Haskell, California Historical Society Library, Ms. 952, January 2, 1885.

47. *Times-Telephone*, February 3, 1884.

48. *Humboldt Standard*, February 7, 1884.

49. *Times-Telephone*, February 15, 1884.

50. *Industrial Worker*, December 7, 1911.

51. *Times-Telephone*, February 20, 1884.

52. *Humboldt Standard*, May 12, 1884.

53. *Labor News*, June 27, 1914.

54. *Times-Telephone*, August 15, 1884.

55. *Industrial Worker*, December 7, 1911.

56. *Humboldt Standard*, July 23, 1884.

57. *Truth*, August 1884, pp. 193–194.

58. *Times-Telephone*, August 15, 1884.

59. *Labor News*, June 27, 1914.

60. As noted, Sweasey joined Robert Owen in New Harmony, Indiana, in the 1840s. Speed, like Keller, was a founding member of the Kaweah Cooperative Colony. Cronin, after a colorful career in the labor movement in Oregon

and Washington in the mid-1880s, lived out his life on a commune in Oregon. See Carlos A. Schwantes, "Protest in a Promised Land: Unemployment, Disinheritance, and the Origin of Labor Militancy in the Pacific Northwest, 1885–1886," *Western Historical Quarterly* 13 (October 1982): 373–390. Alfred Cridge was an IWA member and for a time in the early 1870s was a member of a colony in Riverside, California. He edited the Humboldt Knights' organ, the *Western Watchman* from 1884 to 1886. *The Star* (San Francisco), January 18, 1902.

Chapter 5

1. Only in recent years have the Knights begun to receive the scholarly attention commensurate with their importance. Before the late 1970s, the most important works dealing with the Knights were Norman J. Ware, *The Labor Movement in the United States, 1860–1890* (New York: Knopf, 1929); and Gerald N. Grob, *Workers and Utopia: A Study of Ideological Conflict in the American Labor Movement, 1865–1900* (Evanston: Northwestern University Press, 1961). Among the most important recent studies of the Knights of Labor are Melton McLaurin, *The Knights of Labor in the South* (Westport, Conn.: Greenwood Press, 1978); Bryan D. Palmer and Gregory S. Kealey, *Dreaming of What Might Be: The Knights of Labor in Ontario, 1880–1900* (Cambridge, England: Cambridge University Press, 1982); Leon Fink, *Workingmen's Democracy: The Knights of Labor and American Politics* (Urbana: University of Illinois Press, 1983); Steven J. Ross, *Workers on the Edge: Work, Leisure, and Politics in Industrializing Cincinatti, 1788–1890* (New York: Columbia University Press, 1985); Richard J. Oestreicher, *Solidarity and Fragmentation: Working People and Class Consciousness in Detroit, 1875–1900* (Urbana: University of Illinois Press, 1986); David Brundage, "The Making of Working-Class Radicalism in the Mountain West: Denver, Colorado, 1880–1903," doctoral dissertation, University of California, Los Angeles, 1982; Richard Schneirov, "The Knights of Labor in the Chicago Labor Movement and in Municipal Politics, 1877–1887," doctoral dissertation, Northern Illinois University, 1984. On the Knights of Labor in the Pacific Northwest, see Carlos A. Schwantes, *Radical Heritage: Labor, Socialism, and Reform in Washington and British Columbia, 1885–1917* (Seattle: University of Washington Press, 1979).

2. Jonathan Garlock, comp., *Guide to the Local Assemblies of the Knights of Labor* (Westport, Conn.: Greenwood Press, 1982), pp. 22–23. Reference was found in the county press to two assemblies not listed by Garlock. Membership data are based on recollections of Millard Gardner, *Humboldt Times*, December 31, 1909; and George Speed, *Industrial Worker*, June 21, 1924.

3. *Times-Telephone*, August 9, 1884.

4. *Pacific Coast Wood and Iron* 32 (December 1899):209, reprinted in *Humboldt Standard*, December 13, 1899.

5. *Humboldt Standard*, April 15, 1885.

6. *Times-Telephone*, April 24, 1885.

7. *San Francisco Chronicle*, May 1, 1885.

8. *Humboldt Standard*, April 27, 1885.

9. *Times-Telephone* and *Humboldt Standard*, May 8, 1885.

10. *Humboldt Standard*, May 11, 1885.

11. According to the *Labor Enquirer* of Denver, the paper began as "a six column folio, all home print." *Labor Enquirer*, November 8, 1884. Unfortunately, no issues of the *Western Watchman* are extant before September 18, 1886.

12. Diary of James Beith, vol. 7, p. 149, May 10, 1885.

13. Ibid., vol. 8, p. 11, July 18, 1886.

14. *Times-Telephone*, May 23, 1886.

15. *Western Watchman*, October 9, 1886.

16. Ibid., October 2, 1886.

17. Ibid., September 25, 1886.

18. *Labor Enquirer*, April 18, 1886.

19. *Ferndale Enterprise*, September 2, 1887.

20. The Knights of Labor records, although they contain an abundance of correspondence and records of proceedings, do not contain membership lists. Because of the fear of blacklisting and reprisals, Knights in Humboldt County and elsewhere often did not sign their names to correspondence. Most of the names of the leading Knights in Humboldt were obtained from their correspondence with Powderly and the recollections of Gardner and Speed; some came from the county press. Furthermore, in the mid-1880s, an increasing proportion of the local assemblies were designated as "mixed," even if they were composed primarily of one occupational group.

21. *Labor Enquirer*, January 24, 1885.

22. *Humboldt Standard*, October 11, 1886.

23. Thus Point 7 of the Declaration of Principles stated that the Knights sought "the recognition by incorporation of trades' unions . . . to improve their condition and protect their rights." Point 21 asserted that it was the goal of the Knights "to shorten the hours of labor by a general refusal to work for more than eight hours."

24. The first two planks of the Knights' Declaration of Principles stated that the aim was "to make industrial and moral worth, not wealth, the true standard of individual and National greatness" and to "secure to the workers the full enjoyment of the wealth they create, sufficient leisure in which to develop their intellectual, moral, and social faculties." And the last point stated that the Order sought "to persuade employers to agree to arbitrate all differences which may arise between them, in order that the bonds of sympathy may be strengthened and that strikes may be rendered unnecessary."

25. Mrs. W. S. Johnson to Powderly, March 25, 1886, Powderly Papers, Catholic University of America, Washington D.C.

26. *Industrial Worker*, June 21, 1924. McClaurin, *Knights of Labor in the South*, stresses the pervasiveness of factionalism within the Knights and the extent to which the Order attracted people of different occupational back-

grounds (pp. 40–42). Fink, *Workingmen's Democracy*, agrees that the Knights were often very inclusive in terms of their composition, but does not see this as a source of weakness or of ideological confusion.

27. Charles Devlin to Powderly, September 26, 1886, Powderly Papers.
28. *Labor Enquirer*, April 10, 1886.
29. *Industrial Worker*, June 21, 1924. Cronin played an active role among the Knights in Oregon after leaving Humboldt. Powderly received a stream of letters from Oregon Knights complaining that he was a socialist and an anarchist using the Knights as a vehicle to expand the influence of the IWA. Powderly wrote a succession of letters to Cronin in mid-1886 asking him to respond to the charges. Cronin was a leading figure in fermenting anti-Chinese riots in Oregon and Washington. See Schwantes, "Protest in a Promised Land."
30. *Arcata Union*, September 25, 1886.
31. Diary of James Beith, vol. 7, pp. 156–157, May 31, 1885.
32. *Humboldt Standard*, February 15, 1886.
33. Millard Gardner to Powderly, July 20, 1886, Powderly Papers.
34. *Western Watchman*, December 18, 1886.
35. Ibid.
36. Ibid., March 19, 1887.
37. Ibid., June 4, 1887.
38. *Ferndale Enterprise*, June 17, 1887.
39. *Western Watchman*, June 18, 1887.
40. Ibid., June 4, 1887.
41. *Labor News*, June 27, 1914.
42. *Western Watchman*, June 4, 1887.
43. Garlock, *Guide to the Local Assemblies of the Knights of Labor*, p. 23.
44. *Western Watchman*, October 1, 1887.
45. Ibid.
46. Ibid., December 18, 1887.
47. Ibid., March 19, 1887.
48. Ibid., November 27, 1886.
49. *Times-Telephone*, January 23, 1887.
50. *Western Watchman*, January 8, 1887.
51. Ibid., November 20, 1886, and March 5 and April 30, 1887.
52. In a letter to the *Times-Telephone*, "Citizen" ridiculed the idea and stated that an initial capital of $50,000 would be required. *Times-Telephone*, January 27, 1887.
53. On the Knights and temperance, see Samuel Walker, "Terence V. Powderly, the Knights of Labor and the Temperance Issue," *Societas* 5 (Autumn 1975): 279–293; and David Brundage, "The Producing Classes and the Saloon: Denver in the 1880s," *Labor History* 26 (Winter 1985): 29–52.
54. *Western Watchman*, December 11, 1886.
55. Ibid., February 19, 1887.
56. Ibid., March 19, 1887.
57. *Times-Telephone*, July 21, 1886.

58. *Ferndale Enterprise*, August 7, 1886.

59. *Western Watchman*, July 9, 1887.

60. Hyman Weintraub, *Andrew Furuseth: Emancipator of the Seamen* (Berkeley: University of California Press, 1959). On the organization of sailors and longshoremen on the West Coast in the late nineteenth and early twentieth centuries, see also Paul S. Taylor, *The Sailors' Union of the Pacific* (New York: Ronald Press, 1923); and Stephen Schwartz, *Brotherhood of the Sea: A History of the Sailors' Union of the Pacific* (New Brunswick: Transaction Books, 1986). The CSU merged with the Steamshipmen's Union in 1891 to form the Sailors' Union of the Pacific.

61. *Humboldt Standard*, November 3, 1885.

62. *Times-Telephone*, September 14, 1886.

63. *Coast Seamen's Journal*, November 2, 1887; *Third Biennial Report, California Bureau of Labor Statistics, 1886–1888* (Sacramento: State Printing Office, 1888), p. 665.

64. Marcelle Ann Olsen, "The Scandinavian Immigrants in Humboldt County" (unpublished Ms., December 1973), copy in possession of author.

65. *Humboldt County Historical Society Newsletter* 8 (January 1960): 3.

66. *Industrial Worker*, September 16, 1922, and June 25, 1924.

67. *Humboldt Standard*, September 2, 1886.

68. *Arcata Union*, October 2, 1886.

69. *Labor Enquirer*, November 20, 1886.

70. *Arcata Union*, September 25, 1886.

71. *Labor Enquirer*, November 20, 1886.

72. *Industrial Worker*, June 25, 1924.

73. *Western Watchman*, June 25, 1887.

74. *Labor Enquirer*, March 6, 1886. Cridge was not opposed to electoral participation per se by the labor movement, but he did believe that for it to be effective and meaningful, a more representative electoral system should be devised. Animated by the failure of the California Workingmen's party to secure better representation in the late 1870s, he became an influential advocate of electoral reform. His ideas were discussed quite often by the western labor press. His original work, *Voting Not Representation: A Demand for Definite Democracy and Political Evolution* (San Francisco: published by author, 1880) went through several editions. Cridge was born in Newton, England, in 1824, and emigrated with his family to Canada in 1836. By the 1840s, he was active in the Abolitionist movement in Ohio and continued to be throughout the 1850s. During the Civil War, he worked for the U.S. Secret Service, but later became chief clerk of the Inspection Division of the Quartermaster-General's office. He refused to become an American citizen until the Emancipation Proclamation. In 1877, he came to San Francisco, where he spent most of the remainder of his life as a journalist. Before his death in 1902, he spent stints in Eureka, Stockton, and San Jose as a journalist and editor. *The Star* (San Francisco), January 18, 1902.

75. *Humboldt Times*, June 15, 1886.

76. *Arcata Union*, August 14, 1886.

77. *Humboldt Standard*, August 10, 1886.

78. *Arcata Union*, August 14, 1886.

79. J. W. Timmons to Powderly, July 20, 1886; E. C. Bonstell to Powderly, July 26, 1886; George Georgeson to Powderly, July 28, 1886; Powderly Papers.

80. *Arcata Union*, August 28, 1886.

81. *Humboldt Times*, October 7, 1886.

82. *Western Watchman*, December 25, 1886.

83. Ibid., May 26, 1888.

84. Ibid., July 9, 1887.

85. Ibid., June 25, 1888.

86. Ibid., December 17, 1887.

87. Ibid., March 17, October 25, and November 8, 1890.

88. Calculated from Garlock, *Guide to the Local Assemblies of the Knights of Labor*. This undoubtedly understates the scope and number of lumber workers who joined the Knights, since many joined mixed assemblies.

89. Ibid.

90. *Western Watchman*, January 8, 1887.

91. Diary of James Beith, vol. 8, pp. 67–68, August 25, 1887.

92. *Coast Seamen's Journal*, December 4, 1889.

Chapter 6

1. The role of paternalism and deference in shaping labor relations has received relatively little attention from American social historians. The subject has been treated in depth in studies of North American slavery, notably Eugene Genovese, *Roll, Jordan, Roll: The World Slaves Made* (New York: Pantheon, 1974). Among the works dealing with the topic of paternalism and deference are Thomas Dublin, *Women at Work: The Transformation of Work and Community in Lowell, Massachusetts, 1826–1860* (New York: Columbia University Press, 1979); Melton McLaurin, *Paternalism and Protest* (Westport, Conn.: Greenwood Press, 1971); Anthony F. C. Wallace, *Rockdale, The Growth of an American Village in the Early Industrial Revolution* (New York: Random House, 1978); Jonathan Prude, *The Coming of Industrial Order: Town and Factory in Rural Massachusetts, 1810–1860* (Cambridge, England: Cambridge University Press, 1983); Stanley Buder, *Pullman: An Experiment in Industrial Order and Community Planning, 1880–1930* (New York: Oxford University Press, 1967); Philip Scranton, "Varieties of Paternalism: Industrial Structures and the Social Relations of Production in American Textiles," *American Quarterly* 36 (Summer 1984): 235–257. British social historians have studied paternalism and deference in more depth. Especially notable for their breadth and depth are Howard Newby, *The Deferential Worker: A Study of Farm Workers in East Anglia* (London: Penguin, 1977), and Patrick Joyce, *Work, Society, and Politics: The Culture of the Factory in Later Victorian England* (London: Harvester Press, 1980).

2. *Humboldt Times*, February 11, 1882.

3. Ibid.

4. *Humboldt Standard*, June 26, 1908.

5. *Western Watchman*, July 18, 1896.

6. *Humboldt Standard*, September 2, 1890; *Humboldt Times*, September 2, 1890.

7. *Coast Seamen's Journal*, September 10, 1890.

8. *Industrial Worker*, June 25, 1924.

9. *Western Watchman*, June 11, 1892.

10. *Humboldt Standard*, August 27, 1890.

11. Ibid., September 2, 1890.

12. *Western Watchman*, September 6, 1890.

13. Ibid.

14. Ibid., September 2, 1881.

15. Eugene B. Fountain, *The Story of Blue Lake* (n.p., n.d), vol. 2, p. 228.

16. J. C. Blake, "Pioneers I Remember," *Humboldt County Historical Society Newsletter* 11 (July–August 1963): 5–7.

17. On the important and integrative role played by fraternal orders, see Don H. Doyle, *The Social Order of a Frontier Community: Jacksonville, Illinois, 1825–1870* (Urbana: University of Illinois Press, 1978), and his article, "The Social Functions of Voluntary Associations in a Nineteenth-Century American Town," *Social Science History* 1 (Spring 1977): 333–355.

18. *Times-Telephone*, December 1, 1883: *Humboldt Times*, September 14, 1889, and September 9, 1895; *Humboldt Standard*, July 25, 1893.

19. *Humboldt Times*, September 14, 1889.

20. *Humboldt Standard*, April 26, 1919.

21. Ibid., June 23, 1899.

22. Ibid., August 6, 1907.

23. Ibid., September 2, 1899.

24. Ralph C. Frost, "Boyhood Memories of the Elk River," *Humboldt County Historical Society Newsletter* 13 (March–April 1965): 5–7.

25. Roy Rosenzweig concludes that in Worcester, Massachusetts, although Independence Day was an occasion for the working class to affirm the values of mutuality, reciprocity, collectivity, and community, it was also an event at which workers affirmed their ethnic and religious autonomy and behaved in a boisterous and unruly fashion. Roy Rosenzweig, *Eight Hours for What We Will: Workers and Leisure in an Industrial City, 1870–1920* (Cambridge, England: Cambridge University Press, 1983). There is no evidence that this was the case in Humboldt County.

26. *Democratic Standard*, May 29, 1880.

27. *Humboldt Times*, May 2, 1881.

28. *Western Watchman*, June 1, 1889.

29. Ibid., July 5, 1890.

30. *Humboldt Times*, July 11, 1874.

31. *Humboldt Standard*, July 2, 1898.

32. *Arcata Union*, September 22, 1888.

33. *Humboldt Standard*, June 16, 1899.

34. Genovese, *Roll, Jordan, Roll.*

35. *Humboldt Standard*, June 16, 1899.

36. Dolbeer and Carson Records, Bancroft Library.

37. Dolbeer and Carson Records, vol. 27, p. 229, letter of Milton Carson, December 20, 1913.

38. *Humboldt Standard*, December 24, 1904.

39. Dolbeer and Carson Records, vol. 31, p. 20; letter of William Carson, December 23, 1903.

40. Ibid., vol. 26, p. 3, letter of William Carson, October 12, 1909.

41. Ibid., vol. 33, p. 140, letter of Milton Carson, February 21, 1911.

42. *Humboldt Standard*, February 20, 1912.

43. Ibid., February 20 and 27, 1912.

44. Fountain, *Story of Blue Lake*, vol. 4, pp. 665–666.

45. *Humboldt Times*, October 15, 1897.

46. Ibid., December 2, 1897.

47. Ibid., May 6, 1904.

48. *Western Watchman*, July 30, 1892.

49. *Humboldt Standard*, September 12, 1890.

50. *Humboldt Times*, April 30, May 6, 1892.

51. *Western Watchman*, May 7, 1892.

52. Ibid.

53. *Nerve*, April 27, 1892.

54. *Western Watchman*, May 21, 1892.

55. *Humboldt Times*, May 15, 1892.

56. *Western Watchman*, May 21, 1892.

57. Ibid.

58. *Coast Seamen's Journal*, May 25, 1892.

59. *Humboldt Times*, January 26, 1893.

60. Stephen Mallory White Papers, Stanford University, Ms. 35, Folder 35, F. A. Cutler to White, October 28, 1890.

61. John Gaventa, *Power and Powerlessness: Quiescence and Rebellion in an Appalachian Valley* (Oxford, England: Clarendon Press, 1980), p. 255.

Chapter 7

1. There is relatively little published work on California Populism in spite of the fact that the Populists attained considerable support in the state, electing several congressmen and more than 20 representatives to the state legislature between 1892 and 1896. The two major works are unpublished: Harold Francis Taggart, "The Free Silver Movement in California," doctoral dissertation, Stanford University, 1936; and Donald E. Walters, "Populism in California," doctoral dissertation, University of California, Berkeley, 1952. Two books on California history and politics contain useful chapters on California

Populism: Royce D. Delmatier, Clarence F. McIntosh, and Earl G. Waters, *The Rumble of California Politics, 1848–1970* (New York: Wiley, 1970); and Michael P. Rogin and John L. Shover, *Political Change in California: Critical Elections and Social Movements, 1890–1966* (Westport, Conn.: Greenwood Press, 1969). By contrast, a host of studies of the national Populist movement and in various states, too numerous to cite in full, have been published. Among the most recent and useful studies published are Robert C. McMath, *Populist Vanguard: A History of the Southern Farmers' Alliance* (Chapel Hill: University of North Carolina Press, 1975); Lawrence Goodwyn, *Democratic Promise: The Populist Moment in America* (New York: Oxford University Press, 1976); Bruce Palmer, *"Man Over Money": The Southern Populist Critique of American Capitalism* (Chapel Hill: University of North Carolina Press, 1980); Steven Hahn, *The Roots of Southern Populism: Yeoman Farmers and the Transformation of the Georgia Upcountry, 1850–1890* (New York: Oxford University Press, 1983). For a critical review of the recent literature on American Populism, see James Turner, "Understanding the Populists," *Journal of American History* 67 (September 1980): 354–373.

2. California contained between one-third and one-half of the Nationalist Clubs in America. In May 1889, 48 of the 113 Nationalist Clubs in the nation were in California. See Walters, "Populism in California," p. 20.

3. *Arcata Union*, January 11, 1890.

4. *Western Watchman*, January 18, 1890.

5. *Coast Seamen's Journal*, December 4, 1889, and February 12, 1890.

6. *Western Watchman*, June 21, 1890.

7. Ibid., November 29, 1890.

8. Ibid., January 10, 1891.

9. *Humboldt Times*, February 14, 1891; *Western Watchman*, February 21, 1891.

10. *Nerve*, April 16, 1892.

11. U.S. Bureau of the Census, *Report on Real Estate Mortgages in the United States at the Eleventh Census, 1890* (Washington, D.C.: GPO, 1895), vol. 12, table 56, p. 135.

12. U.S. Bureau of the Census, *Report on Farms and Homes: Proprietorship and Indedtedness in the United States at the Eleventh Census, 1890* (Washington, D.C.: GPO, 1896), vol. 13, table 108, p. 432.

13. In 1880, however, in a similar journey through the county, Ayres regaled his readers with tales of the farmers' hardships.

14. *Western Watchman*, August 13, 1892; February 23 and May 18, 1895.

15. E. J. Wickson, "Dairying in California," U.S. Department of Agriculture, Bulletin 14 (Washington, D.C.: GPO, 1896).

16. *Transactions of the California State Agriculture Society During the Year 1895* (Sacramento: State Printing Office, 1896), p. 20.

17. *Humboldt Times*, January 3, 1895.

18. *Humboldt County Souvenir* (Eureka: Times Publishing, 1904), p. 96.

19. Goodwyn, *Democratic Promise*, p. 541.

20. For an article critical of Goodwyn's thesis, see **Stanley B. Parsons et al.**, "The Role of Cooperatives in the Development of the Movement Culture of Populism," *Journal of American History* 69 (March 1983): 866–885.

21. *Western Watchman*, June 20, 1891.

22. Ibid., July 16, 1891.

23. Ibid., January 2 and May 7, 1892.

24. Ibid., December 19, 1891.

25. Ibid., January 16, 1892.

26. Ibid., February 16, 1895.

27. Ibid., June 20, 1891.

28. Ibid., April 22, 1893.

29. All four essays were reprinted in the *Western Watchman*, February 13, 1892.

30. *Western Watchman*, April 16, 1892.

31. Ibid., June 2, 1894.

32. Ibid., July 21, 1894.

33. Alexander B. Callow, "The Legislature of a Thousand Scandals," *Historical Society of Southern California Quarterly* 9 (December 1957): 332–344.

34. *Pacific Rural Press*, October 24, 1891.

35. *Western Watchman*, July 23, 1892.

36. Besides Willsie and Ayres, several Greenbackers occupied leadership positions in the county Alliance and People's party.

37. A biographical sketch of all Populist candidates appeared in the *Western Watchman*, August 20, 1892.

38. *Western Watchman*, July 30, 1892; *Nerve*, October 29, 1892.

39. The official election results were published in the *Western Watchman*, November 19, 1892. Voting statistics for other California counties were calculated from data in Walter Dean Burnham, *Presidential Ballots, 1836–1892* (Baltimore: Johns Hopkins University Press, 1955).

40. *Western Watchman*, December 28, 1889.

41. Ibid., January 11, 1890.

42. *Nerve*, October 29, 1892.

43. *Humboldt Times*, December 28, 1893.

44. *Nerve*, July 9, 1892.

45. *Western Watchman*, April 30, 1892.

46. Ibid., August 5, 1893.

47. *Humboldt Standard*, August 2, 1893.

48. *Arcata Union*, August 5, 1893.

49. *Humboldt Standard*, May 4, 1894.

50. *Western Watchman*, November 28, 1896, and June 16, 1897; *Humboldt Times*, July 1, 1896.

51. *Western Watchman*, May 12, 1894.

52. Ibid., August 19, 1893.

53. *Humboldt Standard*, January 15, 1895.

54. Ibid., December 21, 1894.

55. *Western Watchman*, July 14, 1894.
56. *Humboldt Times*, July 13, 1894; *Humboldt Standard*, July 12, 1894.
57. *Western Watchman*, July 14, 1894.
58. Ibid.
59. Ibid., November 10, 1894.
60. Ibid., January 27, 1894.
61. Ibid., August 18, 1894.
62. Ibid., September 1, 1894.
63. Ibid., April 1, 1893.
64. Delmatier et al., *Rumble of California Politics*, p. 115.
65. Walters, "Populism in California," p. 299.
66. *Western Watchman*, January 19, 1895.
67. Ibid., February 22, 1896.
68. Ibid., January 21, 1893.
69. *Humboldt Times*, October 7, 1892.
70. *Times-Telephone*, August 22, 1888.
71. Ibid., April 4, 1888.
72. Ibid., September 1, 1888.
73. Ibid., October 13, 1888.
74. *Humboldt Times*, December 31, 1893 and November 2, 1894.
75. Ibid., August 28, 29; October 1, 10, 11, and 17, 1896.
76. Ibid., September 24, 1896.
77. Ibid., October 15, 1896.
78. The Humboldt County Republicans broke with the California Republican party by opposing free silver. All three parties in California favored free silver. See Harold F. Taggart, "California and the Silver Question in 1895," *Pacific Historical Review* 6 (September 1937): 249–269.
79. *Western Watchman*, August 29, 1896.
80. Ibid., October 31, 1896.
81. *Humboldt Times*, August 14 and 22, 1896; *Humboldt Standard*, October 5, 1896.
82. *Humboldt Standard*, September 12, 1896.
83. *Humboldt Times*, September 22, 1896.
84. Ibid., September 24, 1896.
85. Ibid., October 15, 1896.
86. Ibid., September 1, 1896.
87. *Humboldt Standard*, September 11, 1896.
88. *Western Watchman*, November 14, 1896.
89. Ibid., February 27, 1897.

Chapter 8

1. Between 1897 and 1904, membership in American trade unions increased from 440,000 to 2,067,000. The growth of the California labor move-

ment was even more spectacular. Between 1900 and 1904 alone, the number of unions in California increased from 217 to 805, and union membership went from 30,000 to an estimated 110,000. *Tenth Biennial Report, California Bureau of Labor Statistics, 1901–1902* (Sacramento: State Printing Office, 1902), pp. 77–78; *Eleventh Biennial Report, California Bureau of Labor Statistics, 1902–1904* (Sacramento: State Printing Office, 1904), p. 48. Studies of California labor history have focused primarily on San Francisco and Los Angeles, although in recent years a significant amount of work on California agriculture and related industries has appeared, often in unpublished form. Much work remains to be done on California's labor movement outside its two great metropolises. On the San Francisco labor movement in the twentieth century, see Robert Knight, *Industrial Relations in the San Francisco Bay Area, 1900–1918* (Berkeley: University of California Press, 1960); Michael Kazin, *Barons of Labor: The San Francisco Building Trades and Union Power in the Progressive Era* (Urbana: University of Illinois Press, 1987). On the Los Angeles labor movement, see Richard S. Perry, *A History of the Los Angeles Labor Movement, 1911–1941* (Los Angeles: Institute of Industrial Relations, 1963); and Grace H. Stimson, *Rise of the Labor Movement in Los Angeles* (Berkeley: University of California Press, 1955). For a recent article focusing primarily, but not exclusively, on the history of the labor movement in San Francisco and Los Angeles, see Michael Kazin, "The Great Exception Revisited: Organized Labor and Politics in San Francisco and Los Angeles, 1870–1940," *Pacific Historical Review* 55 (August 1986): 371–402.

2. U.S. Bureau of the Census, *Twelfth Census of the United States, 1900, Statistics of Population* (Washington, D.C.: GPO, 1901), vol. 1, table 4, p. 11.

3. Ibid., table 34, pp. 738–739.

4. Eureka City Census. Findings reprinted in the *Humboldt Times*, January 13 and February 3, 1904.

5. U.S. Bureau of the Census, *Fourteenth Census of the United States, 1920, Statistics of Population* (Washington, D.C.: GPO, 1921), vol. 1, table 12, pp. 123–124.

6. Eureka City Census, 1904.

7. *Humboldt Times*, July 7, 1903.

8. Eureka City Census, 1904; *Humboldt Standard*, January 1, 1907.

9. Leigh H. Irvine, *History of Humboldt County, California* (Los Angeles: Historic Record Co., 1915), p. 113.

10. U.S. Bureau of the Census, *Twelfth Census of the United States, 1900, Statistics of Agriculture* (Washington, D.C.: GPO, 1902), vol. 5, table 44, p. 592; idem, *Thirteenth Census of the United States, 1910, Agriculture* (Washington, D.C.: GPO, 1913), vol. 5, p. 823.

11. *Humboldt Standard*, October 6, 1902. Seventeen unions were founded by early October 1902. At least three more unions formed by the end of 1902.

12. *Humboldt Times*, August 24, 1902.

13. *Oakland Enquirer*, September 23, 1902.

14. *Labor News*, October 27, 1906.

15. *Humboldt Times*, February 20, 1903.

16. Ibid., July 28, 1901, and July 31, 1902.

17. Ibid., October 11, 1902.

18. The reports of the California Bureau of Labor Statistics during the early twentieth century are a good source for comparing wage rates by occupation in different California localities.

19. Dolbeer and Carson Records, vol. 24, p. 407, letter of William Carson, July 20, 1906.

20. Elk River Mill and Lumber Company Records, vol. 25, p. 218, letter of Irving Harpster, July 20, 1906.

21. *Humboldt Standard*, February 26, 27 and March 1, 3, 1903.

22. Ibid., January 16, 1903; *Humboldt Times*, April 2, 1903; January 26 and October 25, 1904. Knight, *Industrial Relations in the San Francisco Bay Area*, provides examples of similar practices.

23. There are two good articles, however, analyzing the role of republican ideology in the Homestead strike of 1892: Linda Schneider, "The Citizen Striker: Worker Ideology in the Homestead Strike of 1892," *Labor History* 23 (Winter 1982): 47–66; Paul Krause, "Labor Republicanism and 'Za Chlebom': Anglo-American and Slavic Solidarity in Homestead," in *"Struggle a Hard Battle": Essays on Working-Class Immigrants*, ed. Dirk Hoerder (DeKalb: Northern Illinois University Press, 1986), pp. 143–169.

24. *Humboldt Times*, March 29, 1903.

25. Ibid.

26. Ibid.

27. *Arcata Union*, March 21, 1906.

28. *Labor News*, July 7, 1906.

29. Ibid.

30. Ibid.

31. Ibid., October 7, 1905.

32. Ibid., July 7, 1906.

33. Ibid.

34. Ibid., December 15, 1906.

35. Ibid., December 1, 1906.

36. Ibid., January 20, 1906.

37. *Humboldt Standard*, July 11, 1906.

38. *Labor News*, May 12, 1906.

39. Ibid., December 29, 1906.

40. Ibid., December 23, 1905.

41. Ibid., October 28, 1905.

42. *Humboldt Times*, September 5, 1905; *Labor News*, September 9, 1905.

43. *Labor News*, May 6, 1905. *Labor News* reported that by May 1905, 1,500 lumber workers were union members "with 1,102 obligated." In 1906, there is little doubt that the IBWSW increased its membership.

44. A good example of such a contract was reprinted in *Labor News*, June 9, 1906.

45. *Humboldt Times*, July 3, 1903; *Labor News*, June 9, 1906.

46. *Humboldt Times*, August 2, 1901.

47. *Labor News*, April 1, 1905.

48. *Humboldt Times*, September 23, 1902.

49. *Humboldt Standard*, August 3, 1906; *Labor News*, August 4, 1906.

50. *Humboldt Standard*, January 9, 1905.

51. Ibid., December 21, 1903.

52. *Humboldt Times*, June 28, 1904.

53. Ibid., December 28, 1902.

54. *Humboldt Standard*, June 13, 1904.

55. *Labor News*, December 29, 1906.

56. Ibid., March 3, 1906.

57. Ibid., March 10, 1906.

58. *Humboldt Standard*, September 9, 1903.

59. Minutes of the Eureka Trades Council, June 3, 1909.

60. *Humboldt Times*, January 4, 1905; *Labor News*, February 25, November 25, and December 30, 1905.

61. *Labor News*, July 22, 1905.

62. Ibid., April 15 and November 25, 1905.

63. Ibid., November 25, 1905.

64. Ibid.

65. *Humboldt Times*, August 24, 1902.

66. Ibid., October 5 and 9, 1902.

67. Ibid., January 13, 1903.

68. Ibid., February 20, 1903.

69. *Humboldt Standard*, April 20, 1903.

70. *Humboldt Times*, May 6, 1903.

71. Ibid.

72. Ibid., May 8 and June 27, 1903.

73. *Humboldt Standard*, June 9, 1903.

74. *Humboldt Times*, June 16, 1905.

75. *Labor News*, June 24, 1905.

76. Ibid., September 4, 1906.

77. *Labor News*, November 11, 1905.

78. Ibid.

79. *Humboldt Times*, April 3, 1906.

80. Ibid., October 17, 1906.

Chapter 9

1. This does not include the narrow-based International Shingle Weavers Union of America, which was chartered on March 3, 1903.

2. The historical literature on American lumber unionism and workers is comparatively limited in view of the industry's importance, and much of it is

dated. Among the most important monographs are Ruth A. Allen, *East Texas Lumber Workers: An Economic Picture, 1870–1950* (Austin: University of Texas Press, 1961); Charlotte Todes, *Labor and Lumber* (New York: International Publishers, 1931); Vernon Jensen, *Lumber and Labor* (New York: Holt, Rinehart & Winston, 1945); Jerry Lembcke and William M. Tattam, *One Union in Wood: A Political History of the International Woodworkers of America* (New York: International Publishers, 1984); Norman H. Clark, *Mill Town: A Social History of Everett, Washington, from Its Earliest Beginnings on the Shores of the Puget Sound to the Tragic and Infamous Event Known as the Everett Massacre* (Seattle: University of Washington Press, 1970). The tendency of books and articles on lumber workers has been to romanticize them (especially in histories of the IWW) and to portray them as both militant and excellent union material while ignoring the overall weakness of lumber trade unionism and the reasons for it. For data on the number of lumber workers organized between 1897 and 1934, see *Historical Statistics of the United States: Colonial Times to 1970* (Washington, D.C.: GPO, 1975), pt. 1, p. 178. In this period, the total number of lumber workers organized in any one year never exceeded 52,000 (1904), while the number employed annually, until at least the mid-twentieth century, exceeded 500,000. Even in 1940, after the renaissance of the American labor movement during the New Deal, and some gains by both AFL and CIO lumber unions, only 11.5 percent of the total lumber workforce was organized. George Bain and Robert Price, *Profiles of Union Growth: A Comparative Statistical Portrait of Eight Countries* (Oxford, England: Basil Blackwell, 1980), p. 95. On the incidence of strikes in the lumber industry itself, and in comparison to other industries, see Florence Peterson, *Strikes in the United States, 1880–1936* (Washington D.C.: Department of Labor Bulletin 651, 1938) and the Postcript of this book.

3. On company towns, see James B. Allen, *The Company Town in the American West* (Norman: University of Oklahoma Press, 1966).

4. Estimates of the size of the lumber workforce in Humboldt County during the early twentieth century vary from 4,000 to 5,000. An article in the *Portland Oregonian*, reprinted in the *Humboldt Times*, October 10, 1903, put the figure at 5,000, as did the *Oakland Enquirer*, September 23, 1902. The *Humboldt Standard*, in a major feature edition on the county's lumber industry, put the number at closer to 4,000. *Humboldt Standard*, January 1, 1907.

5. *Humboldt Standard*, January 1, 1907.

6. U.S. Bureau of the Census, *Census of Manufacturing, 1905* (Washington, D.C.: GPO, 1908), pt. 111, pp. 644–645.

7. Statistics compiled from *Humboldt County Souvenir* (Eureka: Times Publishing, 1904). Howard Brett Melendy, "One Hundred Years of the Redwood Lumber Industry, 1850–1950," doctoral dissertation, Stanford University, 1952, pp. 100–117, has a good account of the consolidation of the industry.

8. Dolbeer and Carson Records, vol. 23, p. 125, letter of William Carson, December 30, 1904.

9. The most comprehensive work on Hammond and the Hammond Lum-

ber Company is Lowell S. Mengell, "A History of the Samoa Division and Its Predecessors, 1853–1973" (unpublished manuscript, 1974, Humboldt State University Library). See also Gage McKinney, "A. B. Hammond, West Coast Lumberman," *Journal of Forest History* 28 (October 1984): 196–203. Additional information on Hammond, the early years of the Hammond Lumber Company, and Samoa was obtained from *Humboldt Times*, August 31, 1900, May 17, 1902, October 28, 1903, and a series of articles on Samoa in January 1904; *Humboldt Standard*, July 16 and September 23, 1901; *Arcata Union*, May 4, 1901; *American Lumberman* 73 (January 9, 1904): 18–20; ibid., 74 (May 21, 1904): 22–23.

10. *American Lumberman* 73 (February 20, 1904): 19–21.

11. Useful descriptions of the Pacific Lumber Company and its operations in the early twentieth century were obtained from the following sources: Ben Shannon Allen, "From the Penobscot to the Eel" (unpublished ms., 1949, Humboldt State University Library); W. H. Wilde, "Chronology of the Pacific Lumber Company, 1869–1945" (unpublished ms., n.d., Bancroft Library, University of California, Berkeley); *Pacific Coast Wood and Iron* 34 (November 1900): 169–170; *American Lumberman* 73 (February 20, 1904): 19–21; *Humboldt Times*, January 15, 1909. See also Hugh Wilkerson and John Van Der Zee, *Life in the Peace Zone: An American Company Town* (New York: Collier Books, 1971); Jack Held, "Scotia: The Town of Concern," *Pacific Historian* 16 (Summer 1972): 76–92.

12. U.S. Bureau of the Census, *Eleventh Census of the United States, 1890, Report on Population of the United States* (Washington, D.C.: 1895), vol. 1, pt. 1, table 5, p. 70; idem, *Fourteenth Census of the United States, 1920, Population* (Washington, D.C.: GPO, 1921), vol. 1, table 53, p. 353.

13. *Humboldt Times*, March 26, 1913.

14. For general descriptions of the operations of the Northern Redwood Lumber Company and the town of Korbel, see *Humboldt Times*, February 3 and November 26, 1903; *American Lumberman* 73 (March 5, 1904): 16: *Pacific Coast Wood and Iron* 48 (August 1907): 11: "Korbel: The Way It Was in 1912," *Humboldt Historian* 24 (September–October 1976): 1, 4.

15. *Humboldt Times*, September 16, 17, 19, 23, and 30, 1902; *Humboldt Standard*, September 22 and October 20, 1902.

16. *Humboldt Times*, September 19 and October 15, 1902.

17. *Labor News*, September 18, 1909.

18. *Humboldt Times*, February 14, 1904.

19. Ibid., October 24, 1903.

20. Ibid., January 14, 1904.

21. Ibid., February 16, 1904.

22. *Labor News*, September 18, 1909.

23. Ibid., February 25, 1905.

24. *Humboldt Times*, January 4, 1905.

25. *Labor News*, June 17, 1905.

26. *Arcata Union*, April 19, 1905.

27. *Labor News*, April 22, 1905.

28. Elk River Mill and Lumber Company Records, vol. 23, p. 192, unsigned letter, April 15, 1905.

29. Dolbeer and Carson Records, vol. 23, p. 141, letter of William Carson, January 11, 1905.

30. *Labor News*, March 4, 1905.

31. Ibid., April 22, 1905.

32. Ibid., March 25, 1905.

33. Ibid., April 29, 1905. ⸱

34. Ibid.

35. *Humboldt Times*, April 20, 1905.

36. *Labor News*, April 1, 1905.

37. Ibid., December 30, 1905.

38. Ibid., April 29, 1905.

39. *Humboldt Standard*, June 12, 1905.

40. *Labor News*, April 21 and May 19, 26, 1906.

41. Ibid., June 2, 1906.

42. Ibid., December 5, 1905; February 3 and August 4, 1906.

43. Ibid., September 15, 1906.

44. *Proceedings of the Sixth Annual Convention of the California State Federation of Labor*, 1906, p. 54; *Labor News*, January 13, 1906.

45. *Labor News*, August 26, 1905.

46. Ibid., September 2, 1905.

47. Ibid., May 16, 1906.

48. Ibid., June 16, 1906.

49. Ibid., March 9, 1907.

50. Ibid., April 13, 1907.

51. Ibid.

52. Ibid., April 27, 1907.

53. Ibid., August 4, 1906.

54. Ibid., September 22 and 29, 1906.

55. Ibid., November 3, 1906.

56. *Humboldt Standard*, July 24 and 25, 1906; *Humboldt Times*, July 25 and 28, 1906; *Labor News*, July 28, 1906.

57. *Labor News*, August 4, 1906.

58. Ibid., December 15, 1906.

59. *American Federationist* 14 (February 1907): 107.

60. *Labor News*, November 17, 1906.

61. *Humboldt Standard*, February 11, 1907.

62. *Labor News*, February 23, 1907.

63. Hammond resided in San Francisco and was a leading member of the city's antiunion San Francisco Citizens' Alliance.

64. *Labor News*, April 14, 1906.

65. Ibid., November 17, 1906.

66. Ibid., November 10, 1906.

67. For a good narrative account of the strike, see Richard G. Willis, "The Labor Movement in Humboldt County, 1883–1910: Its Origins, Character, and Impact," master's thesis, Humboldt State University, 1970.

68. *Humboldt Times*, February 28 and April 28, 1907; *Labor News*, March 9, 1907.

69. *Labor News*, March 23 and 30, 1907; *Humboldt Times*, April 4, 1907.

70. *Labor News*, April 20, 1907.

71. Susie Baker Fountain Papers, vol. 47, p. 384, extract from *Blue Lake Advocate*, March 30, 1907.

72. Dolbeer and Carson Records, vol. 25, p. 19, letter of William Carson, April 27, 1907.

73. Ibid.

74. Elk River Mill and Lumber Company Records, vol. 26, p. 323, letter of Irving Harpster, May 2, 1907.

75. Ibid., vol. 26, p. 299, letter of Irving Harpster, April 22, 1907.

76. *Humboldt Standard*, April 29, 1907.

77. *Labor News*, May 4, 1907. The failure of the union movement to take root at the pioneer lumbering concerns was noted as early as 1905. *Labor News*, April 17, 1905.

78. *Humboldt Times*, May 2, 1907; *Arcata Union*, May 4, 1907.

79. *Humboldt Times*, May 2, 1907.

80. Dolbeer and Carson Records, vol. 25, p. 32, letter of William Carson, May 22, 1907.

81. *Humboldt Times*, May 3, 1907.

82. *Coast Seamen's Journal*, May 22, 1907.

83. *Humboldt Times*, May 23, 1907.

84. On the IWW in Humboldt County, see Jerry Willis, "The Story of the IWW in Humboldt County, 1905–1924" (unpublished ms., 1969, Humboldt State University Library).

85. *Labor News*, May 4, 1907.

86. *Industrial Union Bulletin*, May 25, 1907.

87. Ibid., June 15, 1907. For a biography of Williams, see Warren R. Van Tine, "Ben H. Williams, Wobbly Editor," master's thesis, Northern Illinois University, 1967.

88. *Humboldt Times*, May 22, 1907; *Humboldt Standard*, May 22, 1907.

89. *Humboldt Times*, May 24, 1907; *Labor News*, May 25, 1907.

90. *Humboldt Times*, May 26, 1907; *Industrial Union Bulletin*, June 15, 1907.

91. *Humboldt Times*, May 23, 30, 1907; *Humboldt Standard*, May 23, 1907; *Labor News*, May 25 and June 1, 1907.

92. *Humboldt Times*, May 23, 1907.

93. *Industrial Union Bulletin*, May 25, 1907.

94. Ibid., June 15, 1907.

95. *Labor News*, June 1, 1907.

96. *Labor News*, May 11, 1907.

97. *Humboldt Times*, May 9, 1907; *Labor News*, May 25, 1907.

98. *Labor News*, June 1, 1907.

99. *Humboldt Times*, May 29, 1907.

100. *Labor News*, June 8, 1907.

101. *Humboldt Times*, June 5, 1907.

102. Ibid.

103. *Labor News*, June 29, 1907.

104. Ibid., July 20, 1907.

105. Ibid., September 7, 1907.

106. Ibid.

107. Ibid., September 18, 1909.

108. Gary M. Fink, *Labor Unions* (Westport, Conn.: Greenwood Press, 1977), p. 390.

Chapter 10

1. *Labor News*, June 8, 1907.

2. Ibid., September 7, 1907.

3. Ibid., November 9, 1907.

4. Ibid., September 28, 1907.

5. Leigh H. Irvine, *History of Humboldt County* (Los Angeles: Historic Record Co., 1915), p. 113.

6. Ibid.

7. *Labor News*, February 15 and March 7, 1908; *Humboldt Standard*, March 23, 1908.

8. *Labor News*, February 15, 1908.

9. Ibid., May 2 and June 13, 1908.

10. Dolbeer and Carson Records, vol. 25, p. 218, letter of William Carson, February 19, 1908.

11. Ibid., vol. 25, p. 228, letter of William Carson, March 5, 1908.

12. *Labor News*, August 31 and September 7, 1907.

13. Ibid., August 28, 1909.

14. The Pacific Lumber Company announced it would build its own hospital, while the Hammond and Northern Redwood companies offered an insurance plan using the county's existing hospital facilities.

15. Dolbeer and Carson Records, vol. 25, p. 228, letter of William Carson, March 5, 1908.

16. *Humboldt Times*, May 1, 1908; *Labor News*, November 19, 1910. In spite of the decision, the Union Labor Hospital flourished for many years.

17. *Labor News*, July 3, 1909.

18. *Arcata Union*, September 9, 1920.

19. *Labor News*, May 30, 1908; July 23, 1910; September 30, 1911.

20. Ibid., September 30, 1911.

21. *Industrial Worker*, May 15, 1913.

22. Ibid., September 17, 1910; July 20, 1911; and December 26, 1912.

23. *Labor News*, April 30, 1910.

24. Ibid., March 12, 1910.

25. Ibid., January 8, 1910, and July 12, 1913; *Arcata Union*, April 22, 1910.

26. *American Federationist* 14 (September 1907): 691.

27. *Industrial Worker*, November 16, 1911; January 4 and August 11, 1912; May 1 and 15, 1913.

28. Ibid., January 4, 1912.

29. *Labor News*, October 8, 1910.

30. Ibid., July 12, 1913.

31. Ibid., March 19, 1910. Unfortunately, there are no data on money wage rates in the Humboldt County lumber industry in the twentieth century. Wage increases and cuts were sometimes reported in the local press. There are no reports of general increases in lumber workers' wages before 1917. Given the steady rate of inflation in the Progressive era, it seems almost certain that real wages declined.

32. *Labor News*, January 16, 1909.

33. Ibid., May 30, 1908.

34. Ibid., July 29, 1911.

35. Ibid., May 2 and 16, 1908; July 10, 1909; August 20 and October 1, 1910; January 7 and April 15, 1911.

36. Eureka's population grew from 7,327 in 1900 to 11,111 in 1904, and to 12,147 by 1908. The population of Eureka in 1904 and 1908 was determined by city censuses. The results were published in the *Humboldt Times*, January 13, 1904, and January 15, 1908.

37. *Labor News*, May 9, 1908.

38. Ibid., May 22, 1909.

39. Ibid., May 15, 1909.

40. *Humboldt Times*, June 1, 2, 3, and 4, 1909.

41. Ibid., June 2, 1909.

42. *Labor News*, July 10, 1909; *Humboldt Times*, July 4, 1909.

43. *Humboldt County Souvenir* (Eureka: Times Publishing, 1904), pp. 194–198.

44. *Humboldt Times*, July 4, 1909; *Labor News*, July 10, 1909.

45. *Labor News*, August 21, 1909.

46. *Eureka Herald*, September 7 and 10, 1909.

47. *Humboldt Times*, October 5, 1909.

48. *Eureka Herald*, February 25, 1910.

49. *Labor News*, January 29, 1910.

50. Ibid., July 23, 1910.

51. Minutes of the Eureka Trades Council, July 15, 1909.

52. *Labor News*, July 10, 1909.

53. Ibid., September 11, 1909.

54. Ibid., December 18, 1909.

55. *Humboldt Times*, January 5, 1911.

56. Ibid., January 6, 1911.

57. Ibid., January 8, 1911.

58. *Proceedings of the Thirteenth Annual Convention of the California State Federation of Labor*, 1912, pp. 85–86.

59. On California politics in the Progressive era, see Michael Rogin and John L. Shover, *Political Change in California: Critical Elections and Social Movements, 1890–1966* (Westport, Conn.: Greenwood Press, 1970), 35–89; Royce Delmatier et al., *The Rumble of California Politics, 1848–1970* (New York: Wiley, 1970), pp. 165–191; Michael Kazin, *Barons of Labor: The San Francisco Building Trades and Union Power in the Progressive Era* (Urbana: University of Illinois Press, 1987).

60. *Labor News*, September 12, 1908.

61. Ibid., October 31, 1908.

62. Ibid., October 29 and November 5, 1910.

63. In tabulating the Socialists by occupation, more than 100 occupational categories were listed in the Register of Voters, most of them working-class occupations. The table, therefore, understates the number of working-class people who registered as Socialists.

64. Besides strong branches of the Socialist party in Eureka, Arcata, and Fortuna, reference was found to branches in the rural townships of Loleta, Falk, Petrolia, and Shower's Pass.

65. *Eureka Herald*, January 19, 1910.

66. *Industrial Worker*, September 28, 1911.

67. Ibid.

68. Ibid., November 2, 1910.

69. *Humboldt Standard*, May 14, 1914.

70. *Labor News*, September 23, October 28, and December 2, 1911.

71. *Humboldt Times*, December 5, 1911.

72. *Humboldt Standard*, June 23, 1909.

73. *Humboldt Times*, June 21, 1911.

74. *Labor News*, April 20, 1912.

75. Ibid., May 18, 1912.

76. Ibid., March 4, 1911.

77. Ibid., December 17, 1910.

78. Ibid., June 15 and July 27, 1912.

79. Ibid., January 6, 1912.

80. *Humboldt Times*, April 4, 1912.

81. Ibid., August 7, 1912.

82. Ibid., October 16, 1912.

83. Ibid., July 10, 1912.

84. *Humboldt Beacon*, June 28, 1912.

85. *Labor News*, October 5, 1912.

86. Ibid., November 30, 1912.

87. For a biographical sketch of Elijah Falk, see Irvine, *History of Humboldt County*, pp. 339–340.

88. *Labor News*, July 17, 1915.

89. Ibid.

90. *Humboldt Standard*, April 10, 1915.

91. Ibid., April 15, 1915.

92. *Labor News*, December 1, 1916.

Chapter 11

1. *Proceedings of the Thirteenth Annual Convention of the California State Federation of Labor*, 1912, p. 82.

2. *Proceedings of the Fourteenth Annual Convention of the California State Federation of Labor*, 1913, p. 67.

3. *Labor News*, May 24, 1913.

4. Ibid., March 6, 1915.

5. Ibid.

6. Ibid., October 16, 1915.

7. *Industrial Worker*, August 27, 1910.

8. Ibid.

9. Ibid., October 8 and November 2, 1910.

10. Ibid., January 5, 1911.

11. Ibid., February 2, 1911.

12. Ibid., July 6, 1911.

13. Ibid., December 26, 1912.

14. Ibid., May 29, 1913.

15. According to the *Industrial Worker*, the largest response to the strike call came from 1,000 paper mill workers in Oregon. Elsewhere, isolated groups of a few hundred lumber workers struck. The strike was called off on July 3, 1913. See *Industrial Worker*, July 10, 1913. Philip Foner, who at one point describes the lumber industry as "an ideal field for the IWW" (p. 218), acknowledges that the strike was a failure. Philip S. Foner, *The Industrial Workers of the World, 1905–1917* (New York: International Publishers, 1965), pp. 219–227.

16. *Labor News*, August 2, 1913.

17. *Humboldt Standard*, March 20, 1903; *Humboldt Times*, May 21, 1904.

18. Manuscript Census, Humboldt County Census of Population, 1910. Lumber workers residing in Hydesville and Cuddeback towns were excluded, as they almost certainly were outside the geographical orbit of the Pacific Lumber Company.

19. Archives of the Georgia-Pacific Lumber Company, Portland, Oregon, unmarked folder.

20. *Humboldt Times*, January 8, 1911.

21. Hans C. Palmer, "Italian Immigration and the Development of California Agriculture," doctoral dissertation, University of California, Berkeley, 1965, p. 155.

22. *Industrial Worker*, June 15, 1911.

23. James J. Hudson, "The McCloud River Affair of 1909: A Study in the Use of State Troops," *California Historical Quarterly* 35 (March 1956): 29–35.

24. *Sixteenth Biennial Report of the California Bureau of Labor Statistics, 1913–1914* (Sacramento: State Printing Office, 1914), pp. 74–76.

25. *Pioneer Western Lumberman* (San Francisco) 56 (July 15, 1911): 21.

26. *Proceedings of the Twelfth Annual Convention of the California State Federation of Labor*, 1911, pp. 64–65.

27. *Proceedings of the Thirteenth Annual Convention of the California State Federation of Labor*, 1912, p. 61.

28. *Sixteenth Biennial Report of the California Bureau of Labor Statistics, 1913–1914*, p. 74.

29. *Labor News*, January 8, 1910.

30. Hudson, "The McCloud River Affair of 1909."

31. Edwin Fenton, *Immigrants and Unions, a Case Study: Italians and American Labor, 1870–1920* (New York: Arno Press, 1975); Steve Fraser, "Dress Rehearsal for the New Deal: Shop Floor Insurgents, Political Elites, and Industrial Democracy in the Amalgamated Clothing Workers Union," in *Working Class America: Essays on Labor, Community, and American Society*, ed. Michael H. Frisch and Daniel J. Walkowitz (Urbana: University of Illinois Press, 1983), pp. 212–255. Despite the fact that the San Francisco labor movement was among the most powerful in the nation in the first decade of the twentieth century and that Italians were a significant segment of the population, they do not appear to have joined the labor movement in very large numbers. See Robert Knight, *Industrial Relations in the San Francisco Bay Area, 1900–1918* (Berkeley: University of California Press, 1960); Dino Cinel, *From Italy to San Francisco: The Immigrant Experience* (Stanford: Stanford University Press, 1982).

32. Julio J. Rovai, *Rio Dell–(Wildwood): As I Saw It in the Early Twenties* (published by author, 1979), pp. 5–7. Aileen Kraditor has argued forcefully that many American immigrant groups accepted employer hegemony in return for "relative autonomy" in their ethnic enclaves. Insofar as the argument has merit, it may fit the Italians better than most immigrant groups. Aileen Kraditor, *The Radical Persuasion, 1880–1917: Aspects of the Intellectual History and Historiography of Three American Radical Organizations* (Baton Rouge: Louisiana State University Press, 1981).

33. *Labor News*, May 3, 1913; *Industrial Worker*, May 15, 1913.

34. *Industrial Worker*, November 25, 1922.

35. Cinel, *From Italy to San Francisco*, p. 63.

36. *Labor News*, January 8 and July 23, 1910; July 12, 1913; February 28, 1914. *Sixteenth Biennial Report of the California Bureau of Labor Statistics, 1913–1914*, p. 66.

37. *Pioneer Western Lumberman* 56 (July 15, 1911): 21.

38. *Pioneer Western Lumberman* 62 (December 15, 1914): 16–17.

39. *Proceedings of the Sixth Annual Session, Pacific Logging Congress, 1914*, p. 3. Labor historians have given relatively little attention to the introduction of incentive and piece-rate systems of wage payment in the 1910s and

1920s. See, however, Ronald W. Schatz, *The Electrical Workers: A History of Labor at General Electric and Westinghouse, 1923–60* (Urbana: University of Illinois Press, 1983), pp. 22–23. The contemporary literature on these new bonus plans is fascinating: J. K. Louden, *Wage Incentives* (New York: Wiley, 1944); Stewart M. Lowry, Harold B. Maynard, and G. J. Stegemerten, *Time and Motion Study and Formulas for Wage Incentives* (New York: McGraw-Hill, 1927); *Financial Incentives: A Study of Methods for Stimulating Achievement in Industry* (New York: National Industrial Conference Board, 1935).

40. *Proceedings of the Eighth Annual Session, Pacific Logging Congress, 1916*, pp. 9–10.

41. Ibid., p. 31.

42. *Labor News*, July 20, 1918.

43. *Proceedings of the Fourteenth Annual Session, Pacific Logging Congress, 1923*, p. 35.

44. *Labor News*, July 20, 1918; *Labor Clarion*, August 16, 1918.

45. *Proceedings of the Fourteenth Annual Session, Pacific Logging Congress, 1923*, pp. 35–36.

46. *Proceedings of the Fourth Annual Session, Pacific Logging Congress, 1912*, p. 5.

47. The secondary literature on welfare capitalism is sparse, but see Stuart D. Brandes, *American Welfare Capitalism, 1880–1940* (Chicago: University of Chicago Press, 1976); and David Brody, "The Rise and Decline of Welfare Capitalism," in John Braeman et al., *Change and Continuity in Twentieth Century America* (Columbus: Ohio University Press, 1968), pp. 147–178. On the subjects of welfare capitalism, ethnic clannishness, and the brittleness of trade unionism, see Tamara K. Hareven and Randolph Langenbach, *Amoskeag: Life and Work in an American Factory-City* (New York: Pantheon, 1978).

48. *Proceedings of the Second Annual Session, Pacific Logging Congress, 1910*, p. 28.

49. *Proceedings of the Fourth Annual Session, Pacific Logging Congress, 1912*, p. 18.

50. Edwin Van Sycle, *They Tried to Cut It All: Grays Harbor—Turbulent Years of Greed and Greatness* (Seattle: Pacific Search Press, 1980), p. 77.

51. *Pioneer Western Lumberman* 72 (November 15, 1919): 17.

52. *Pioneer Western Lumberman* 62 (November 15, 1914): 25.

53. *Industrial Worker*, January 30, 1913.

54. *Pioneer Western Lumberman* 56 (July 15, 1911): 21.

55. Ibid.

56. Records of the Pacific Lumber Company, Bancroft Library, C-G 95, carton 4, "Calendar of Events in the History of the Pacific Lumber Company."

57. *Collier's National Weekly* 50 (March 15, 1913): 28.

58. *Humboldt Beacon*, September 8, 1916.

59. Pacific Lumber Company, *Scotia: The Model Town* (Pacific Lumber Company, Scotia, 1929).

60. *Humboldt Times*, April 1, 1909.

61. *Eureka Herald*, March 3, 1910; Records of the Pacific Lumber Company, Carton 3, Folder 2.

62. *Humboldt Beacon*, December 8, 1911.

63. *Pioneer Western Lumberman* 65 (April 1, 1916): 15.

64. *American Lumberman* 73 (January 9, 1904); *Humboldt Times*, October 28, 1903, and January 7, 12, 16, 17, and 26, 1904.

65. Recollections of Elsie Miller, 1953, transcripts, Bancroft Library.

66. *Humboldt Standard*, January 13, 1921.

67. *Humboldt Beacon*, August 8, 1913.

68. *Humboldt Times*, July 6, 1914.

69. Ibid., November 23, 1917.

70. Ibid., March 13, 1918.

71. One study estimated that it cost $75 per replacement. *Four L Bulletin*, February 1922 *et seq.*, F. B. Gibson, "What Does Labor Turnover Cost." Cited in Cloice R. Howd, *Industrial Relations in the West Coast Lumber Industry*, Bureau of Labor Statistics, Bulletin 349 (Washington, D.C.: GPO, 1924), p. 39.

72. In the late 1910s and the 1920s, labor turnover became an increasing concern of employers. This is partially reflected in the secondary-source literature written on the subject: Paul F. Brissenden and Emil Frankel, *Labor Turnover in Industry: A Statistical Analysis* (New York: Macmillan, 1922); Sumner H. Slichter, *The Turnover of Factory Labor* (New York: Appleton, 1919).

73. *Sixteenth Biennial Report of the California Bureau of Labor Statistics, 1913–1914*, p. 64.

74. Howd, *Industrial Relations in the West Coast Lumber Industry*, p. 38.

75. Harold M. Hyman, *Soldiers of Spruce: Origins of the Loyal Legion of Loggers and Lumbermen* (Los Angeles: Institute of Industrial Relations, University of California, 1963), p. 112.

76. *Humboldt Beacon*, June 28, 1918.

77. Claudia Wood, "History of the Pacific Lumber Company, 1862–1955" (unpublished ms., 1956, Humboldt State University Library); Ben Shannon Allen, "From the Penobscot to the Eel" (unpublished ms., 1949, San Francisco), chap. 26, p. 7.

78. *Industrial Worker*, November 25, 1922.

79. *Proceedings of the Third Annual Session, Pacific Logging Congress, 1911*, pp. 50–51.

80. *Proceedings of the Fourth Annual Session, Pacific Logging Congress, 1912*, p. 18.

81. *Humboldt Times*, July 18, 1913; *Labor News*, July 19, 1913.

82. *Humboldt Times*, July 6, 1919.

83. Ibid., June 18, 1920.

84. Ibid., May 13, 1920.

85. Ibid., January 4, 1921.

86. Daniel Nelson, *Managers and Workers: The Origins of the New Factory System in the United States, 1880–1920* (Madison: University of Wisconsin Press, 1975), p. 137.

87. The Camp Sanitation Act of 1913 stated that bunkhouses, tents, and other sleeping places were to be kept in a "cleanly state," free from vermin "and matter of an infectious and contagious nature." Every bunkhouse had to be well ventilated and the bunks made of iron or canvas.

88. *Sixteenth Biennial Report of the California Bureau of Labor Statistics, 1913–1914*, pp. 53–54.

89. Ibid., pp. 138–139.

90. Ibid., p. 140.

91. The records of the Commission are housed at Bancroft Library.

92. *American Federationist* 25 (October 1918): 891–893.

93. *Humboldt Times*, March 17, 1920.

94. Letter from Director of Camp Sanitation (unsigned) to H. W. Cole, December 19, 1921, Records of the California Commission of Immigration and Housing, carton 18, folder 12.

95. *Ninth Annual Report of the California Commission of Immigration and Housing* (Sacramento: State Printing Office, 1923), pp. 32–33.

96. Ibid.

97. *Humboldt Times*, March 17, 1920.

98. *Fifth Annual Report of the California Commission of Immigration and Housing* (Sacramento: State Printing Office, 1919), p. 31.

99. *Humboldt Times*, March 17, 1920.

100. See Samuel E. Wood, "The California Commission of Immigration and Housing: A Study of Administrative Organization and the Growth of Function," doctoral dissertation, University of California, Berkeley, 1942.

101. *American Federationist* 25 (October 1918): 891–893.

102. Hyman, *Soldiers of Spruce*; Robert Ficken, "The Wobbly Horrors: Pacific Northwest Lumbermen and the IWW, 1917–1918," *Labor History* 24 (Summer 1983): 325–341.

103. On the IWW's efforts to organize the lumber workers of the Pacific Northwest, see Robert L. Tyler, *Rebels of the Woods: The IWW in the Pacific Northwest* (Eugene: University of Oregon Books, 1967). The repression of the IWW is well described in Melvyn Dubofsky, *We Shall Be All: A History of the IWW* (New York: Quadrangle, 1967); William Preston, Jr., *Aliens and Dissenters: Federal Suppression of Radicals, 1903–1933* (Cambridge: Harvard University Press, 1963); Robert J. Goldstein, *Political Repression in Modern America: 1870 to the Present* (New York: Schenkman, 1978). Virtually nothing has been written about the activities of the IUTW in this period.

104. Julio Rovai, *Wildwood–Rio Dell: After the 1928 Fire* (published by author, 1981), pp. 3–4.

105. David M. Gordon, Richard Edwards, and Michael Reich, *Segmented Work, Divided Workers: The Historical Transformation of Labor in the United States* (New York: Cambridge University Press, 1982).

106. Elizabeth Fones-Wolf, "Industrial Recreation, the Second World War, and the Revival of Welfare Capitalism, 1934–1960," *Business History Review* 60 (Summer 1986): 232–257.

Postscript

1. *Labor News*, May 5, 1917.

2. Ibid.

3. Ibid., September 8, 1917.

4. The World War I shipbuilding venture of James Rolph alone employed 1,000 workers. Lynwood Carranco, *Redwood Lumber Industry* (San Marino, Calif.: Golden West Books, 1982), p. 99. In addition, Andrew Hammond expanded his shipbuilding labor force during the war by several hundred men.

5. *Humboldt Times*, April 30, 1917.

6. *Northern California Union Labor Gazetteer* (Eureka: Labor News Press, 1918). Copy in Bancroft Library, University of California, Berkeley.

7. See Valerie Jean Conner, *The National War Labor Board: Stability, Social Justice and the Voluntary State in World War I* (Chapel Hill: University of North Carolina Press, 1983).

8. *Industrial Worker*, July 30, 1917.

9. *Humboldt Standard*, March 1, 1918.

10. *American Federationist* 25 (June 1918): 498.

11. *Labor News*, March 15, April 26, and May 3, 1919.

12. Ibid., June 28, 1919.

13. *Labor News*, *Humboldt Times*, and *Humboldt Standard* provided detailed accounts of the strike.

14. *Humboldt Times*, January 1, 1920.

15. *Labor News*, February 3, 1920.

16. In the early 1920s, eight Wobblies were convicted and sent to prison by the Humboldt County courts and others were arrested and tried. On the persecution of the IWW there, see Jerry Willis, "The Story of the IWW in Humboldt County, 1905–1924" (unpublished ms. at Humboldt State University Library, 1969).

17. *Industrial Worker*, July 29, 1922.

18. Ibid., October 6, 1923.

19. *Industrial Pioneer* 4 (April 1924): 19–21.

20. Ibid. (June 1924): 23 and 26.

21. *Industrial Worker*, July 29, 1922.

22. Ibid., November 22, 1924.

23. Florence Peterson, *Strikes in the United States, 1880–1936* (Washington, D.C.: Department of Labor Bulletin 651, 1938), p. 38.

24. Ibid., p. 95.

25. Frank Onstine, *The Great Lumber Strike of Humboldt County 1935* (Arcata: Mercurial Enterprises, 1980).

26. The information on labor relations in Humboldt and Mendocino counties in the 1930s is from Howard Brett Melendy, "One Hundred Years of the Redwood Lumber Industry, 1850–1950," doctoral dissertation, Stanford University, 1952, pp. 331–352.

27. The fullest accounts of the IWA and the STWU's organizing efforts

are to be found in Vernon Jensen, *Lumber and Labor* (New York: Farrar & Rinehart, 1945); and Jerry Lembcke and William M. Tattam, *One Union in Wood: A Political History of the International Woodworkers of America* (New York: International Publishers, 1984).

28. See William G. Robbins, "Timber and War: An Oral History of Coos Bay, Oregon, 1940–1945," *Journal of the West* 25 (July 1986): 35–43.

29. For a brief account of the 1946–1948 strike, see Melendy, "One Hundred Years of Redwood Lumber," pp. 353–362.

30. George S. Bain and Robert Price, *Profiles of Union Growth: A Comparative Statistical Portrait of Eight Countries* (Oxford, England: Basil Blackwell, 1980), p. 95. In a frequently cited article, Clark Kerr and Abraham Siegel, "The Interindustry Propensity to Strike—An International Comparison," in *Industrial Conflict* ed. A. Kornhauser, R. Budin, and A. M. Ross (New York: McGraw-Hill, 1954), pp. 189–212, the authors put the U.S. lumber industry in the "medium-high" category for the propensity to strike in the period from 1927 to 1941 and 1942 to 1948. This assessment must be treated with some caution. The 1927 to 1941 time frame was broad and did not distinguish between the propensity to strike from 1927 to the mid-1930s and the later years when strike activity undoubtedly increased. Furthermore, Kerr and Siegel used man-days lost due to strikes as their statistical criterion. The potential for one or several major strikes to distort the picture using this criterion is obvious. It would be useful to know both the absolute number of strikes in an industry and especially the number of days lost in relation to the number of workers employed in the industry. Paul Edwards, in his book, *Strikes in the United States, 1881–1974* (New York: St. Martin's Press, 1981), uses a variety of indices to measure the incidence of strikes between 1950 and 1972. With respect to the lumber industry, of the four indices established by Edwards, only in one, the number of days lost per worker involved in strikes, could the industry be described as ranking in the "medium-high" category. See pp. 192–193.

Select Bibliography

Manuscripts

All manuscripts are in the Bancroft Library, University of California, Berkeley, unless otherwise noted.

Beith, James. Letter Book and Diary.
California Commission of Immigration and Housing. Records.
Dolbeer and Carson Lumber Company. Records.
Elk River Mill and Lumber Company. Records.
Eureka Trades Council. Official Minutes, 1909–1918. Eureka Labor Temple, Eureka, California. Copy in possession of author.
Hammond Lumber Company. Records. Oregon State Historical Society, and Archives of the Louisiana-Pacific Lumber Company, Portland, Oregon.
Haskell, Burnette. Diaries and Papers. Bancroft Library and California Historical Society Library, San Francisco.
International Workingmen's Association. Collection.
Pacific Lumber Company. Records.
Powderly Papers. Catholic University, Washington, D.C.
U.S. Bureau of the Census, Schedules of Manufactures for Humboldt County, California, 1860–1880.
U.S. Bureau of the Census, Schedules of Population for Humboldt County, California, 1860–1910.
White, Stephen Mallory. Papers. Stanford University Library.

Public Documents and Convention Proceedings

California. Bureau of Labor Statistics. *Biennial Reports*. Sacramento: State Printing Office, 1883–1926.
California. *California Commission of Immigration and Housing Annual Reports*. Sacramento: State Printing Office, 1914–1924.
California. Surveyor General's Office. *Reports of the Surveyor General*. Sacramento: State Printing Office, 1854–1882.
Great Register of Voters for Humboldt County, California. 1871–1920. Complete set of records at California State Library, Sacramento.
Proceedings of the California State Federation of Labor, 1900–1926.

Proceedings of the Pacific Logging Congress, 1910–1926.
U.S. Bureau of the Census. *Historical Statistics of the United States: Colonial Times to 1970*. Washington, D.C.: GPO, 1975.
————. *Agricultural Statistics*. Washington, D.C.: GPO, various censuses.
————. *Census of Manufacturing*. Washington, D.C.: GPO, various censuses.
————. *Statistics of Population*. Washington, D.C.: GPO, 1860–1920.
————. Land Office. *Reports of the Commissioner of the General Land Office*. Washington, D.C.: GPO, 1880–1890.

Newspapers and Journals

American Federationist (Washington, D.C.), 1900–1925.
American Lumberman (Chicago), 1900–1908.
Arcata Leader, 1879–1881.
Arcata Union, 1886–1922.
Coast Seamen's Journal (San Francisco), 1887–1920.
Daily Evening Signal (Eureka), 1876–1880.
Democratic Standard (Eureka), 1877–1883.
Eureka Herald, 1908–1912.
Ferndale Enterprise, 1878–1910.
Humboldt Beacon (Fortuna), 1907–1922.
Humboldt Standard (Eureka), 1875–1922.
Humboldt Times (Eureka), 1854–1885 and 1887–1920; *Times-Telephone*, 1885–1886.
Industrial Pioneer (Chicago), 1921–1926.
Industrial Worker (Seattle), 1909–1926.
Journal of United Labor (Washington, D.C.), 1882–1890.
Labor Clarion (San Francisco), 1906–1920.
Labor Enquirer (Denver), 1882–1888.
Labor News (Eureka), 1905–1925.
Mendocino Beacon, 1883–1888.
Nerve (Eureka), 1892–1895.
Northern Independent (Eureka), 1869–1872.
Pacific Coast Wood and Iron/Pioneer Western Lumberman (San Francisco), 1884–1920.
Pacific Rural Press (San Francisco), 1873–1896.
Seattle Union Record, 1903–1921.
Shingleweaver (Everett), 1905–1910.
Truth (San Francisco), 1882–1884.
West Coast Signal (Eureka), 1871–1880.
Western Watchman (Eureka), 1886–1898.
Workmen's Advocate (New Haven), 1885–1888.

Secondary Sources

Allen, James B. *The Company Town in the American West*. Norman: University of Oklahoma Press, 1966.

Allen, Ruth A. *East Texas Lumber Workers: An Economic and Social Picture*. Austin: University of Texas Press, 1961.

Andrews, Ralph W. *Redwood Classic*. Seattle: Superior Publishing, 1958.

Bender, Thomas. *Community and Social Change in America*. New Brunswick: Rutgers University Press, 1978.

Brandes, Stuart D. *American Welfare Capitalism, 1880–1940*. Chicago: University of Chicago Press, 1976.

Brody, David. "The Rise and Decline of Welfare Capitalism." In *Change and Continuity in Twentieth Century America*, edited by John Braeman, pp. 147–178. Columbus: Ohio University Press, 1968.

————. *Workers in Industrial America: Essays on the Twentieth Century Struggle*. New York: Oxford University Press, 1980.

Buhle, Paul, and Alan Dawley, eds. *Working for Democracy: American Workers from the Revolution to the Present*. Urbana: University of Illinois Press, 1985.

Carr, Ezra. *The Patrons of Husbandry on the West Coast*. San Francisco: A. L. Bancroft, 1875.

Carr, John. *Pioneer Days in California*. Eureka: Times Publishing, 1891.

Carranco, Lynwood, and John T. Labbe. *Logging the Redwoods*. Caldwell, Idaho: Caxton Printers, 1975.

Carranco, Lynwood, ed. *The Redwood Country: History, Language, Folklore*. Dubuque, Iowa: Kendall & Hunt, 1971.

————. *Redwood Lumber Industry*. San Marino, Calif.: Golden West Books, 1982.

Cherry, Edgar. *Redwood and Lumbering in California Forests*. San Francisco: Edgar Cherry, 1884.

Cinel, Dino. *From Italy to San Francisco: The Immigrant Experience*. Stanford: Stanford University Press, 1982.

Clark, Norman H. *Mill Town: A Social History of Everett, Washington*. Seattle: University of Washington Press, 1970.

Conlin, Joseph. "'Old Boy, Did You Get Enough of Pie': A Social History of Food in Logging Camps." *Journal of Forest History* 23 (October 1979): 165–185.

Cox, Thomas R. *Mills and Markets: A History of the Pacific Coast Lumber Industry to 1900*. Seattle: University of Washington Press, 1974.

Cox, Thomas R., Robert S. Maxwell, Phillip D. Thomas, and Joseph J. Malone. *This Well-Wooded Land: Americans and Their Forests from Colonial Times to the Present*. Lincoln: University of Nebraska Press, 1985.

Coy, Owen C. *The Humboldt Bay Region, 1850–1875*. Los Angeles: California State Historical Association, 1929.

Cross, Ira B. *A History of the Labor Movement in California*. Berkeley: University of California Press, 1935.

Daniel, Cletus A. *Bitter Harvest: A History of California Farmworkers, 1870–1941*. Ithaca: Cornell University Press, 1981.

Davis, Richard C., ed. *Encyclopedia of American Forest and Conservation History*. New York: Macmillan, 1983.

———. *North American Forest History: A Guide to Archives and Manuscripts in the United States and Canada*. Santa Barbara: A.B.C., Clio Press, 1977.

Dawley, Alan. *Class and Community: The Industrial Revolution in Lynn*. Cambridge: Harvard University Press, 1976.

Delmatier, Royce D., et al. *The Rumble of California Politics, 1848–1970*. New York: Wiley, 1970.

Doyle, Don Harrison. *The Social Order of a Frontier Community: Jacksonville, Illinois, 1825–1870*. Urbana: University of Illinois Press, 1978.

Dublin, Thomas. *Women at Work: The Transformation of Work and Community in Lowell, Massachusetts, 1826–1860*. New York: Columbia University Press, 1979.

Dubofsky, Melvyn. "The Origins of Western Working Class Radicalism, 1890–1905." *Labor History* 7 (Spring 1966): 131–154.

———. *We Shall Be All: A History of the IWW*. New York: Quadrangle, 1967.

Elliott, W. W., & Co. *History of Humboldt County, California*. San Francisco: W. W. Elliott, 1881.

Fahl, Ronald, J. *North American Forest and Conservation History: A Bibliography*. Santa Barbara: A.B.C., Clio Press, 1977.

Fenton, Edwin. *Immigrants and Unions, A Case Study: Italians and American Labor, 1870–1920*. New York: Arno Press, 1975.

Faler, Paul, and Alan Dawley. "Working Class Culture and Politics in the Industrial Revolution: Sources of Loyalism and Rebellion." *Journal of Social History* 9 (June 1976): 466–480.

Faler, Paul G. *Mechanics and Manufacturers in the Early Industrial Revolution, 1780–1860*. Albany: State University of New York Press, 1981.

Ficken, Robert E. "The Wobbly Horrors: Pacific Northwest Lumbermen and the Industrial Workers of the World, 1917–1918." *Labor History* 24 (Summer 1983): 325–341.

Fine, Nathan, *Labor and Farm Parties in the United States, 1828–1928*. New York: Rand School of Social Science, 1928.

Fink, Leon. *Workingmen's Democracy: The Knights of Labor and American Politics*. Urbana: University of Illinois Press, 1983.

Foner, Eric. *Free Soil, Free Men, Free Labor: The Ideology of the Republican Party Before the Civil War*. New York: Oxford University Press, 1970.

———. *Tom Paine and Revolutionary America*. New York: Oxford University Press, 1976.

Foner, Philip S. *History of the Labor Movement in the United States*. 1947–1986. 7 vols. New York: International Publishers.

Frisch, Michael H., and Daniel J. Walkowitz, eds. *Working Class America: Essays on Labor, Community, and American Society*. Urbana: University of Illinois Press, 1983.

Fritz, Emmanuel, comp. *California Coast Redwoods: An Annotated Bibliography to and Including 1955.* San Francisco: Foundation for American Resource Management, 1957.

Garlock, Jonathan. *Guide to the Local Assemblies of the Knights of Labor.* Westport, Conn.: Greenwood Press, 1982.

Genovese, Eugene. *Roll, Jordan, Roll: The World Slaves Made.* New York: Pantheon, 1974.

Goodwyn, Lawrence. *Democratic Promise: The Populist Moment in America.* New York: Oxford University Press, 1976.

Gordon, David M., et al. *Segmented Work, Divided Workers: The Historical Transformation of Labor in the United States.* New York: Cambridge University Press, 1982.

Grassman, Curtis E. "Prologue to Progressivism: Senator Stephen M. White and the California Reform Impulse, 1875–1905." Doctoral dissertation, University of California, Los Angeles, 1970.

Green, James R. "The Brotherhood of Timber Workers, 1910–1913: A Radical Response to Industrial Capitalism in the Southern U.S.A." *Past and Present* 60 (August 1973): 161–200.

———. *The World of the Worker: Labor in Twentieth Century America.* New York: Hill & Wang, 1980.

Griffiths, David. "Anti-Monopoly Movements in California, 1873–1898." *Southern California Quarterly* 52 (June 1970): 93–121.

Grob, Gerald N. *Workers and Utopia: A Study of Ideological Conflict in the American Labor Movement, 1865–1900.* Evanston: Northwestern University Press, 1961.

Gutman, Herbert G. *Work, Culture, and Society in Industrializing America.* New York: Knopf, 1976.

Hahn, Steven. *The Roots of Southern Populism: Yeoman Farmers and the Transformation of the Georgia Upcountry, 1850–1890.* New York: Oxford University Press, 1983.

Hahn, Steven, and Jonathan Prude, eds. *The Countryside in the Age of Capitalist Transformation: Essays in the Social History of Rural America.* Chapel Hill: University of North Carolina Press, 1985.

Hareven, Tamara K., and Randolph Langenbach. *Amoskeag: Life and Work in an American Factory-City.* New York: Pantheon, 1978.

Hine, Robert V. *California's Utopian Colonies.* San Marino: Henry E. Huntington Library, 1953.

———. *Community on the American Frontier: Separate but Not Alone.* Norman: University of Oklahoma Press, 1980.

Hirsch, Susan E. *Roots of the America Working Class: The Industrialization of Crafts in Newark, 1800–1860.* Philadelphia: University of Pennsylvania Press, 1978.

Hoerder, Dirk, ed. *"Struggle a Hard Battle": Essays on Working-Class Immigrants.* DeKalb: Northern Illinois University Press, 1986.

Holbrook, Stewart H. *Holy Old Mackinaw: A Natural History of the American Lumberjack.* New York: Macmillan, 1938.

Howd, Cloice R. *Industrial Relations in the West Coast Lumber Industry.* U.S.

Bureau of Labor Statistics, Bulletin 349. Washington, D.C.: GPO, 1924.

Hyman, Harold M. *Soldiers of Spruce: Origins of the Loyal Legion of Loggers and Lumbermen*. Los Angeles: Institute of Industrial Relations, 1963.

Industrial Workers of the World. *The Lumber Industry and Its Workers*. Chicago, n.d.

Irvine, Leigh H. *History of Humboldt County, California with Biographical Sketches*. Los Angeles: Historic Record, 1915.

Ise, John. *United States Forest Policy*. New Haven: Yale University Press, 1920.

Jensen, Vernon. *Lumber and Labor*. New York: Holt, Rinehart, & Winston, 1945.

Joyce, Patrick. *Work, Society and Politics: The Culture of the Factory in Later Victorian England*. London: Harvester Press, 1980.

Katz, Michael B., et al. *The Social Organization of Early Industrial Capitalism*. Cambridge: Harvard University Press, 1982.

Kazin, Michael. *Barons of Labor: The San Francisco Building Trades and Union Power in the Progressive Era*. Urbana: University of Illinois Press, 1987.

Knight, Robert E. *Industrial Relations in the San Francisco Bay Area, 1900–1918*. Berkeley: University of California Press, 1960.

Laurie, Bruce. *Working People of Philadelphia, 1800–1850*. Philadelphia: Temple University Press, 1980.

Leab, Daniel J., ed. *The Labor History Reader*. Urbana: University of Illinois Press, 1985.

Lembcke, Jerry, and William M. Tattam. *One Union in Wood: A Political History of the International Woodworkers of America*. New York: International Publishers, 1984.

McLaurin, Melton A. *The Knights of Labor in the South*. Westport, Conn.: Greenwood Press, 1978.

McMath, Robert C. *Populist Vanguard: A History of the Southern Farmers' Alliance*. Chapel Hill: University of North Carolina Press, 1975.

Mann, Ralph. *After the Gold Rush: Society in Grass Valley and Nevada City, California, 1849–1870*. Stanford: Stanford University Press, 1982.

Melendy, Howard Brett. "One Hundred Years of the Redwood Lumber Industry, 1850–1950." Doctoral dissertation, Stanford University, 1952.

Montgomery, David. *Beyond Equality: Labor and the Radical Republicans, 1862–1872*. New York: Knopf, 1967.

——— . "Gutman's Nineteenth Century America." *Labor History* 19 (Summer 1978): 416–429.

——— . "Labor and the Republic in Industrial America: 1860–1920." *Le Mouvement Social* (April–June 1980): 201–215.

——— . "To Study the People: The American Working Class." *Labor History* 21 (Fall 1980): 485–512.

——— . *Workers' Control in America*. New York: Cambridge University Press, 1979.

Morgan, H. Wayne, ed. *The Gilded Age*. Syracuse: Syracuse University Press, 1970.

Nash, Gerald. *State Government and Economic Development: A History of Administrative Policies in California, 1849–1933.* Berkeley: Institute of Governmental Studies, 1964.

Nelson, Daniel. *Managers and Workers: The Origins of the New Factory System in the United States, 1880–1920.* Madison: University of Wisconsin Press, 1975.

Newby, Howard. *The Deferential Worker: A Study of Farm Workers in East Anglia.* London: Penguin, 1977.

Nugent, Walter T. K. *Money and American Society, 1865–1880.* New York: Free Press, 1968.

Oestreicher, Richard J. *Solidarity and Fragmentation: Working People and Class Consciousness in Detroit, 1875–1900.* Urbana: University of Illinois Press, 1986.

Palmer, Bruce, *"Man Over Money": The Southern Populist Critique of American Capitalism.* Chapel Hill: University of North Carolina Press, 1980.

Palmer, Bryan D., and Gregory S. Kealey. *Dreaming of What Might Be: The Knights of Labor in Ontario, 1880–1900.* New York: Cambridge University Press, 1982.

Pessen, Edward. *Most Uncommon Jacksonians: The Radical Leaders of the Early Labor Movement.* Albany: State University of New York Press, 1967.

Petersen, Eric F. "California Politics, 1870–1894." Doctoral dissertation, University of California, Los Angeles, 1968.

Prude, Jonathan. *The Coming of Industrial Order: Town and Factory in Rural Massachusetts, 1810–1860.* New York: Cambridge University Press, 1983.

Robbins, William G. *Lumberjacks and Legislators: Political Economy of the United States Lumber Industry, 1890–1941.* College Station: Texas A & M University Press, 1982.

Rogin, Michael P., and John L. Shover. *Political Change in California: Critical Elections and Social Movements, 1890–1966.* Westport, Conn.: Greenwood Press, 1970.

Rosenzweig, Roy. *Eight Hours for What We Will: Workers and Leisure in an Industrial City, 1870–1920.* New York: Cambridge University Press, 1983.

Ross, Steven J. *Workers on the Edge: Work, Leisure, and Politics in Industrializing Cincinatti, 1788–1890.* New York: Columbia University Press, 1985.

Salvatore, Nick. *Eugene V. Debs: Citizen and Socialist.* Urbana: University of Illinois Press, 1982.

Saxton, Alexander. *The Indispensable Enemy: Labor and the Anti-Chinese Movement in California.* Berkeley: University of California Press, 1971.

Schwantes, Carlos A. *Radical Heritage: Labor, Socialism, and Reform in Washington and British Columbia, 1885–1917.* Seattle: University of Washington Press, 1979.

Sharkey, Robert. *Money, Class, and Party: An Economic Study of Civil War and Reconstruction.* Baltimore: Johns Hopkins University Press, 1959.

Slobodek, Mitchell. *A Selective Bibliography of California Labor History.* Los

Angeles: Institute of Industrial Relations, 1964.

Smith, David C. *A History of Lumbering in Maine, 1861–1960*. Orono: University of Maine Press, 1972.

Stephenson, Charles, and Robert Asher, eds. *Life and Labor: Dimensions of American Working Class History*. Albany: State University of New York Press, 1986.

Taft, Philip. *Labor Politics American Style: The California State Federation of Labor*. Cambridge: Harvard University Press, 1968.

Taggart, Harold F. "The Free Silver Movement in California." Doctoral dissertation, Stanford University, 1936.

Thernstrom, Stephan. *Poverty and Progress: Social Mobility in a Nineteenth Century City*. Cambridge: Harvard University Press, 1964.

Thompson, Edward P. *The Making of the English Working Class*. London: Penguin, 1963.

Todes, Charlotte. *Labor and Lumber*. New York: International Publishers, 1931.

Tyler, Robert L. *Rebels of the Woods: The IWW in the Pacific Northwest*. Eugene: University of Oregon Books, 1967.

Unger, Irwin. *The Greenback Era: A Social and Political History of American Finance, 1865–1879*. Princeton: Princeton University Press, 1964.

Varcados, Richard. "Labor and Politics in San Francisco, 1880–1892." Doctoral dissertation, University of California, Berkeley, 1968.

Walkowitz, Daniel J. *Worker City, Company Town: Iron and Cotton Worker Protest in Troy and Cohoes, New York, 1855–1884*. Urbana: University of Illinois Press, 1978.

Wallace, Anthony F. C. *Rockdale: The Growth of an American Village in the Early Industrial Revolution*. New York: Knopf, 1978.

Walters, Donald E. "Populism in California." Doctoral dissertation, University of California, Berkeley, 1952.

Ware, Norman J. *The Labor Movement in the United States, 1860–1890*. New York: Knopf, 1929.

Weinstein, James. *The Decline of Socialism in America, 1912–1925*. New York: Knopf, 1967.

Wiebe, Robert. *The Search for Order, 1877–1920*. New York: Hill & Wang, 1967.

Wilentz, Sean. *Chants Democratic: New York City and the Rise of the American Working Class, 1788–1850*. New York: Oxford University Press, 1984.

Willis, Richard G. "The Labor Movement in Humboldt County, 1883–1910: Its Origins, Character, and Impact." Master's thesis, Humboldt State University, California, 1970.

Wood, Richard G. *A History of Lumbering in Maine, 1820–1861*. Orono: University of Maine Press, 1935.

Wood, Samuel E. "The California Commission of Immigration and Housing: A Study in Administrative Organization and the Growth of Function." Doctoral dissertation, University of California, Berkeley, 1942.

Wynn, Graeme. *Timber Colony: A Historical Geography of Early Nineteenth Century New Brunswick*. Toronto: University of Toronto Press, 1981.

Index